Wilderness Mum

Wilderness Mum

How I Left City Life Behind to Raise a Family in Nature

KATE BARRON

MACMILLAN

First published 2026 by Macmillan
an imprint of Pan Macmillan
The Smithson, 6 Briset Street, London EC1M 5NR
EU *representative*: Macmillan Publishers Ireland Ltd, 1st Floor,
The Liffey Trust Centre, 117–126 Sheriff Street Upper,
Dublin 1 D01 YC43
Associated companies throughout the world

ISBN 978-1-0350-6851-7

Copyright © Kate Barron 2026

The right of Kate Barron to be identified as the
author of this work has been asserted in accordance with
the Copyright, Designs and Patents Act 1988.

All plate section photographs courtesy of the author except section 2,
page 5 bottom © Ben Birchall/PA Images

All rights reserved. No part of this publication may be reproduced,
stored in a retrieval system, or transmitted, in any form, or by any means
(including, without limitation, electronic, mechanical, photocopying, recording
or otherwise) without the prior written permission of the publisher.

Pan Macmillan does not have any control over, or any responsibility for,
any author or third-party websites (including, without limitation, URLs,
emails and QR codes) referred to in or on this book.

3 5 7 9 8 6 4 2

A CIP catalogue record for this book is available from the British Library.

Illustrations by Kate Barron

Typeset by Palimpsest Book Production Limited, Falkirk, Stirlingshire
Printed and bound in the UK using 100% Renewable Electricity by CPI Group (UK) Ltd

This book is sold subject to the condition that it shall not, by way of
trade or otherwise, be lent, hired out, or otherwise circulated without
the publisher's prior consent in any form of binding or cover other than
that in which it is published and without a similar condition including this
condition being imposed on the subsequent purchaser. The publisher does not
authorize the use or reproduction of any part of this book in any manner
for the purpose of training artificial intelligence technologies or systems.
The publisher expressly reserves this book from the Text and Data Mining
exception in accordance with Article 4(3) of the European Union
Digital Single Market Directive 2019/790.

Visit **www.panmacmillan.com** to read more about
all our books and to buy them.

For Magnus, my greatest adventure . . .
May you be bold in your dreams and wild in your heart.
Above all, may you always pursue what makes you happy.

Contents

Prologue		1
1	Going Solo	5
2	A New Direction	13
3	Some Hard Lessons	20
4	Teaching the Way Forward	29
5	The Call of the Wild	41
6	Revelations	50
7	Afghan Bound	58
8	A Leap of Faith	68
9	Finding My Feet	79
10	Getting in Step	87
11	Lockdown in the Woods	95
12	By Some Fiendish Stroke of Luck	105
13	Shellshock	110
14	Piped Over the Border: Leaving Scotland	120

15	The Birth of a New Plan	131
16	Urban Maul	140
17	Haystack Hotel	148
18	Early Days	159
19	Cold That Numbs Your Bones	166
20	You Can't Buy These Experiences, You Have to Walk for Them	176
21	The Good Doctor	182
22	The Hope of a Sunrise	193
23	A Small Tartan Pouch	199
24	Birth Part 1	206
25	Birth Part 2	213
26	Bloody, Blistered and Blanched	221
27	Go with the Flow	232
28	At Dancing Ledge	244
29	Blonde Hedgehogs	251
30	Sod's Law	261
31	Birthday in the Scillies	269
32	Salted and Sun-Kissed	276
33	There and Back Again	285
34	Cool Your Jets	291
35	No Judgement, No Questions, Just Love	303
36	Wow	308
37	New Horizons	318
38	Puffins	326
39	My Soul and My Song	336
Acknowledgements		340

Prologue

Had you told me ten years ago that I would leave London, throw in my job and my hard-earned, decade-long career, meet a homeless man at the bottom of a cliff and join him on a walk that meant living outside in a tent for three years, I would never have believed it. Had you also told me I'd choose to have a baby while on that walk and to continue living outdoors with my son as a newborn, I would have laughed out loud. But now, I can't envisage any other way of living.

To me, a life full of adventure is one of the greatest gifts we can give a child – adventure builds self-assurance and resilience, offers problem-solving challenges and teaches them to persevere through setbacks, cope with uncertainty and adapt to new environments. It fosters independence and the confidence to give things a go. To discover new passions and capabilities, prepare for the unexpected, assess and take risks and trust in one's instincts, as well as bringing the obvious benefits of nurturing lifelong physical and mental health. It's also the basis of strong family bonding, memories and experiences that will shape your child's story . . .

1

Going Solo

The five-seater plane touched down deep in the Colombian jungle. With no roads for hundreds of miles, the only way in was by foot, horseback or small aircraft. As I stepped out, an intense wave of heat hit me, leaving me momentarily breathless. *Wow, straight into the furnace,* I thought. I watched as a horse-drawn cart trundled across a field with my backpack.

From the air, I'd seen nothing but a dense sea of emerald green, like endless broccoli florets, interrupted only by plunging waterfalls and a snaking white river. I felt like I was about to be dropped straight into the middle of Jurassic Park. Instead, the vast canopy below, the size of Switzerland, had for decades provided cover for the illicit drugs trade and raging civil conflict, making the region a no-go zone for tourists until it reopened to the public in 2009. Now, it was August 2018, and my first visit here.

I had landed in La Macarena, a tiny, remote outpost that had once been the stronghold of FARC (Revolutionary Armed Forces of Colombia), Colombia's largest rebel group. FARC began as rural guerrillas demanding land rights and fighting against a small elite that controlled most of the country's wealth. In the eighties, they shifted tactics, funding their movement through kidnappings, ransoms, illegal mining and cocaine production. By the 1990s, they had grown into Latin America's most powerful guerrilla force. Their involvement in the drugs trade made the region inaccessible for decades, but by 2009 their influence had weakened sufficiently that it was able to reopen to the public. It was now deemed safe for tourists and I was excited to venture into this incredibly beautiful hidden backwater with such a complex and fascinating history.

I breezed through the airport, a small building in a field with next to no security, and located my guide, who turned out to be a nineteen-year-old called Alberto who had come to pick me up on his motorbike. Visitors were prohibited from accessing the area without a local guide; if I'd tried, I'd have almost certainly been picked up by the armed guards that I would soon notice still patrolling parts of the riverbanks here.

'Have you got a helmet?' I asked in Spanish.

'No, we don't wear helmets here. No one does – it's so people can see who we are.'

'Right! Okay then. Let's hope you've passed your driving test!'

It was nothing less than I should have expected given my risky journey to get here, which had included taking the Colombian equivalent of a four-hour Uber Pool at 1 a.m. – alongside three total strangers – along a single-track road nestled between the Andean mountains, known for landslides. Until I landed in La Macarena, I had been volunteering for a social educational enterprise, creating training resources for local teachers in Bogotá, and this was my first excursion further inland after two weeks of being in the country.

When you travel alone as a female, you have to make so many snap judgement calls, and in countries with a reputation for crime and danger, making those calls when you're put on the spot can feel very intense. One error in judgement can potentially cost you your life. I've definitely done a lot of things on the riskier end of the spectrum in my time; everyone's boundaries when it comes to risk are different. I guess, the more I travelled, the higher my threshold for risk became. And so far, my experience of Colombia had only challenged the stereotypes of its violent past – yes, I'd kept my wits about me and taken on board local advice, but I had already fallen in love with the country's vibrant culture, stunning beauty and incredibly warm hospitality.

Careering away from La Macarena airport along a rugged, dusty track, I clung onto Alberto for dear life. He was taking me to a local guesthouse, my base for the next few days.

'Sorry about the bumps!' he shouted. 'The roads we use for the tourists were originally built by the FARC to transport drugs, so they're in pretty bad condition, but they're the only roads we've got.'

When the road was too pot-holed or too swamped with mud for his motorbike to contend with, I found myself balanced precariously on the back rim of a 4x4 pick-up truck!

My guesthouse was rustic, but the Latin hospitality was second to none. It really was a case of, 'mi casa es su casa', the kind of warm open-armed welcome that makes you feel like a member of the family. I spent the next four days trekking, horseback riding and wild swimming through and around the winding waterways of one of the most uniquely stunning water phenomena in the world: Caño Cristales, otherwise known as the 'Liquid Rainbow' or 'The River that Escaped from Paradise'. The colours appear vividly when an aquatic plant called *Macarenia clavigera* is in bloom. This riverweed produces a pigment that covers the riverbed, radiating intense colours when hit by sunlight. It exists nowhere else on Earth.

I had been lucky enough with my timing to meet the triad

of criteria needed to witness this spectacle at its best, and it was truly otherworldly. The display of colours was so varied and vivid, almost psychedelic – a canvas of bright magenta splattered with splodges of lime green and neon yellow, with cascading white water against a backdrop of black rock, forest green and blue sky. It was a living work of art by Mother Nature.

Over the past few years, I'd come to learn that it was in nature I found my kicks, where I found beauty, wonder and adventure. It was where I felt most stimulated, present, alive, and where I found those unique experiences that set a life apart. As I swam in the colourful waters, I pondered that, if I were to be handed a sketchbook of my life as an old lady, I'd want to see one painting after another of me on incredible adventures, immersed in the most wildly unique and beautiful landscapes the natural world had to offer, hopefully one day with the added figures of a partner and children alongside me. And I wanted that sketchbook to be bulging!

So, what was I still doing living and working in London? It was a question I'd asked myself a lot over the past few years, and one that would hound me for the rest of this trip. The problem was it was a question that came with so many other questions attached. I'd been teaching in London for nearly a decade, during which time I'd lived all over the city with a combination of friends, colleagues and complete strangers. I had been a head of English for the past seven years, including three years in my current school, where I was now teaching Year 6. Teaching was all I knew and I was deeply committed to the profession. Not only that, but I'd worked so hard to get where I was. The notion of packing it all in to take off and travel the world often felt overwhelming. Was it naive and foolish to leave my career behind? I couldn't just travel and live off thin air either – how would I earn money to keep myself afloat? Would travel provide enough meaning to replace the sense of larger purpose and fulfilment that teaching gave me? There was a lot of fear around diverting from a conventional career path that I'd been steered towards my whole life.

But, deep down, I felt I was heading for a crossroads and I knew which road I wanted to take; I just needed to muster up the courage to follow that road when I got there!

From the depths of the jungle, I then headed to the majesty of the mountains. Colombia is so diverse in its landscapes and I wanted to witness as many of its contrasts as I could. I spent the next few days trekking to the summit of an active, glacier-capped volcano in the Central Cordillera belt of the Colombian Andes, the 4,950-metre peak of Nevado de Santa Isabel.

I felt as if I'd reached a point in my life where I could identify with the pull of forever wandering. The more I travelled, the more the urge to wander and explore pulled me in and I knew it would be with me for ever. Aged twenty, as part of my degree course, I had spent a year teaching in Mexico with the British Council, an experience that truly cemented my desire to see the world; I went on to explore parts of India, Africa and Argentina, to name but a few destinations. Travel had got under my skin, into my bones even. It was a part of me, and there was no shaking it off.

The temperatures in the base camps at night were absolutely freezing, a far cry from the heat of the jungle. The summit push involved an early start in the dark with crampons (spiked ice shoes), ice axes, helmets, head torches and harnesses, moving over the glacier through a blanket of white. The mist never cleared on the summit to give me a sunrise view over the mountains, but, in dealing with the cold and the altitude, I had made it through a pretty physically and mentally demanding few days and felt a real sense of triumph on that summit.

For the rest of that week, solo and exhilarated, I tackled demanding hikes through the heavy rain and thick, swirling mist of the Cocora Valley, where hundreds of giant wax palms, Colombia's national tree, soar into the sky. It was enchanting, mystical and mysterious. The power of exploring on foot was taking me to some truly amazing places which could only be accessed if I was willing to put in the physical effort to get there. I was falling in love with this way of seeing the world. It was action-packed yet slow enough to give me time to really notice and appreciate what I saw. I wanted to take my time and really get under the skin of a place. To me, that was what meaningful travel was all about. Relaxing on sun loungers did nothing for me, they left me restless – but throwing myself into trips that were active, physically demanding and action-packed made me far more energized and reinvigorated when I returned. On every trip, I was building myself up to take on more and more extreme physical and mentally gruelling feats. If I wanted to start adventuring on a more serious level, I needed to test my limits to see if I had what it took. Each time I challenged myself, I better understood what I was capable of.

From the Colombian Andes, I headed to the Pacific coast, stopping in Calí for the twenty-second annual El Petronio festival, a celebration of Afro-Colombian culture that attracts hundreds of thousands of people. The festival honours a community with a long history of struggle – descendants of enslaved African people, who remain among Colombia's most impoverished, neglected and isolated citizens. The festival is seen as a symbol of endurance and resistance for its people and an important means of promoting and preserving their rich history and culture.

El Petronio was a riot of music, food, fashion and crafts fuelled by 'Viche', a potent, locally cultivated, home-brewed spirit, once an illegal moonshine. I felt like I'd spent three days at one giant, crazy street party, culminating in wild nights of pulsating drumbeats, salsa rhythms and a heaving, gyrating, sweaty, chanting crowd.

It struck me that too many of us are living to work, not working to live, chasing material success instead of what truly matters: health, family, friends, nature and enriching experiences. I knew there was great personal reward, value and joy in having a hard-earned career, but the balance between that and other things in my life was undeniably off-kilter. Being out here reminded me that I needed to 'let go' in a larger sense.

My final stop would take me to an altogether different scene on the Pacific coast, El Parque Nacional Natural Uramba Bahía Málaga, a national park famous for the humpback whales who make the 5,000-mile migration from their polar feeding grounds of Antarctica to the warmer breeding areas of the region between July and November. It was a mission to get to but without doubt one of the most magical places I have ever laid eyes on. After a bus ride to Buenaventura, where I'd been warned to take care as the area had a bad reputation, I waited four hours for my boat to Juanchaco, a remote fishing village located within the national park. It was only accessible by boat, which takes about an hour from Buenaventura and had been delayed due to bad weather. As one of the wettest regions in the world, torrential downpours are common, but I was excited to witness the whale migration nevertheless.

The accommodation options in the national park were limited and very rustic. After the boat docked at Juanchaco pier, it was too dark for me to walk to my hostel on the other side of the island and I was given a ride on the back of a teenage lad's motorbike. I hopped on, my 65-litre backpack balanced across his lap. Five minutes in, his headlight gave out and we ended up driving across the beach, mostly through the water, in pitch-black darkness, crashing into driftwood and any other washed-up item we happened to bump into!

KATE BARRON

I spent my thirty-second birthday watching humpback whales breach and spin against a backdrop of untamed coastline – jungle-tufted bluffs and waterfalls plunging into emerald-green pools. I came to learn that these whales are often referred to as 'nannies of the deep' because of their incredibly protective maternal instincts, nursing their calves for up to a year, swimming closely alongside them, teaching them how to navigate, dive and communicate. Humpbacks have even been known to protect other species from predators such as orcas and sharks, tactfully positioning themselves between predator and prey, even lifting vulnerable animals out of the water. I knew places like this where nature still reigns supreme and untamed were increasingly rare in our world, and I felt a real sense of urgency to see them before they disappeared. I wasn't just travelling to see and experience new places and cultures any more: I was actively seeking out these wild spaces that held the power to leave me in awe and make me feel free. After five weeks in Colombia, the wild had left its mark on me.

2

A New Direction

I'd barely unpacked before I was swept up in the back-to-school frenzy. Normally, after a summer away, I'd feel totally re-energized and full of excitement to dive in, eager to meet my new class and bring fresh ideas to life. I hadn't completely lost that feeling, and was still determined to show up for my pupils and give teaching my all, but this time there was another sensation alongside it – a quiet frustration, as if I'd let myself down by putting my dreams on hold for another year.

The idea of leaving teaching to build my life around my passion for adventure, rather than squeezing it into weekends and holidays, had taken root in my mind a few years ago and grown steadily. I'd spent most of the previous year going endlessly back and forth, wondering whether to take the decision to hand in my notice. I came so close but, in the end, I let myself get talked into taking another leadership role and, with that, I was committed to another year.

It was September 2018 and by this point I'd been teaching full-time in east London for nearly a decade. I entered the profession after leaving university, through Teach First, a fast-track 'sink or swim' programme. It catapulted me from the small scenic bubble of St Andrews on Scotland's east coast to the mega metropolis of London. I was twenty-three, bright-eyed and bushy-tailed, full of ambition and determined to make a difference.

As trainees, we were thrust into the huge responsibility and overwhelming reality of full-time classroom teaching, while studying for a PGCE during evenings and weekends. It was like being thrown into the lion's den. Our first schools were chosen for us and mine was a community primary school in Tower Hamlets. Not only did it very quickly become apparent that I had absolutely no idea what I was doing but I also became acutely aware of how inexperienced I was amid a sea of staff who'd all spent three years or more gaining degrees in education; how naive I must have looked to them before I got the hang of things!

Clichéd though it may sound, I went into teaching to make a difference and, more often than not, I felt I was doing just that. I taught primary-age children and, for me, teaching was truly a vocation. I loved the creativity, variety and challenges of teaching and I was passionate about bringing subjects to life, particularly English. When I'd first started, I'd found English the hardest subject to teach, and so I invested so much time and effort into it that it soon became my favourite and then my specialism. Stories open up endless worlds of wonder and imagination for pupils, and I loved diving into those worlds with them.

We put on surprise immersive stagings of works of literature such as 'The Highwayman', whereby pupils would enter a space that immediately transported them into the world of the poem; teachers in full costume, a soundscape of galloping horse hooves, a projected landscape of moonlit moorland and all sorts of clues to discover and piece together, including a genuine Victorian musket and pistol we'd sourced (unloaded, of course!). There really is nothing quite like it when all the stars align in a lesson and the classroom is buzzing with excitement, curiosity and focus. On days like those, I felt I had the best job in the world.

But it also went so much deeper than that. I became fascinated by the 'how' of teaching: the challenge of how best to deliver lessons in ways that would most engage and inspire every one of my students. Beyond that, I really valued feeling like I was a significant figure in their lives, particularly as a primary teacher, where you spend almost six hours a day, every day, with the same children for an entire academic year. The connections we make, the relationships we build and the sense of community we nurture as teachers meant I felt I was having a hand in building their characters and supporting their development in a way that went far beyond just their learning. Teaching is one of those jobs where you can face the entire spectrum of human emotion in a single day; but no matter what, I always wanted to do my very best by every child I taught.

There were so many moments that made me well up in tears and beam with pride as a teacher. One relates to a whole primary-school Shakespeare storytelling project I'd led over the autumn term, entitled 'Shaking Up Shakespeare', which culminated in every year group delivering a performance in the iconic Union Chapel in Islington, London – a Victorian architectural gem with exceptional acoustics, often used as a concert space. Watching primary children from Year 1 upwards deliver such confident, powerful performances of Shakespeare, combining song, poetry, storytelling, even rap, in front of a packed audience has to be one of my favourite moments in my teaching career. In whatever way I'd made a difference to a child's life – whether it was helping them achieve something they couldn't do before; watching them beam with pride and self-worth at the progress they'd made; or something as simple as making a face light up, a spark ignite or an idea take shape – it all held so much value.

I had worked my absolute socks off to get where I was, which came with a big emotional attachment. My first school in Tower Hamlets ended up failing its Ofsted inspection and going into Special Measures during my NQT (newly qualified teacher) year. Consequently, the headteacher was replaced and I ended up being promoted to the school's Literacy Lead. I was extremely keen but very inexperienced, and what followed was an onslaught of visits from the local authority and frequent interim inspections from Ofsted; it was a really hard year. Our final inspection sixteen months later redefined us as 'Outstanding', one of four in 56,000 schools to have managed such a feat, a testament to the true dedication and skill of all the teaching staff. I'd had a tough start there but it was a fantastic school and I stayed for six years, making some great friends and great memories along the way.

When I decided it was time to move on, I made a choice that certainly wasn't going to make my life any easier. I moved to a recently opened four-to-eighteen free school in Newham, another of London's most deprived areas. Free schools are funded by the government, not run by the local authority, and therefore have more control over how they operate. The school was looking to revolutionize the education system, and my new colleagues were full of inspiring and innovative ideas. I learned so much and felt proud to be a part of an organization beginning to make powerful change on a national level. However, the school had not long since opened and, as a result, everything had to be created from scratch year upon year, which was a mammoth task.

The more the years passed by, the more leadership roles I took on. I'd always been told that, gradually, as the years progressed, the workload should get lighter, but that just didn't seem to be my experience – although part of that was down to my own decisions and the pathways I'd chosen. Before I knew it, the best part of a decade had gone and other dreams for my life seemed to be passing me by. I'd seen too many female colleagues pour everything into their classrooms, only to realize too late they'd missed their chance to have children of their own. I didn't want to wake up in my forties full of regret.

If I'd never met someone that I wanted to have children with, I'm almost certain I would have pursued other options: a sperm donor or adoption. I felt strongly that I could be enough for a child on my own if it came to that. I set myself a mental deadline of around thirty-eight before I'd start looking into it more seriously. That still felt far off, so I focused instead on building the life I wanted for myself.

By then, I was well respected in my work, with various promotions under my belt, and so it was daunting to give all of that up. I was scared to let it go. Yet there's a reason that 40 per cent of teachers quit the profession after five years. I'd made it to nearly double that, but nine years in and the truth was I was paying too high a personal price to continue full-time in the classroom. I felt as if I were juggling more balls than I could ever hope to catch. I'd even developed debilitating migraines, which I had never had before.

Travelling had opened up a world of possibilities to me and I was constantly questioning whether full-time teaching was what I really wanted to do and where I wanted to be long-term. Was I happy to keep sailing along on familiar smooth seas or was it time to rock the boat? I knew I was determined and resilient enough to keep going for maybe another five, ten, twenty years, but what would my life look like all those years down the line if I did? Yes, I'd have taught hundreds of children and there'd be significant reward in that, but what would I have had to sacrifice on a personal level? I had other dreams to travel the world, expand my adventurous horizons and support the development of education on a wider, even global scale, all of which would hopefully one day include meeting someone and starting a family. I felt, if I allowed myself to stay, those dreams would most likely fall by the wayside.

My social life was fun and varied where I made time to fit it in; I loved my friends and they were great respite at weekends, but I began to find the same weekly routine suffocating and restrictive. My travel experiences had made me crave spontaneity and the excitement of never knowing what was around the corner.

Colombia had been just one of many incredible journeys I'd taken over the past decade. My twenties were spent saving every penny during term time and then jetting off with teacher friends to far-flung destinations whenever possible. The school holidays were spent going on safari in Tanzania, swimming the palm-fringed waters of Zanzibar, basking on Sierra Leone's golden sands, skiing in France and travelling the length of Vietnam. We roamed ancient temples in Cambodia, dived into India's colourful chaos, hiked Patagonia's mountains, trekked Argentina's glaciers, wandered Oman's canyons and rode camels across Abu Dhabi's Empty Quarter.

However, by the time I reached my thirties, most of my friends had married and begun to have children. They were 'settling down' and were no longer free to join me on my ventures. That's when I decided to really embrace solo travelling. I had spent some time alone abroad before – in Spain as a teenager and on my year teaching in Mexico – but my first big solo trip, during which I turned thirty-one, was a month travelling around Belize followed by a week back in Mexico. It was liberating and exhilarating and I left full of confidence, excited to plan the next trip.

By May 2019, with SATs exam stress mounting, the constant focus on results felt like a betrayal of the reasons I'd gone into teaching in the first place. I fundamentally disagree with the current exam culture of our education system, which I think is outdated and fails to equip pupils with the kind of skills they need to thrive in life. The school's vision to do things differently, which had so inspired me, was now being thwarted under government pressure to get results. At times, I felt like it was beginning to lose its sense of what it had set out to do. To me, it felt like the school's hands were tied and it made me realize that mine weren't. I kept thinking back to Colombia, as I had many times over the course of that year. Deep down, I knew I couldn't afford to waste any more time. I didn't want to sit tight on calm seas any longer. It was time to jump.

3

Some Hard Lessons

I returned after the May half-term with a resignation letter in my bag. Walking into my headteacher's office was one of the most nerve-wracking moments of my life. Handing in that letter meant I couldn't just daydream or talk about forging a new path any longer; I was actually going to have to do it. Once that letter changed hands, I became accountable to myself for doing everything in my power to make it work, and suddenly there was a timeframe. This decision set a wave of other choices in motion. Where would I go? How would I fund it? My hand shook as I passed over the letter, but it was now done. I'd taken a first step away from everything I knew, my old life left behind.

In that moment, I felt a huge sense of relief wash over me and an overwhelming excitement at having my future at my feet without a clue as to what was going to come next. There was no more schedule, no more routine and no real plan. It was scary, invigorating and just so liberating. In July 2019, I walked out of the school gates for the last time. I was ready to leave London and live out of my backpack full-time. My new life plan was finally in motion!

Soon enough, I found a way to lead the life I wanted without having to sacrifice one path for another. Rather than having to choose between my passions, I could weave them together in a way that gave my path ahead even greater possibility and meaning. Alongside general teaching, for the previous seven years or so, I'd worked my way up to the position of senior trainer with an organization called Storytelling Schools, whose approach is to put oral storytelling at the heart of learning. In order for me to develop on this path, I had negotiated release from my full-time classroom for about ten days over the year so I could deliver storytelling training in other schools around the country. In all my years in the profession, Storytelling Schools' approach had the single most transformational impact on my classroom practice and I was really passionate about it. I had never been interested in moving up the school hierarchical ladder to become a deputy or a headteacher; I'd always wanted to reach a position where I could have a more far-reaching impact than on just one school, and this allowed me to do that.

Now, with my resignation handed in and accepted, and as I contemplated and plotted what I wanted to do with my new-found freedom, it struck me that perhaps I didn't need to sacrifice one passion for another – maybe I could combine them? Storytelling Schools already worked with several schools throughout the UK and I was keen to help expand its work abroad. I had the experience of my year spent teaching in Mexico, and I had spent a brief stint working with teachers in villages in Sierra Leone, which had given me a glimpse into how much good could be achieved. Better access to and better quality of education is a huge factor in tackling so many of the world's problems.

Storytelling Schools also partnered with Malta's government and – in what proved to be a case of perfect timing – in October 2019, I agreed a three-year contract with its National

Literacy Agency to bring positive change to teaching and learning in Malta and Gozo. I'd be flown out four times a year, with visits lasting two to three weeks, to train their specialist English teachers to become accredited in our method – using fun, dynamic and inclusive techniques to help children tell stories from memory. By engaging deeply and creatively with a story first, students are then ready to write with confidence and enthusiasm. We applied this approach across all areas of the curriculum, making stories a powerful springboard for developing communication skills and learning subject content in any discipline. Introducing large-scale educational reform in another culture was challenging but the breakthroughs were incredibly rewarding. When I wasn't working, I wandered the cobbled streets of ancient cities or hiked the scenic coastal trails on Gozo.

The role suited my new life plan perfectly as it freed up months in between my commitments. It paid well too, so I could use the money I earned to fund longer adventures, travelling for two to three months at a time, far beyond the limits of my classroom teaching days. With work spaced throughout the year, the only question I had to answer was, *Where to next?*

I wanted to get serious about adventuring and build the skills for larger-scale expeditions. But how would I enter into a world that still felt like the First-Class Smoking Room in the film *Titanic* – an elite club dominated by men in some mahogany-clad drawing room under gilded portraits of other celebrated men who had come before them?

I was aware that stereotype was changing, but it still felt like I'd have to climb Everest just to be given a key! It was about time there were more women adventurers and, as far as I saw it, why couldn't I be one of them? Where were the women adventurers speaking in sell-out venues around the country or making a name on television? There was a phrase I was starting to hear a lot – 'You can't be what you can't see.' Well, my view was you can, it might just take a bit of effort.

I was determined to push my adventures to expedition level, even though I knew it would be a long road. From what I'd seen, expeditions were astronomically costly, between the specialist training, gear and insurance. In my mind, I needed to secure sponsorship, but I didn't know where to start and I worried that I lacked the credentials to even get a foot in the door.

Nevertheless, I was happy. My new lifestyle was coming together. I had the best of both worlds – I'd found a way to spend most of the year adventuring, while maintaining a rewarding career in education and staying afloat financially. My decision to jump had paid off.

I began the next phase of my travels with a five-week exploration of the Hawaiian islands. Soon enough, I found myself touching down on these jewels in the Pacific and my first stop was Maui. Here, I'd planned to do a multi-day backpacking route, hiking and camping on the Haleakalā volcano, the world's largest dormant volcano, which rises to 3,055 metres. I set off early and began the 10-mile hike to Palikū, the most remote camping area in the crater. That would be the last time I saw another human until my return.

The first leg began with a 900-metre winding descent down a trail known as Sliding Sands, covered in red Mars-like sand and volcanic black rock. It opened out onto grassy plains and I marched on towards the lush green mountains in the distance. At 2 p.m. I arrived at a tiny locked wooden hut and pitched my tent nearby. I stood back and admired my work. There it was – my little red tent, a striking blob of colour nestled in the grass against the backdrop of mountains. It looked like a tiny red ant on a huge lily pad. There was no one around for miles and miles, and I was excited to be all alone.

Nothing about my background suggested I might one day end up living a life in the wild. I grew up in a secure home with loving, supportive parents, and I have wonderful memories of my childhood, but ours was not an adventurous family by any stretch. Sure, we spent time outdoors, and a Sunday morning walk was a family ritual, but other than that, we were about as wild as house cats. Tents, bikes and kayaks were unknown features of another lifestyle altogether.

I was also never really very sporty; I loved tennis and enjoyed lobbing a ball during a game of cricket or rounders. But beyond that? Not really. I certainly wasn't athletic – when I was young, that word was reserved for those who won everything at sports day, and, as I got older, for the ultrarunners, hardened expeditioners and iron men and women pushing themselves at elite level. I was none of those. I was never tall, long-limbed or agile. But, despite my background, here I was, fully embracing this wild, unconventional life on the road.

When I reached the 'Garden Island' of Kauai, I had my sights set on the Kalalau Trail in the Nā Pali Coast Wilderness Park. The trail is the only land access to this incredibly rugged, sacred, untouched coastline. I had no idea at the time, but with its challenging terrain, perilous drops and flash floods, this trek has earned itself a reputation as one of the most dangerous in the world.

The initial two-mile ascent was very muddy, rocky and steep. Reaching the top, I was rewarded with my first view of the spectacular undulating coastline before me and the sweet pungent scent of wild guavas. At Ke'e Beach, I took a short break and some water to relieve myself from the muggy heat, before crossing the unavoidable knee-high stream – a crossing notorious for flash floods on this coast, known to have washed unsuspecting hikers out to sea.

As I continued, I quickly realized I'd wildly underestimated the difficulty of this hike. Very steep climbs, intense heat and narrow, exposed cliffs pushed me much harder than I'd anticipated. The path wound along sharp sea cliffs with heart-stopping drops, and I knew I'd need to dig deep to reach camp.

At Hanakāpi'ai Falls, a sign saying 'Six-Mile Campground' revealed my first mistake: I hadn't allowed enough time to complete the hike. My permit only allowed two days, meaning I had to cover the 11 miles to Kalalau Beach on the first, camp overnight and then cover the same return distance the next day. 11 miles had sounded completely doable when I booked my national-park permit, but now I was neck-deep in the demanding reality of the trail. After a very early start and a three-hour drive to reach the park, it seemed I must have been the last hiker to leave the trailhead that morning, setting off at 9.30 a.m., and my backpack felt painfully heavy with my 5-kilo tent, weighed down even more since I'd had to pack it away still soaking wet from the previous night's downpour. I was already exhausted with half the trail still to go. I had to ration my food and water and forgo exploring the waterfalls, feeling exasperated by my lack of research. Obviously, I still had a lot to learn about hiking!

But, as I ploughed on, I was soon distracted by the jaw-dropping beauty of the Nā Pali coast. This time, I really had landed in Jurassic Park: this coastline was the actual setting for the film's fictitious Isla Nublar, and I could see why. With lush green cliffs soaring to 1,200 metres, fluted with deep-carved valleys and razor-sharp ridges, it was the first time I'd been moved to tears by nature.

At the infamous Crawler's Ledge, I suddenly found myself on a very precarious stretch where the path narrowed in places to not much more than the width of both my feet. Slowly, I edged along, the cliff face pressing against my shoulder, all too aware that my heavy pack might throw me off balance. Below me was a 100-metre drop into surging waves which charged at the cliff like a salivating sea monster. My eyes scanned for any sign of a lifeline below, in case I fell, but there was nothing: no crevice to grip onto, no ledge to find. Instead, I spied abandoned hiking poles that lay strewn across the rocks. Like some kind of offering in exchange for safe passage, they had been thrown by previous hikers in an attempt to gain even just a centimetre of extra room. It was the ultimate in shedding excess baggage, and now I understood why the couple I'd crossed paths with 2 miles back had stopped me and insisted I remove my tent, which was strapped horizontally along the bottom of my backpack, and reattach it vertically.

So far, I'd been blessed with blazing sunshine, but this was a place where the weather could change at the drop of a hat and, just as my luck would have it, the heavens opened again. Within seconds, I was soaked through. Scared to move for fear of slipping, all I could do was stop in my tracks and focus completely on staying absolutely rooted to the spot. I stood like that for fifteen minutes and it felt like an eternity. As soon as I made it onto wider ground, I sighed with huge relief that I had survived Crawler's Ledge in a downpour!

Shortly after, and having just crossed another stream, I realized I was struggling to make out the trail. I pushed on, thinking I saw a path, only to find myself climbing over fallen trees in dense jungle. I had no satellite on me to call for emergency help, no signal on my phone, no map and no compass. My phone only had half a tank of battery left and nobody knew where I was. Given I was only camping for one night, I'd decided to save on weight and not bother bringing a gas stove or any pots in which to cook a proper meal. I was also sure that there was no one else behind me. I had left far too late in the day for a hike this demanding. I had been reckless not to have done more research about what I was getting myself into.

I reckoned I had an hour left before it got dark. I tried to retrace my steps and find the trail again but I couldn't. Panic began to get the better of me, but once I'd composed myself, I hiked back again, slowly piecing together landmarks until I made it to the stream and breathed an immense sigh of relief as I rejoined the trail. I now had less than one hour to walk another two very steep miles to Kalalau Beach, so I really had to move!

I finally arrived with only a very short spell of light left to enjoy the day. I hurriedly pitched my tent and mustered the energy to head off to the waterfall that cascades from cliffs at the end of the beach. It's illegal for any boat to land on this beach, so the only way to get to it is on foot. When I got there, I was glad I'd made the effort. I had made it, and after my struggles on the trail it seemed all the more special; I really had stumbled upon paradise.

The next day, I set off early, bracing for the challenge of retracing my steps on limited food and little rest. When I eventually made it back at the end of the day, the trail completed, I was utterly exhausted. The Nā Pali trek had been well worth the effort, easily the most jaw-droppingly beautiful place I had ever seen, truly the trek of a lifetime, but it had also taught me true adventure isn't about chasing thrills at any cost, or tackling rugged landscapes on a whim. It's about understanding and respecting the wildness of a place. If I was going to take adventuring seriously, I needed to take safety seriously and prioritize being better prepared.

With Hawaii and another stint in Malta completed, in February 2020 I took off for a month in Nepal. I was on my own at first, volunteering to train a group of teachers in Kathmandu for a local charity, before I joined a group to climb the mountain of Mardi Himal on a five-day trek in the Himalayas. From there, I was meant to be going solo but had no set plans, so ended up embarking on a very impromptu, eventful adventure with four other ladies I'd met on that trek. We were in a car whose engine was tied together with an iPhone charger! Needless to say, it broke down several times. One of our group's bags even slipped from the roof-rack and vanished over the edge of the cliff, tumbling a heart-stopping 4,000 metres into the abyss below – we just prayed we wouldn't be next!

We spent an incredible week exploring on foot the extremely remote, snow-dusted region of Mustang on the border of Tibet. On my return, I decided my next adventure would be going in search of Japan's wilderness and I booked return flights for a month-long trip in April, when I planned to solo-hike around the mountainous region of Hokkaido in the far north.

Then, almost overnight, everything changed.

4

Teaching the Way Forward

In March 2020, having just completed my third stint of teacher training in Malta for two weeks and returned to the UK to celebrate my nanna's 102nd birthday, Covid-19 suddenly swept through the world and the first national lockdown was announced.

I was at a real loss for what to do. I couldn't believe what was happening. It had taken me so long to get to where I was now; finally everything was taking shape and I could see a new future beginning to emerge before me. Then, bam, in the blink of an eye, without any warning, the rug had been pulled from beneath my feet. I had no idea what I was going to do. As the situation progressed, the contract with Malta looked like it was going to be cancelled. I now had no job, no income, no home; I had no choice but to move in with my mum, who has been disabled since 2008 after being diagnosed with an extremely rare condition called a spinal dural arterio-venous fistula, which was fortunately treated with an operation. However, the condition caused the nerves in her spinal cord to be damaged, leaving her with constant neurological pain and considerable limitations to her mobility; she is only able to walk short distances, even with the aid of walking sticks.

Mum had always wanted to travel, but as a young woman she didn't have the courage to go against what was expected of her, so she got a job, saved for a house, built a life. She married my dad, had two children, became a working mum and put her dreams of exploring the world on hold. Since her diagnosis she has shown herself to be endlessly resilient and incredibly brave. Mum is well aware that many people suffer far worse conditions, and therefore refuses to feel sorry for herself. She simply pushes through each day, managing the pain, adapting to her reality and making the best of her situation. Yet her story is a constant reminder that time is not a given. We never know what's around the corner. The future is not promised and we cannot afford to take it for granted. She inspires me in so many ways, but what happened to her always sits quietly in the back of my mind, giving me a little nudge and urging me to just go for it; live for the now and don't wait.

I tried to make the best of lockdown by busying myself teaching some of my ex-pupils for free online. I also started an education vlog called EduKate and got stuck into co-writing some books for Storytelling Schools. By May, I had my name on two publications: *147 Storytelling Games* and *The Storytelling Schools Method Handbook for Teachers*. I also began writing my own teaching handbook centred around teaching 'Shakespeare through Storytelling'. It was a project that never got finished because of a surprising call I received. I was asked to work on a huge national project making a series of teaching videos on behalf of Storytelling Schools for Oak National Academy, an initiative created in response to the pandemic to provide free online resources for teachers in the form of high-quality teacher-made lessons and resources, so that the lessons could still take place remotely during school closures. It was an urgent call-to-arms whirlwind of a project, which saw a legion of educators from across the country work from home to create an entire year's curriculum for every subject and every age group as an online-classroom support resource for parents and educators post-lockdown.

I was asked to be the English Subject Lead for Early Years and Key Stage One on behalf of Storytelling Schools, which entailed designing a year-long progressive curriculum for each year group. With the help of ten other teachers, we produced more than 600 fully resourced teaching videos in just three weeks! I was hugely proud of what we had created in such a short space of time and saw it as a very worthwhile social endeavour.

By the time I had signed off on my last video, it was mid-August 2020, the first lockdown had been lifted and the nation had finally been released after months of solitary confinement. I, like everybody else, was bursting at the seams to get out. Restrictions meant that foreign travel was pretty much off the cards, but I was able to weigh up my options for an adventure on home soil.

For me, there was only one thing I wanted to do with my new-found freedom. I wanted the rush of adventure, the solitude of the wilderness and the awe-inspiring beauty of the mountains. In my mind, there was only one place where I was going to find it: the wild and rugged Scottish Highlands. Despite having studied at the University of St Andrews on the east coast of Scotland for four years, I had regrettably never really travelled further than my university bubble, and was excited to finally make amends for that. Little did I know that this trip would set in motion a chain of events that would change the course of my life.

The pull of what Scotland could offer was so great that, within twenty-four hours of first hatching the idea, I was on my way north. I had no actual plan other than to hike and wild camp. I hired a car in Inverness and, while waiting at some traffic lights, I decided to head west on a total whim to do my own off-the-beaten track version of the North Coast 500, a 516-mile scenic route and, allegedly, the ultimate in British road trips.

It was now my thirty-fourth birthday, which I celebrated by climbing Stac Pollaidh, a mountain north of Ullapool that's known for its resemblance to a porcupine. On the way, I'd stopped in Ullapool to visit a friend of a friend who worked in the art gallery there, and she had scribbled down the name of a place near Wick for me to visit later on in my trip. I thought little of it and shoved the napkin in my pocket, ready to look at again at a later date. Over the next few days, I explored the north coast, including the beautifully remote Sandwood Bay and Smoo Cave, and Ben Hope, Scotland's northernmost Munro, among other areas.

I had really fallen in love with the mystery and majesty of Scotland by now – everywhere felt so steeped in rugged beauty, legend and fascinating history. No matter which way I looked, the scenery was simply breathtaking. I couldn't believe I'd left it until my thirties to choose to adventure here. I was already hooked and knew this would be the first of many more visits to Scotland.

Although I'd wild camped on my own around Hawaii, that had mostly been in national-park territory – access was only obtainable with a permit-approved pass, which perhaps gave the illusion of an extra layer of security. Out here, that wasn't the case, and I found wild camping on my own at night unnerving to begin with – the places I pitched in were isolated, quiet and completely out of signal. My gear was very basic and old-hat too, which meant I was often cold. The only sounds were those of owls hooting, twigs snapping and animals walking past, all of which had me on high alert as I lay awake at night hoping I wouldn't be trampled in my sleep by a Highland cow! It wasn't the animals that scared me most, though; it was the thought of crossing paths with someone who may not have the best intentions. Yet it was very unlikely I was going to meet someone out here, and I knew it was just my inner fear talking because I wasn't used to feeling this exposed or vulnerable, or experiencing this level of silence. I was simply out of my comfort zone and I just had to push through it. And that was partly why I was here – to push myself to embrace more discomfort, more solitude and more uncertainty. As the nights went by, I began to get used to the solitude and enjoyed the fact that it quietened my mind and allowed me to refocus, appreciate my surroundings and live in the moment.

I was lucky enough to have a few spells of glorious sunshine, but it wouldn't have been a trip to Scotland without having my fair share of downpours and strong winds. They say Scotland is a great place to visit for two weeks of the year, you just never know which two weeks! I was really getting into the swing of my solo adventure in the wilds of Scotland and already wishing my time here didn't have to end.

Towards the end of August, after walking to the dramatic sea stacks at Duncansby Head and exploring the ghostly remains of Keiss Castle, I randomly pulled out a crumpled paper napkin from my pocket and saw the words 'Whaligoe Steps' scribbled in black marker: the place the woman in the art gallery had recommended.

It must be worth the effort if she bothered to write it down for me, I surmised. I didn't really have time, given it was late in the day, but what the heck!

So, I found myself, late in the afternoon, about 7 miles outside the small town of Wick, turning down a narrow track past a row of terraced council bungalows into a tiny parking area. There was no sign from the road and, if you didn't know what you were looking for, you'd miss it entirely, but here I was at the top of the Whaligoe Steps, a rocky inlet surrounded by sheer cliffs, with 365 flagstone steps, built around 1792, that lead to an old natural harbour below.

As I steadied myself on top of the windblown cliffs, I chuckled to myself. 'Just another summer's day on the north coast of Scotland, then!' I was standing there debating what to do when a cold, sharp blast in the face reminded me that I didn't have time to dawdle. This was going to be a close call, as I had no idea where I was going to camp that night. It had been a very windy day with multiple downpours and I knew the sensible option would be to make sure I was set up for the night in case the weather turned again.

As I began winding my way down the 365 uneven flagstone steps to the bottom of the cliff face, I couldn't help but laugh at my situation. Sunset was around 8.30 p.m., so I only had about three hours of daylight left. Making the call to risk this final feat of exploration meant I'd condemned myself to the almost certain fate of scrambling around alone in the dark Highland wilderness trying to find a spot where I'd feel safe pitching my tent for the night. Despite what had happened in Hawaii, I was still more of the 'happy-go-lucky, make it up as you go along' type of adventurer, with a 'live for the now and deal with the repercussions later' philosophy.

My style of solo travel was instinctive, spontaneous and action-packed. I had a sort of blind faith that everything would turn out alright no matter how crazy the antic, and, to be honest, in my experience, it always had. So, true to form, I decided to make time and continue on down the cliff with the faith that something would work itself out somehow or other.

The flagstone steps, precarious in places, zig-zag round five hairpin bends, and I stopped briefly to take in the view. I already felt so exposed to the elements here. This was a place where waterfalls were blown backwards by the force of the wind and sea spray shot right up over the cliffs as the waves whipped into a frothing frenzy, crashing mightily against the rocks below. There was something about this place I could already feel and, there and then, I knew I'd made the right call.

As I reached the natural harbour at the bottom of the steps and was contemplating the rugged, imposing cliffs that towered 75 metres high over it, I spotted a man with a very distinct, untamed look about him. He had a scraggly beard and was wearing a ripped kilt, tweed tartan gilet, worn-out wetsuit boots, patterned bandana, and had a knife strapped to his side. He didn't see me; he was busy tying a knot with a makeshift strap to keep a broken tent pole together in an attempt to hold up his very battered, mud-covered tent. Aside from the fact that he looked like he'd stepped straight out of the Battle of Culloden, I could tell he wasn't your average part-time camper. He caught my interest immediately. There was a wildness about him which made him fit perfectly into the surrounding landscape. *What's this guy about?* I thought. *And why the hell would someone pitch their tent down here in this wind?* It seemed like a bold choice given how exposed this place felt. *He's bound to take a bit of a beating in that thing tonight.*

Just then, an elderly gentleman brushed past me on my right and said, 'What do you reckon? He's either nuts or SAS!'

'Haha – probably both!' I replied.

My first thought was that he was homeless, but something didn't quite add up on that front and I didn't want to judge a book by its cover. I knew I couldn't leave here without finding out a little more about his story. The state of his attire made me think he'd been doing this for some time. He appeared resourceful: despite his broken, battered gear, he was soldiering on and making the best of a challenging situation. He was clearly more well-practised at the art of outdoor living than I was, having chosen to pitch up at the bottom of this cliff face. A curiosity had stirred within me and I made up my mind to go and talk to him before I left.

I wandered around, snapping away with my camera, and quickly found a favourite spot, watching the waves crash dramatically against the cliff edge. I'd been keeping an eye on the rugged man and his tent behind me and saw he was now engaged in conversation with a woman who looked a similar age to me. The wind had died down somewhat and it had suddenly got pretty busy with tourists at the bottom of these steps, so I decided to head off. But I didn't want to leave without having spoken to him; I knew I'd regret it. I waited it out for another ten minutes or so, but he and the woman were still chatting animatedly. In the end, my impatience got the better of me. I felt a little awkward about interrupting them, but I knew I couldn't leave without saying something.

'Hi! I'm so sorry for interrupting,' I said in a rush. 'Please excuse me, it's just I'm in a real hurry so have to take off now, but I couldn't help but notice you here and just had to ask what it is you're doing – hope you don't mind!'

The man was obliging and polite. 'Sure, no worries. I was just explaining to this lady that I'm walking the entire UK coastline, raising money for a veteran's charity, SSAFA. I started in Wales and have been walking for just over three years now.'

SSAFA, I later learned, stood for Soldiers, Sailors, Airmen and Families Association. Founded in 1985, it's the UK's oldest charity for veterans.

I was blown away. This man, who told me his name was Chris, spoke to the avid adventurer inside me and my intrigue rocketed. 'Wow,' I said. 'That's some adventure! Incredible! What made you decide to do that?'

It was at this point that I noticed he had a beautiful white lurcher with him, peering out from inside the tent, tucked up cosily in a sleeping bag.

'I'd been in a bit of a bad place with depression and anxiety before I left, but this journey has really restored my faith in humanity.'

There was so much I wanted to ask, but instead I simply replied, 'What an amazing thing to have restored! Sounds like this walk's already worked wonders and given you back so much.' I then asked if he wouldn't mind if I took his photo for a bit of portrait practice while I was there. I knew I'd stumbled upon someone truly unique and remarkable, on an equally unique and remarkable journey – definitely worthy of a portrait, I decided! He again happily obliged and crouched down as I positioned myself to include the tent and the crumbled ruins of an old salt house as his backdrop.

'Oops, might help if I take the lens cap off!' I said, and we both laughed. He smiled when I explained I was a novice, and I quickly took a few shots, not wanting to appear intrusive.

'Well, it sounds like a real once-in-a-lifetime adventure and I'm sure there'll be plenty more magic in store for you! Good luck with the rest of it and nice to meet you! Bye!'

Hurriedly, I made my way back up the cliffs with a spring in my step, glad that I hadn't shied away from approaching him and missed an opportunity to learn a little about his unusual story. It was no more than a three-minute exchange, but I was struck by his comment about this walk restoring his faith in humanity. It was a very deep and profoundly personal thing to share with a stranger, and I wondered what had happened to make him lose faith in the first place.

I made it back to my hire car and focused on my next mission – finding my own wild camping spot for the night, preferably a bit further south. The next day, I would have to head back to the south of England for work. I scoured the map quickly with the aim of scouting an ideal place to pitch for the night, but decided I'd just wait and see what cropped up along the way.

As I drove further and further away, my thoughts kept wandering back to this man I'd just met and the epic journey he was on. Our encounter had been so random and so brief but it had really struck a chord with me. For one, I was bowled over by the sheer scale of his undertaking. I had no idea at this point how many miles made up the UK coastline. It wasn't actually the distance that grabbed my attention, however, so much as the longevity. He said he'd been walking continuously for over three years.

Three years! That is serious commitment!

Most modern-day expeditions span several weeks or months at most and I personally hadn't heard of any in recent times that had involved anywhere near this length of time. Chris had mentioned he'd set off from Wales, so he still had a long way to go! I kept wondering, *How on earth does he manage to keep going for so long without stopping to work? How the hell does he fund himself?* As somebody who was looking to start doing longer, more extreme adventures and eventually dive into the expedition world, these were questions to which I just had to know the answers.

Suddenly it dawned on me that I'd just spent the past half an hour thinking about Chris, with questions running riot in my head. Obviously, there was a lot about the nature of what he was doing that caught my attention, but there was something about *his* nature too. There was a humbling confidence about him that I really liked. He could have waxed lyrical about his achievement so far, but he'd quickly brushed over that part to tell a complete stranger something very personal about how his journey had changed him. I liked the fact that he'd felt able to allude to his mental health struggles to someone he'd only just met – to me, it showed someone who wasn't afraid to open up and be honest about his vulnerabilities. There was also a really positive energy about him to which I was drawn. Chris seemed to have a real love for the way he now lived, so much so that it had become a part of him, and it was physically evident from the lines on his face and the dirt on his hands.

I liked that he clearly didn't give two hoots what he looked like and was more than comfortable in his own skin: the take-me-as-I-am kind of bloke, especially given that his attire meant he was bound to turn a few heads. In this day and age, people are all too quick to conform and I admired the fact that he wasn't afraid to stand out from the crowd. His authenticity was attractive in itself.

Most of all, I immediately trusted him. As a woman used to travelling on her own, I knew all too well the risks that came with the all-important decisions of whether to trust a complete stranger you've only just met. I'd had to do this so many times and it only takes one bad call for the tide to turn. There were two things that made me trust him: first, at the risk of sounding cheesy, I felt he had kind eyes; and second, the way he looked after his dog, whose name, I had learned, was Jet. It hadn't escaped my attention that his dog had been very cosily wrapped up inside the tent. I've always agreed with the old adage that you can tell a lot about a man by the way he treats his dog, and here was a man who clearly put his first.

I had to hand it to the guy – in just three minutes, he'd managed to make a pretty strong impression. Either that, or I'd just watched too many episodes of *Vikings* during the first lockdown and figured Chris was about as close as I was going to get to meeting one!

Suddenly there was a lay-by coming up and, almost without thinking, I found myself braking and doing a U-turn. I was going back! Deciding that Chris might be hungry, I found the nearest fish and chip shop, pulled up and bought two dinners, two cans of Tennent's and a sausage for the dog. With a grin on my face, I got in the car and headed back to the steps. It was a snap decision that would change everything.

5

The Call of the Wild

I trundled down the Whaligoe Steps laden with my backpack and tent and an overstuffed carrier bag. It was about six thirty in the evening and still light; the sombre sky's spirits had started to lift, it seemed.

'Chris?' I called out hesitantly. 'It's me, Kate – the girl from earlier.'

He poked his head out of the tent. 'Hi! Everything okay?'

'It'll be getting dark soon and I have nowhere to camp. Would it be okay with you if I pitched next to you for the night, since you obviously know what you're doing? I also thought you might be hungry, so I got us both some fish and chips, with a couple of cans of Tennent's to wash it down and a sausage for Jet!'

'Ah, thank you – that's so kind of you!' he replied. 'Jet is gonna love that sausage! And camping here is no problem at all, Kate. You're more than welcome. Can I give you a hand pitching your tent? It's pretty windy!'

'No, don't worry, I've got it,' I insisted.

He thanked me for the fish and chips and offered to set

them to one side so we could eat once I'd finished, although Jet understandably got her sausage immediately!

He sat in the entrance of his tent and I could feel his eyes on me as I wrestled with the billowing tent flaps that kept on trying to take flight, whipping and flapping around me like the sail of a ship. I finally managed to stake each of the four corners down to the ground with metal tent pegs, before jostling with the bending tent poles, threading them through the lining as quickly as possible to lift and secure the arched frame. After about ten minutes, it was ready – no longer a crumpled heap on the floor but my slightly lopsided home for the night.

'Ta-daaa! The Four Seasons awaits!' I joked.

'Honestly – that was painful to watch!' he laughed. As I whipped my sleeping bag out of my backpack to set up my sleeping space, he remarked, 'What the hell is that?'

'It's my sleeping bag! I know, it's awful. I've had it since my first Duke of Edinburgh expedition at school. It's about as good as a hanky. You know the phrase, "All the gear and no idea?" Well, take that and flip it – I'm basically all the ideas and none of the gear! This week, I've been freezing cold, hardly had any sleep and have woken up so stiff I feel about eighty,' I said with a chuckle.

'Some decent kit might be a good start! You can't sleep in that; it's a disgrace. Later, we'll swap and you can have mine for the night. And don't worry about the wind – it's gonna calm down soon, I'm sure of it – we should be in for a pretty nice evening, I reckon.'

'Really? Are you sure? That's so kind!' Looking back now, given his circumstances, I kick myself for being so quick to jump at his offer. He had to sleep in a tent every single night, year in, year out, whereas the next day I was going back to a warm bed indoors. But, at the time, I was just so thrilled at the prospect of getting more than two hours' sleep in a tent for the first time in nine days, I couldn't help myself.

He invited me to join him sitting outside his tent and we shared my 'gourmet' offering of fish and chips washed down with Scotland's finest – a can of Tennent's – and I couldn't help but notice how dotingly he looked after his dog. She was still curled up inside his sleeping bag and he kept checking in on her every few minutes or so, making sure she was warm enough, giving her strokes and kisses – and plenty of his dinner! He clearly loved her to bits and she looked so lovingly at him in return.

I asked whether she'd been with him the whole time.

'No, no – I adopted Jet on the way. I got her in Ayrshire, on the west coast, just before I started the islands, and she has been my best friend ever since. She's incredible. She's stuck by my side through thick and thin on this journey. Never has anyone shown me such loyalty.'

'She's beautiful. Has she always been called Jet?'

'Yes, and it suits her – trust me, you've never seen a dog run as fast as she does! She is an absolute rocket, especially if she sees a rabbit! I'd love to write a children's book about her one day. No other dog has done what she's done and she's had the most amazing adventures along the way!'

The two were obviously inseparable, and that made me warm to Chris even more.

After dinner, I suggested we scramble over some rocks to get a closer look at the churning waves surging in a cauldron of white foam as they smashed against the cliffs. 'Sure, but here,' he said, handing me his hat. 'Take this, I can see you're cold. It's proper Shetland wool, hand-knitted by a lady I met there. Just don't drop it in the water – I'd hate to have to dive in for it!'

For someone with so little, it struck me as unbelievably generous that he'd offered to lend me something of his for the second time. We sat there for a while on the rocks and, sure enough, the wind began to die down.

By the time we got back to where our tents were pitched, although cold, it was now a calm evening. 'Told you,' said Chris. 'One thing I pride myself on is reading the weather. It's one of my specialities! There are no second chances when it comes to Mother Nature, so when you're out in it as much as I am, it's essential to know what you're up against. I learned the hard way, especially during winters in the Outer Hebrides and Shetland.'

Chris looked up at the sky and began pointing out constellations, before sharing stories of encounters with otters, eagles and even orcas. He then launched into an old Shetland folktale about a baby girl snatched by an eagle and taken to its nest, only to be rescued by a brave little boy who climbed down the cliff to retrieve her and later grew up to marry her. Chris had yet to learn how much I loved stories and how big a role they played in my life. As he spoke, I was struck by the deep connections he'd made to the places and people he'd met on his travels. He didn't just walk through these landscapes with a mindset of head down, push on and cover the distance; he forged deep ties to the land and the locals and learned as much as he could about their stories and way of life. It was the kind of attachment that made a journey so worthwhile, in my view.

It was dark now and the stars lay sprinkled across the sky. Chris got out his phone.

'I've never shared this with anyone, but I want you to hear it. A man played this for me on Foula. This is music that has never left that island. He allowed me to record it to remind me of the island once I'd left. The islanders are very protective over their heritage and, trust me, this was a real honour.' We sat and listened in silence, looking up at the stars. It truly was a beautiful piece of music, very pure, and a far cry from the music played in the bars and pubs back in London! It was lilting and slow, quite sad in tone – I could feel the raw emotion in every instrument. For a few moments, I felt transported back a hundred years to life on a harsh, windswept island, beside a lost generation, all clad in their traditional dress, dirty from their chores that day, stone walls their only protection from the severe icy winds outside. As they huddled around a fire to keep warm, they played music and sang together, whiling away the long, dark evenings. It took me a world away from the one I knew. The fact that he'd chosen to share such a personal and precious recording with me, that he clearly had never shared with anyone else, did make me wonder if he was already feeling the same deep connection for me that I was feeling for him.

Our conversation flowed so easily as we exchanged crazy travel stories and compared our favourite explorers. We discussed our mutual love of survival stories and skills, history, geology, Norse legends and Greek mythology. He told me all about his lifestyle on the walk and how he'd headed out with nothing but a borrowed pair of boots, just £10 to his name and a tent with a hole in the top, and how he'd gradually learned to live off the land in order to survive. It was just him, Jet and his tent, walking all day and wild camping each night, in all weathers, year-round. As they'd begun to conquer the Scottish islands, they'd caught the attention and captured the hearts of more and more people, so much so that the kindness of strangers began to follow them everywhere. Despite the fact that Chris had no income and all donations went straight to the charity via his JustGiving page, people found themselves wanting to get behind him and be part of this incredible journey in some way. He had been able to keep going for three years, had found happiness, pride and purpose living in the wilds and raising money for charity as he went, and was absolutely hell-bent on completing his mission.

As the night drew on and we became more comfortable in each other's company, he confided in me a little about his past.

Chris was an ex-paratrooper who had fallen on hard times since leaving the forces. Before he started the walk, he'd been suffering from severe anxiety and depression. He had become extremely insular, often shutting himself away from the outside world for weeks at a time, and he reached a point where he barely recognized himself. His family and friends had watched him crumble before their eyes, at a total loss for how to help him. He'd been swallowed by a black hole and felt completely lost and trapped inside his own mind; a broken man who had hit rock bottom.

The situation had escalated to a point where he realized that, if he didn't do something drastic, things would spiral out of control. He'd managed to leave the house for a surf one day, his only form of escapism, and had an epiphany. Standing on the cliffs on his way back from the beach, he made an impulsive decision there and then to walk the entire UK coastline – and a few days later he was gone. The veterans' charity SSAFA had helped him when he'd run into trouble after leaving the forces, and he wanted to raise funds and awareness for them to show his gratitude. More than that, he made a promise to himself that he would return a happy man – and he was. The walk had been a type of rebirth for him.

It was a lot to take in, and I was taken aback by how open and honest he was; I thought him very brave for being willing to share this with me. He'd clearly had a lot of pain and sadness in his life, but he had somehow found the courage within him at his lowest point to make a change. I found the story of his transformation so powerful and inspiring.

I had never met anybody who had left everything they'd known behind to fulfil a life such as his. It felt like we were two souls both seeking the same path, just by different means.

'It's freezing out here. Come and sit inside the tent,' he said. 'It'll be warmer with the three of us, plus you can cuddle Jet – she's my hot-water bottle!' Then he paused. 'I've never actually invited anyone inside my tent before. This space is sacred, my home. It's always just been me and Jet in here.'

Once inside, I couldn't help myself. 'Wow, it's pretty pungent in here! Now I know the real reason no one's allowed in! There aren't enough air fresheners in the world to cut through that!' I laughed. Then I told him he was in good company. 'I've hardly washed for nine days – and my hair, well, think Edward Scissorhands on a good day!' I took the hat off and freed my hair from its bobble to reveal a giant bird's nest stuck together of its own accord.

'You look like Worzel Gummidge!' he laughed. 'But I love that you don't give a toss. You may be even stinkier than me!' Safe to say, we definitely felt like kindred spirits!

Eventually, I looked at the time. 'It's nearly three a.m.! How did that happen?' We both laughed, and after he handed over his jacket and sleeping bag, having taken mine, I retired to my tent.

As I lay there, I mulled over the things he'd told me. Other than tour assignments as part of his time in the Paras, an elite group of soldiers, Chris had never really travelled abroad. Of the two of us, if we were counting countries, I was definitely the more 'well travelled'. Yet it occurred to me that perhaps Chris embodied the notion far better than I did. To me, the way he was living on his journey had so much purity and integrity; he had detached himself from everything the rest of us cling to, had whittled life down to the absolute bare necessities, and in doing so had found freedom in its truest form. He moved at his own pace, taking his time, dictated to only by the weather and the tides. He was his own man with no one to answer to but himself. He had found strength and joy in a life of simple freedom. This idea of a slower, more meaningful kind of travel had a powerful draw.

To me, adventure had always been synonymous with exotic destinations where I'd get a totally different experience from anything I was used to back home. I enjoyed the rush, shock and challenge of being catapulted into somewhere completely unfamiliar. The thought of adventure travel at home had never even crossed my mind. Somewhere in my subconscious, I'd written it off as inferior and drab in comparison to what I could find elsewhere. But here I was, listening spellbound for hours to a man who had enough incredible stories about his travels along the UK coastline to fill a lifetime.

In the morning, I stretched out my stay as long as I could. It meant I had time to meet Davy, a local who voluntarily looked after the steps and a real character. His wiry white moustache framed his mouth all the way down to the bottom of his chin and he wore a scratchy, green knitted fisherman's jumper with a slightly less traditional baseball cap on his head. To me, it felt like he was so much a part of this place that the salt of the sea ran through his veins, and the lines on his face were his many stories, written by the wind. He shared that the Whaligoe Steps were originally cut from the rock for a total of £8 back in the 1790s to provide access for what would become a thriving harbour during the herring boom of the 1800s. Back then, the women would gut the fish before loading the baskets and hauling them up all 365 steps. These women were renowned for being as burly, strong and sturdy as the men – not only did they haul the huge loads of fish all the way up the cliff face on their backs in handmade willow baskets known as 'caisies', but they then had to walk another 7 miles to Wick just to unload them. These women, who all had about eight children each to look after, would collect water from a nearby well to drink, boil it in a large pot over an open fire, cook all the meals and wash everything by hand. They would milk animals; cut peat; harvest crops; sew, weave and knit; wash, make and mend fishing nets; unload cargo; and salt the fish. Some of them were even known to abseil down the next cliffs along, to collect fish where there were no steps. They really were the original wilderness mums!

When I decided I couldn't delay my departure any longer, Chris and Jet accompanied me back to the clifftop. As we climbed, I kept thinking how tough life must have been for those women back then. They were made of strong stuff, that's for sure – and with that, I pushed on that little bit harder. At the top, we hugged.

'Oh, I almost forgot – your Shetland hat!' I said, pulling it out of my bag.

'No, it's yours,' he insisted. 'I want you to have it. Just take care of it, okay?'

I felt honoured by the gift, thanked him, and asked if he wanted to exchange numbers so we could keep in touch. I knew it was unlikely we'd meet again. But, as I walked out of sight, I really hoped we would.

6

Revelations

There was no doubt that meeting Chris had been a memorable end to my adventure in the Scottish Highlands. I couldn't shake the feeling as I drove home that there was something fated about our encounter. For one thing, if it hadn't been for that lady in the art gallery in Ullapool who'd scribbled the name of the steps on a napkin, I'd never have even heard about them. For another, there was no sign to the steps, just a dirt-road turn-off that I could very easily have missed. It did all feel quite serendipitous.

Stopping for a break on the long drive back to my mum's in Malvern, I was very surprised to see a message from Chris already. I'd got as far as the Lake District before I needed to stop for the night, but, with it being the tail-end of the summer holidays, the place was rammed and there wasn't a single bed in a B&B or Travelodge available anywhere. I ended up sneaking into the corner of a Travelodge car park and sleeping in the back of my car that night. I replied to his message the following morning with a photo of my hair, which was now an exact replica of that of the brown-haired witch from the film *Hocus Pocus*. As the days progressed, Chris and I began messaging more and more, and soon the text messages turned into phone calls. We were getting on like a house on fire and talking constantly.

By the time I headed off on a short surfing trip to Portugal in mid-September, I was wondering if there was more to this chat for me than just friendship, but I wasn't sure whether he felt the same. Perhaps I was simply someone he got along with, a welcome escape from the solitude of his journey with only Jet for company.

Soon after, Chris invited me to attend a prestigious award ceremony in London, where he and Jet would receive a Soldiering On 'Animal Partnership' Award for their journey. This was an award voted for by the public, honouring the unique achievement of a member of the armed forces community, with the support of an animal, celebrating their special relationship. He said he'd sleep rough on the streets afterwards and that I might want to stay with a friend. 'No way,' I replied. 'I'll join you.' The event ended up being cancelled due to a resurgence in Covid cases, but I think my response had surprised him – maybe enough to make him realize that, if I didn't mind sleeping rough, I'd be able to see past his smelly socks!

As the days turned into weeks, we were back and forth on the phone a lot and, the more we kept in touch, the more it became clear to me how much I liked Chris. Aside from his determination and resilience, he was fun, outgoing and very funny, with a dry sense of humour. There was no doubt he was having a hard time every day, but he was so fired up by this profound sense of purpose and love for his way of life that his positivity was infectious. He was confident, spoke with conviction and was always upbeat – he could be freezing cold or soaked to the skin but would always spin it into something to laugh about and I loved this easy-going, fun-loving side of him. My feelings were definitely growing by the day.

It soon began to dawn on me just how much effort he put

into staying in touch so often. By this point in his journey, Chris had amassed a loyal and supportive Facebook following of around 80,000 people. As he moved along the coast, news of his route would be posted onto local community groups, and people would often reach out with offers of help, such as a hot meal, a barn to sleep in or a place to charge up his battery packs if needed. Previously, he'd used any battery he had to capture the coastline or update his followers, but now he'd started to save his battery for our calls. He'd often turn his phone on just once during the day to call me, so I could see where he was, before quickly hanging up to deal with an incoming tide or cliff face; and then he'd walk miles out of his way on top of his daily mileage just to find a place to charge, so he could call me again at night. He was making big sacrifices and huge efforts on my behalf, and I began to realize that he wouldn't be going so out of his way if he didn't have feelings for me, too.

As we became increasingly comfortable talking to each other on the phone, Chris opened up more about his past. He'd had a daughter, Caitlin, at the age of twenty-one with his ex-wife, and, after winning sole custody of her once she was six, had raised her as a single parent. He'd worked multiple jobs to make ends meet, but had never been good with money and frequently ended up falling behind with bills, to the point where debt collectors were knocking on the door.

The anxiety and feelings of failure he harboured as a father who had let down his daughter had affected him so much that he'd suffered with crippling depression, and his daughter felt forced to move out at sixteen, unable to live with him any more. Chris had faced homelessness several times, and it was as another eviction loomed that he had decided he had nothing to lose. His plan for the walk was made on a whim a few days before he actually set off. It was, he told me, a last-ditch, desperate attempt to turn his life around.

These were huge revelations, full of pain, sadness and hardship, and I was almost holding my breath at times as I listened. Being completely honest, there was a part of me that worried, if he'd struggled this badly with mental health in the past, it could potentially resurface and come back to haunt him again. That was a scary prospect, but, at the end of the day, I was an optimist – I was full of admiration for his bravery and honesty in speaking about it all so openly, and I truly believed in the power of his transformation. The man I was getting to know was a far cry from the one he described as his former self.

Chris also admitted he'd been hesitant to mention sooner that he had a child, in case it put me off. It was big news to take in, but I felt so drawn to Chris, and I didn't want the fact that he already had a child to be a barrier to us moving forward. After all, he was forty, and I understood that lots of people by that point in their life had children or were divorced. Also, his daughter was twenty, so it wasn't like I'd be taking on the role of stepmother to a young child, which might have been more daunting. I told him I wished he had felt he could tell me sooner, but that I looked forward to meeting her at some point.

Although it had become evident through our phone calls that our feelings for one another had grown, we had yet to really admit them to each other. In October, six weeks after our first encounter at Whaligoe Steps, we arranged to meet again for a 'first date' to see if our connection felt as real in person. The plan was that I'd fly to Inverness, then we'd head to the Black Isle for a few days to stay in a bothy – basic, remote, free-to-use shelters originally built for rangers and shepherds and now used by outdoor enthusiasts.

The days building up to my departure were so nerve-wracking. I was bursting with excitement to see Chris, but really worried that I'd overplayed our bond and had read too much into things, conjuring up a picture of what I wanted rather than what really existed. I knew it would be a crushing disappointment if it turned out that the picture didn't quite fit the frame.

Nevertheless, I decided to make it as special as possible. That way, even if things didn't work out quite as I was hoping, we'd still have the memory of a really unique date and the foundations for a lasting friendship. So I whipped up a lemon drizzle cake as a treat, grabbed a bottle of port I'd brought back as a gift for him from Portugal and splashed out on some fancy cheeses to go with it.

The night before my flight, I stayed up until three in the morning crafting a 'Chris Walks the UK' board game as a bespoke present for him, finally calling it a night with just a few hours to spare before catching my train to the airport.

Getting off the plane at Inverness, my mind whirled with questions. *What if I don't feel the way I thought I would when I see him? What if I want more and he doesn't – or vice versa? What if it all goes pear-shaped and I'm stuck here, miles from home, for four very awkward days?* I knew there was a lot at stake for us both. For my part, I didn't give my heart away easily and yet here I was, all in.

When I saw Chris standing there in the airport car park waiting for me, I realized he was just as nervous. I ran up, dropped my bags and hugged him. We kissed then and there, and I knew that, whatever happened, I was where I wanted to be. The scary part now was accepting that I had finally met someone I wanted to be with long-term and trying to envisage what that would look like for us moving forward.

One of Chris's followers, a man named Tug, had kindly agreed to pick us up from the airport and drop us at the trailhead leading to the bothy. As we pulled in, Chris and Jet were due on an online video call any second to accept their Animal Partnership Award via Zoom. We raced up a steep hill so we could reach enough phone signal, and while it was very surreal seeing him accept the award via video call in a sloping woodland in the middle of nowhere, I watched proudly, delighted for them both – from all I'd seen, they were very worthy winners!

We wound down through the pine forest to the shore, where Eathie Bothy stood, an empty, dark, stone-walled room with a very basic fireplace and a few faded information boards about its history and the eighteenth-century geologist Hugh Miller, who had hunted fossils nearby. I was thrilled to be here – this place was right up my street.

Over the next four days, I immersed myself in Chris's life on the coast. Our days were a mixture of survival tasks and simply enjoying time together in this beautiful and remote place. We'd collect fallen logs from the forest for firewood, break them down into smaller logs and whittle what we needed for kindling using his knife. That activity took precedence to ensure we would be warm at night. We'd trek to the nearest farm for fresh drinking water, then explore the shoreline, hopping rocks and wading through slippery kelp at low tide for stone-skimming contests. We ran with Jet along the sand, searched for fossils, and Chris showed me how to pry limpets from rocks to forage from the sea. He demonstrated how to get a blazing fire going and distil sea water to drink, if ever necessary. We also practised the more unusual first-date art of knife throwing. Between his military background and the amount of time he'd had to perfect his skills with little else to do in the wild, he had a deadly aim. When it came to my efforts, let's just say I didn't quite make the bullseye but did at least hit the board!

In the evenings, we'd belt out power ballads, a glass of port in hand, dancing by the fire. We told stories, shared adventures and laughed out loud as we feasted on lemon drizzle cake, snuggling up to Jet by the fire.

This was my first-ever experience of sleeping in a bothy. Most are bare to the point of being spartan – no running water, electricity or beds, just the very basics: a fireplace, benches, a table or some sort of rough sleeping platform, and often a pile of wood left behind by the last people to use it, in good bothy etiquette. This one had none of that, just a fireplace and some eight-legged residents. Chris had spent some time clearing it out before I arrived and sweeping away most of the cobwebs and the broken glass to make it usable. He'd often spoken about the bothies he'd slept in on the west coast and the islands, places full of character in the middle of nowhere, surrounded by wilderness, with traces of people who had passed through: trophies picked up on walks, such as whale vertebrae, stag antlers and beachcombed oddities; half-bottles of whisky and scribbled memories in dusty notebooks. These places were like ever-evolving museums in the wild, full of stories. Chris had even left letters in a few with the intention of returning to collect them someday.

This bothy might have been totally bare, but to me it was a doorway – my first foray into the wild world of Scottish bothies – and I was excited. We had no candles for ambience, no extra light other than what the fire and our head torches could offer, and the cold stone floors and thick stone walls, though unforgiving, still made it slightly less biting than sleeping outside. We pitched the inner tent to create an extra cocoon of warmth, and as I lay inside my sleeping bag, my eyes scanned an entire canvas ceiling covered with the names of all the islands Chris had walked, written by him in marker pen – so many places in my own homeland I'd never even heard of, like Eriskay, Gigha, Ulva, Papa Stour and Little Bernera, to name but a few. I pored over the uniqueness of all those island names, even contemplating that one or two might make for an unusual child's name one day; they felt like whole other worlds that I knew I needed to explore for myself. There was also a phrase that read, *Keep going, mate. This was never going to be easy!*

It was about as far from a first date in London as it could get. Truth be told, I'd found the dating scene back home tedious and awkward, so much so that I rarely bothered with it. People call it the dating game and most of the time that's what it felt like – one big game with too many insincere players! Friends would insist on signing me up for the latest dating apps, and at times I would entertain it, but more often than not I wished I'd used the time to see friends, plan lessons or even stay at home and run a bath. Deep down, I'd always hoped to meet someone who shared my love for adventure and who craved the same lifestyle. My philosophy was that I just wanted to get on with doing things that appealed to me and hoped I would bump into the right person along the way!

Now, finally, I felt I had. I told Chris I loved him on that very first night and shed a tear of joy when he replied that he loved me, too. Hidden away in that tiny stone bothy, in that moment, we could have been the only two people in the world. We had finally found each other and now we had a really exciting future ahead of us.

Except, just a few days into our fledgling relationship, I was about to throw a curveball our way. I had to go away again – this time to Afghanistan.

7

Afghan Bound

To say Afghanistan isn't your typical tourist destination would be an understatement. At the time of my planned departure in October 2020, its fall to the Taliban was still ten months away, but the situation there was already unquestionably volatile and incredibly fragile. Decades of war and instability had left it in political, social and economic turmoil. Certainly, mainstream media coverage over the years following the US invasion in 2001 had given the Western world one prevailing image of Afghanistan – that of a frightening, no-go war zone.

However, while undoubtedly risky, there were still pockets of the country deemed stable enough for tourists – and I wanted to see them. Afghanistan had long held magic in my mind. As a child I'd been enthralled by mythical tales of the Middle East and as a teen I'd read the books by Khaled Hosseini depicting the idyllic beauty of the country in its liberal heyday of the 1960s and 1970s. In my twenties, it was ancient civilizations and the historic importance of Afghanistan as a crossroads between the empires of Asia, Eastern Africa and Southern Europe that fascinated me, as described by Peter Frankopan in *The Silk Roads*. Now, in my early thirties, I was inspired by Eric Newby's *A Short Walk in the Hindu Kush*, recounting his experience of packing in his London life at thirty-six to travel to the remote Panjshir Valley.

All of these tales sparked in me a fascination for a country of unforgettable adventure. I wanted to marvel at the snow-capped peaks of those vast and boundless Afghan mountain ranges and watch local artisans keeping their incredible age-old craftsmanship alive, blowing glass, hand-weaving rugs and making jewellery. I wanted to dance to the music of the national instrument, the *rubab*; converse cross-legged on floor cushions while eating freshly fired bread from the tandoor; and take part in traditions that might soon disappear. It may have been a romanticized vision that I was drawn to, but in my mind Afghanistan's culture and history was woven from as many rich and colourful threads as the rugs for which it was so renowned.

I also wanted to venture beyond the headlines and see the side of Afghanistan that wasn't being reported on, convinced there was still so much beauty, heart-warming hospitality and optimism to be found. I wanted to meet, hear and learn from the people who lived there.

Another major reason I was eager to go was my work. Afghanistan had one of the youngest populations in the world, which meant education was vital for both economic growth and democratic development. However, decades of turmoil had massively impeded access to education, especially for women and girls. I connected with an Italian NGO that had set up schools in the city of Bamiyan, hoping to partner with them to launch a teacher-training programme. The plan was to visit the NGO towards the end of my trip. Leading the project would be risky, but I believed it was worth it to make a positive impact in a place where it was clearly needed.

But now, with my departure imminent, I was suddenly no

longer single, which was a new and unanticipated factor. Any partner would have been worried, but, as an ex-paratrooper, Chris knew the reality of what I might be stepping into. Understandably, he hated the idea of me going.

Chris was blunt in his reaction. 'You're mad. This is no joke, Kate. I've spoken to people and it simply isn't safe out there. I know you love to travel and I really do understand the desire to go and explore somewhere so off the beaten track, and I admire your balls, but this is really risky. I know better than most about taking calculated risks, but this isn't calculated, it's crazy.'

Although he'd never served in Afghanistan, Chris had contacts on the ground out there who painted a pretty ugly picture of what it was like. He'd also lost friends there, while others he knew were still struggling in the aftermath of their experience. The guilt of going weighed on me heavily. As if he didn't have enough on his plate, pounding 20 miles on foot all day and living full-time in a tent, outside in the cold! This was only made worse by the fact that he'd opened up and told me that his greatest fear in life was loss.

Although he didn't go into too much detail, given we'd not long since met, he did explain that as a child he'd been hugely affected by his parents splitting up and that he'd gone into survival mode from a young age. As a result, he was reluctant to get too close to anyone for fear of being let down and hurt. He had lost his trust in people and this had followed him throughout his life. This fear had plagued most of his relationships and was a big reason why he'd chosen to remain single for the past decade. Now he'd finally let his guard down and opened himself up to having love in his life, he was terrified that he might lose me.

I felt so guilty that I'd be putting him through so much torturous worry for the weeks I'd be away. Was I being unnecessarily selfish? And not just to him, but to my friends and family, who I also knew were deeply concerned about me going? In fact, whenever I told anyone of my plan, the response was a universal, 'Are you off your rocker?!'

For the first time, I realized how much the pursuit of an adventurous life was essentially a selfish venture and how much it could impact the feelings of those who loved me. But despite Chris's misgivings, and my own, I decided to press ahead with my trip. I'd spent weeks on research, spoken in-depth with the organization and gone through all of the risk-assessment precautions. In my heart of hearts, I knew I wanted to go. At the end of the day, it had to be my call.

Yet Chris's words continued to haunt me right up until the moment I checked in for my flight to the Afghan capital, Kabul. How could I think it was worth it? Here I was, thirty-four years old, having just met a man I'd fallen in love with, and I was about to risk it all by getting on this plane. I felt like I'd spent years creating this beautiful painting of the possible life that lay before me and, having finally added the finishing touches, I was about to grab a knife and slash it right down the middle.

Waiting in the queue to check in, a huge part of me just wanted to call it all off there and then, buy a ticket for the first flight up to Inverness and be reunited with him again. I really was in two minds and just didn't know what to do.

'Miss? Excuse me, miss?'

I looked up. It was my turn. I took a deep breath and stepped forward. I watched my backpack trail off out of reach along the conveyor belt as I took hold of my boarding pass. *Well, that's that*, I thought. *I'm going.*

I had no idea how often I'd be able to contact Chris while I was in Afghanistan, if at all, so I called him one last time as I sat on the plane before take-off. He was just outside Inverness, about to retire to his tent for the evening. 'Everything will be fine,' I reassured him. 'I'll be back before you can say the word "coastline". I love you and I'll see you soon.' And, with that, I took to the skies.

I have to admit that, as the plane touched down in Kabul, I was nervous. The city still saw attacks on a daily basis, usually bombings or shootings. We arrived late afternoon and our group of five travelled by regular 4x4 to a safe house. We drove through the city; it was bustling, the streets packed with people, the traffic chaotic, the smell of exhaust fumes occasionally interrupted by that of charred, smoky meat being cooked by street vendors on the side of the road. The architecture was a jarring juxtaposition of precarious Soviet-built concrete apartment blocks, huge lavish wedding halls, ornately decorated buildings and gated compounds.

I tried to focus on the fact that it was deemed far less risky to be a tourist in Kabul than it was to be a diplomat or an NGO worker. We could blend in more easily, wearing low-profile clothing and using low-profile, everyday cars. On arriving at the safe house there were two gates to get through, both guarded by armed men, and our car was stopped between them for a security sweep, where identities were verified and detectors were moved around under the car to check for any explosive devices. I had never experienced security like this.

Once inside, we were given a tour of the safe house and shown bombproof vests and helmets to put on, as well as the escape exit, in case of an emergency. It took me a while to get to sleep that night, as I lay there contemplating the stark reality of where I was; I'd put myself in the middle of a war zone, and there was no going back now. I thought about Chris, but I trusted in my instinct that all would be well, and finally drifted off.

The next morning, we took a flight to Bamiyan, thus avoiding the Taliban checkpoints along the roads and the 110-mile drive. This is where I'd spend the next two weeks. Cut off from the rest of the country's troubles because of its inaccessible location nestled between the Hindu Kush mountains in central Afghanistan at an altitude of 2,550 metres, Bamiyan was at the time regarded as the safest province in the country – peaceful, calm and quiet. It was home to the Hazara people, Afghanistan's third-largest ethnic group and a Shi'a minority who faced severe persecution under previous Taliban rule. Yet, despite repeated attempts, the Taliban had not managed to infiltrate Bamiyan since they were last driven out, with checkpoints outside still guarded by foreign soldiers.

On the journey to Bamiyan, I did wonder whether I'd be able to enjoy myself at all or if I'd just be on tenterhooks the whole time; but, before long, I found myself with that excited, tingling feeling I'd had so often before when travelling. Out of the window was the most incredible view. Below, spread as far as the eye could see, was a vast golden-brown mountainous desert: the magnificent Koh-e-Baba, the western foothills of the Hindu Kush. I was already hooked, and I couldn't wait to see what else I would discover here.

Autumn had fully embraced the landscape, and it was breathtaking: row upon row of poplar trees lit up the lush green valleys with leaves that shone so bright they looked like gold coins; rivers laced with icicles wound their way like glistening paths from the mountains. It really was a paradise.

While in Bamiyan, I wandered through ancient bazaars, met artisans and explored ruins on red-brown hillsides where Genghis Khan once laid waste to the region. I climbed the cliffs where the famed 'Bamiyan Buddhas' once stood, the oldest and largest carved Buddhas in history, which, after standing sentinel over the valley for more than 1,500 years, had been obliterated by the Taliban in 2001. Now, these vast, empty niches tower over the valley, a tragic example of the power of conflict to reshape and even destroy the world's greatest cultural heritage sites.

I ventured into surrounding caves, where monks once lived and meditated, discovering remnants of the world's oldest oil paintings. In a world which has become so developed, populated and urbanized, to stand in a place where the view had hardly changed in 1,500 years felt pretty mind-blowing. As the sun set, the valley was bathed in gold, and I understood why Bamiyan had earned its reputation as the 'Land of Shining Light'; a ray of hope for a place where darkness has so often prevailed.

It would have been completely perfect but for one thing: I so wished Chris was there with me. I knew he would love the view as much as I did. In the back of my mind I was always wondering how long it would be before we could speak again and I rang him whenever I could. Now, it was my turn to search daily for wi-fi to stay in contact.

Band-e-Amir, Bamiyan's national park, was filled with incredible untouched beauty. Apart from a few local villagers, we had it to ourselves, and it was an utter privilege. The vast fortress of mountains occasionally gave way to reveal deep blue lakes that sat like sapphires set in gold rings. One evening, I watched the sunset transform into moonlight on one of these lakes, the silvered ripples glowing beneath the endless sky. I even took a freezing dip at sunrise, breaking the ice to plunge into the lake's minus-ten-degree water, though it took a painfully long time to warm up afterwards! Hiking around these mountains, even witnessing games of buzkashi – the national sport, a mounted-horse pursuit – were experiences I'll never forget.

One person who left an impression on me was our guide, Sajjad, who was one of the two athletes who'd made the cut for Afghanistan's first-ever Olympic ski team. After spending thirteen years as a refugee in Iran, Sajjad returned to Bamiyan's snowy mountains where, along with another keen skier, Alishah, he began skiing without any resorts, runs or chairlifts. Each day, they hiked four hours up a mountain for just a four-minute descent – two runs at best! A Swiss entrepreneur, noticing Sajjad and Alishah's grit, invited them to train in St Moritz for three seasons, and back in Bamiyan they rigged up a makeshift ski lift from a wheelbarrow, rope and motorbike to maximize their training time. After years of tireless dedication, the pair were invited to the PyeongChang Games in 2018, but missed qualifying by a narrow margin.

When I asked if he'd try again, Sajjad explained how difficult it was without resources, funding or facilities. But, undeterred, he'd founded Afghanistan's first ski club to help others pursue his dream. 'One day,' he said, 'I want an Afghan to stand on that podium.' His resilience reminded me so much of Chris, back in the UK, driven to complete his journey no matter the hardships. Chris had set off with nothing, facing harsh winters and relentless physical strain, day after day. Setbacks never swayed him, and his resolve was one of the things I loved most. Both Sajjad and Chris shared that indomitable spirit, pushing forward no matter what life threw their way.

Cradled in between the mountains, Bamiyan exuded a quiet calm and sense of isolated beauty. It had really shone a light for me on the real Afghanistan beyond the headlines of war: jaw-dropping landscapes, gentle, kind-hearted people and a phenomenal richness in culture and history.

As the last days of my trip approached, I knew Chris was relieved I'd soon be home. In the end, a security warning stopped me from visiting the schools, which I was disappointed about. I consoled myself knowing I'd soon be able to speak to Chris more often. Then, with just twenty-four hours until departure, another, more serious warning came through; all domestic flights were cancelled. My return to Kabul was delayed by two days, meaning I'd also miss my flight home. I managed to call Chris and tried to keep things low-key, but I could hear the worry in his voice.

When we finally made it back to Kabul, our first stop was a medical centre for Covid-19 tests – essential for boarding the flight home. But, on our way there, a bomb exploded at the university, sending the city into high alert. The tense unease I'd felt on my arrival returned. Continuing on to the medical centre felt like a gamble, but if we wanted to get out of the country, we had no choice.

After the tests, I was relieved to be returned to the safe house once again, but we weren't out of the woods yet. We still had to sit and wait nervously over the next few hours for the results. I stayed calm, reminding myself that we were not the target, but I couldn't help but feel we were essentially sitting ducks. Then the tests came back negative and we all breathed a sigh of relief. The thought of one or two of us having to stay back while the others flew home was not a reality anyone wanted to face. Now everyone had the all-clear, it was a mad flurry to get new flights booked.

Having been on the go the whole time and out of wi-fi range, I hadn't had a chance to speak to Chris for a while. I tried to call but it wouldn't connect. Time was ticking by before we had to leave for the airport but I really wanted to get hold of him before I left. Finally, I got through. 'Chris,' I said. 'I'm okay, but a bomb's gone off at the university, so it's all a bit chaotic here. I'm leaving now for the airport. I don't know if I'll be able to contact you, but I'll do everything I can to let you know I get on the plane safely.'

'Kate, Kate,' I heard the others call. 'The car's ready. Let's go, we're leaving. We need to go now!'

'Shit, Chris – I've got to go! I'll try and call you from the airport,' I said, running into the courtyard, immediately losing the wi-fi connection from inside the safe house, cutting off the call mid-sentence.

I kicked myself. Why did I tell him about the bomb? He'd be worried sick.

The regular airport drop-off was blocked by emergency response vehicles, so our car let us out on the roadside, a good five-minute walk from the terminal. We grabbed our bags and walked briskly, heads down, through a concrete walkway. It was very tense. When we finally reached the entrance, we were ushered behind curtains and into small rooms for security checks. With no functioning wi-fi in the airport, contacting Chris again was impossible. It would be at least eight hours before I could speak to him.

The wait to board the plane was nerve-wracking, to say the least – I couldn't shake the feeling that we were a trapped target, sitting in a confined and crowded airport terminal where every minute felt like an hour. I felt a rush of relief when the plane finally took off from Kabul, and even more so once I knew we were safely out of Afghan airspace, heading towards our stopover in Dubai.

Landing back on English soil, I was glad to have made it home safe and sound, but my long radio silence had taken its toll on Chris. When I'd finally been able to reach him on my stopover in Dubai, I could tell he was exhausted with worry. After I'd cleared Heathrow security, I followed the signs to the train station, ready to head back to my mum's house as planned. But just as I was about to buy my ticket, something made me pause. I looked up at the timetables, feeling a pull in a different direction.

8

A Leap of Faith

When I landed in Inverness around six hours later, Chris was there waiting. We wrapped each other in the longest, tightest hug imaginable. I winked at him. 'See, told you it'd all be fine!' Given he'd been living with his heart in his throat the past two weeks, he raised his eyebrows at me for making light of it, but he appreciated my humour and was just glad to have me back. My time in Afghanistan had been a wake-up call. Life was precious, time was precious, and I was so lucky to have been born into a world of privilege and opportunity. I didn't live under a tyrannical regime, nor was I confined to a conflict zone – I was free. I got to choose how I lived my life.

It dawned on me that I didn't want to look back one day and wish I'd had the courage to live differently. I wanted to make each day count. I looked at Chris, this man I loved, who seemed to embody ultimate freedom and adventure. His way of life was working wonders for him, and I wanted a taste of that, too, to live a life of fulfilling adventure on my own terms. This past year, I had certainly made myself freer, but was it enough?

For the next fortnight, our base was a little cabin in the back garden of a wonderful supporter of Chris's called Nicki. She was an absolute gem, her kind offer of accommodation in the small village of Balloch, about 4 miles east of Inverness, giving us the space and quiet time we needed after a tense few weeks apart. The cabin was bigger than I'd expected, with a long narrow kitchen, living room complete with comfy sofas, a table and wide-screen TV, and a bathroom. We slept on a mattress on the living-room floor, with Jet curled up next to us on the sofa, under a blanket. I couldn't believe we were already feeling this level of commitment when, in reality, it was only the third time we'd ever seen each other. Chris halted the walk for a few days so we could spend time together, and to allow me time in that first week to focus on a freelance project and wrap up a Year 6 Global Citizenship textbook I'd been writing for Pearson. It was painful – I was itching to be outside, walking and exploring, diving into the life I'd come here for.

The second week, I joined Chris walking, and we made progress. This was my first real glimpse into what life on this walk was all about, racking up the miles with my home on my back as we moved from A to B each day, and then having to work for our most basic necessities – shelter, food and water.

We picked up the trail where Chris had left off, at Fort George, an eighteenth-century military fortress built to suppress Highland uprisings, home of the Black Watch, a historic Scottish regiment known for its distinguished service. With some sleuth manoeuvring, we gained access to a secluded bit of beach along the estuary just in time to watch the sun go down between the fort's bartizan turrets. After pitching up, I took Jet for some sprints on the beach in the name of bonding, but she mainly just looked up at me in a 'What kind of shocking throw is that?!' way and waited for Chris to come and do the job properly. Given the temperature was two degrees and knowing there was no wood here, Chris had come prepared with peat logs so I could warm up by a fire before my first Scottish November night in a tent. I was eager to learn and watched carefully as Chris got the fire going. He talked to me about the differences between burning peat and wood, and I practised blowing into the fire to keep it fed with oxygen, trying my best to avoid singeing my hair and lips.

Then we sat by it for hours, under the stars, eating toasted marshmallows.

After two days walking through the beautiful fishing towns of Nairn and Findhorn, me gradually finding my feet by the day, we reached Lossiemouth. The weather was overcast but I was in really high spirits, excited to experience another day in the life of Chris's walk. That morning, I accompanied Chris to the armed forces primary school on the RAF base nearby, where he gave a talk outside about his walk to a group of children. Given my teaching experience, this was really up my street. I knew that armed forces children can often have a tougher time than most, with frequent school changes and the emotional strain of having a parent away, sometimes in dangerous situations. For some, there's also the harsh reality of loss and grief at such a young age. I loved watching how natural Chris was with the children; they gravitated to his warm, fun energy so quickly, although of course Jet was the star of the show! It was heart-warming to see Chris, despite all the challenges of his journey, making time to bring joy and inspiration to others, especially kids. There were so many schools we could visit along the way to inspire so many children; it was a unique opportunity to make a real difference.

That night, we pitched the tent at the base of the sand dunes on Lossiemouth beach, a huge expanse of sand with a picturesque lighthouse in the distance.

Once we'd foraged for firewood and cooked dinner, we went

for a sunset stroll at low tide along the rippled sand. As I snapped away, taking photos of the palette of pastels in the sky, Chris suddenly burst into a sprint, with Jet hot on his tail. His limitless energy never ceased to amaze me! She zoomed past him and I stopped to watch the two of them chase each other, bolting up and down the shoreline at a rate of knots and bounding around in circles together. A beaming smile spread across my face. I could've sat and watched the two of them play together all day. From the second I'd met Chris, I'd seen there was a special connection there between this man and his dog, but now I was learning it went far deeper – they were each other's family. He was her world and she was his.

In fact, their bond was closer than anything I'd seen before between human and animal. Jet was more than a companion; she was Chris's anchor, his constant, his joy, and I could tell she had played a major part in helping him put the broken pieces of himself back together again over the past few years. I watched them look at each other and it didn't matter that Jet couldn't talk; they understood each other instantly and instinctively. It was as though each carried a piece of the other's soul around with them. Watching them, I had tears in my eyes. To me, it was more than moving, it was magic – as if the fates had brought out their golden threads especially to weave them together.

Laughing, I broke into a run, indulging in this game of chase, hoping that Jet might start to see me as a new member of her pack, or maybe even play with me or run towards me just once. I kept slapping the front of my thighs, shouting, 'Jet, come on, Jet!' but she would only stop to glance at me. She responded only to Chris, followed only Chris. During my time with them so far, I'd spent every spare moment doting on her, hoping she'd feel safe and comfortable around me, stroking and cuddling her for hours, asking to feed her and keeping her company if Chris ever stepped away for a moment.

I wanted Jet to accept me, and I knew because of her bond with Chris she might not find that easy. She was so used to having him all to herself and now she was suddenly expected to share his attention with someone else, and another female at that. It would take time, I knew, but gaining Jet's trust meant a great deal, and I was determined to keep trying.

I woke up in the morning to a coffee made by Chris in his titanium mug. Despite a very broken night's sleep on another chilly November night, I got out of the tent full of the unexpected joys of early morning, so much so that I started doing a silly dance. There I was in the cold light of dawn doing what can only be described as a combination of the 'funky chicken', 'the sprinkler' and 'reverse the bus'!

'Far too much for this time in the morning!' Chris laughed.

That afternoon, we were due to visit Lossiemouth's RAF base. Nothing could have prepared me for what was in store. Members of the 51 Squadron met us on the beach, escorting us through town to the base. The reception was unbelievable, the turnout like a royal-wedding street party! People lined the streets in their hoards, waving banners they'd made, shouting, clapping and cheering. Some approached with gifts, including a handmade winter coat for Jet, while a photographer snapped away as he walked. I honestly couldn't believe what I was seeing. 'They must have you confused with Harrison Ford!' I laughed, turning to Chris.

Once we reached the base, Chris was swiftly bundled into the military equivalent of a limousine with the captain to go and see the Spitfires (a real honour), while someone figured out what to do with me, this unexpected extra they hadn't accounted for. Chris still cracks up about it to this day: his A-list, red-carpet treatment, while I was left stranded in the car park! I'll never live it down.

Eventually, I was walked down to meet him for a private tour of a Typhoon fighter jet. Given that it had taken me two years to even locate the fuse box in my last flat, I knew this was as close as I was going to get to operating a state-of-the-art piece of machinery on this level. *This is my* Top Gun *moment!* I thought excitedly.

Afterwards, we joined everyone in the officers' mess for dinner and drinks. I was so pleased for Chris that the military bases along the way seemed to be pulling out the stops for him, recognizing his efforts and all he was doing for the armed forces. It felt like the entire town had come out to support him. Having never followed Chris online, I had no idea whatsoever just how many people knew about his journey, never mind felt so invested in it. Frankly, I was shocked. For the first time, it hit me that the walk wasn't just about one man raising money, it was bigger than that. Something about this walk, the mission, Chris, Jet or all of it combined was standing out to people and capturing their hearts and imaginations. He was connecting with the public and bringing people together in a way that was truly beautiful and powerful.

What made it even more astonishing was that Chris didn't seem to realize the extent of it. He was just a bloke on his mission, plodding along each day. He had never mentioned the kind of attention he was receiving, and, given what I'd just seen, I loved him all the more for it. He was humble and focused on the task at hand; he didn't let himself get swept up in having his fifteen minutes of fame, so to speak. He was there to walk for a cause and that always came first. It was evident to me that this walk was a powerful force for changing people's lives in a profoundly positive way, and I felt proud to be with him and to be a small part of it.

Those five days had taken us from Fort George through Nairn, Lossiemouth, Buckie and Cullen. It had been so magical and eye-opening. I now had some idea what the walk entailed on a day-to-day basis. I'd dipped my toe in the water and, despite having had some very uncomfortable nights squashed and freezing in a one-man tent, I felt energized, exhilarated and hungry for more. It had also cemented us as a couple. Our bond felt unshakeable, and I didn't want my time there with him to end.

That evening, having returned to the cabin as Chris prepared dinner for us, I sat at the table twirling my pen around on a blank piece of paper, lost in thought. Something had been niggling away at me – the seed of a thought that had taken root in my mind over the past few hours and was growing fast.

It had taken me years to gain the courage and confidence to find my current path, and the icing on the cake was always to find that perfect match, someone who shared the same values and the same kind of vision for life as me; a kindred spirit who wanted to grab life by the horns and just go for it; a fellow adventurer whom I adored and could share it all with. I had spent years wondering if I would ever find that person.

But there, in that cabin in a back garden in Inverness, I knew the man in the kitchen, stoked to high heaven about the use of an oven, was exactly who I'd been looking for. I didn't want a long-distance relationship, to see him every now and then and spend the time between reunions wishing we were together. I wanted us to embrace the now, embrace each other, and start living the life of adventure we both knew we wanted together. When it came down to it, this man I loved was already on the adventure of a lifetime and I wanted to do it with him.

The thought of how I could do it, or even that I'd be giving up a lifetime's career, didn't matter to me at that moment. Yes, it was sudden and very soon in our relationship to throw all my eggs into one basket, but it felt right. As with the decision to go to Afghanistan, I knew that following my heart and not my head was usually the winning option. Yes, there would be work commitments to sort out and it wouldn't be easy, but I wasn't going to let that stop me. My instinct was telling me to go for it and work the rest out later.

Knowing how much he'd been craving a roast dinner, I'd bought all the ingredients from the nearby Co-op once we'd got back, and now Chris emerged from the kitchen, chuffed to bits with his roast chicken, ready for us to eat. Wracked with nerves, I knew this was the time.

'Chris, can I ask you something?'

He stopped still, holding the plates of food, a look of concern on his face.

'Is everything okay?' he asked.

'I love you,' I said.

'I love you too, Kate.'

'What would you say if I told you I wanted to join you for the rest of the walk, not here and there but full-time? Me with you every day for the rest of this walk and hopefully beyond.'

He stood for a second and just stared into my eyes. Then the warmest smile started to form on his face as he quickly put the plates down. He grabbed my hands and looked at me. He didn't need to say anything. I already knew the answer. He came closer, put his arms around me and whispered softly, 'Let's do this.'

In that moment, I wasn't just committing to the walk but I was making a commitment to him and to a future for us together. I didn't know what the future held but I knew that I was choosing Chris as the man I wanted to be with long-term, and hopefully, in time, even be the father of my children.

9

Finding My Feet

It was 22 November 2020, a week after our conversation, and my first official day walking the UK coastline for SSAFA alongside Chris and Jet. I felt extremely proud to join him in his fundraising efforts for a charity that undoubtedly made a big difference in people's lives, particularly the lives of our veterans who all too often slip under the radar. From what Chris had told me, SSAFA's volunteers had quite literally almost knocked the door down in persevering to help him in his very darkest days. If their volunteers were willing to put in that kind of effort, then so was I! I knew I'd find out more about the charity along the way, but what mattered to me most was feeling that I was still pursuing an endeavour where I was able to help people and make a difference. I knew the charity would become my all-important sense of purpose, as well as my motivation to dig deep and keep putting one foot in front of the other when the going got tough.

I couldn't help but reflect on how Chris and I had come at this walk from such completely opposite ends of the spectrum. When Chris set off, it was in sheer desperation; a last-chance attempt to claw his way out of his black hole and loosen the suffocating grip of his depression and anxiety. The walls of his life had been closing in; he was a broken man at rock bottom and had nothing left to lose. The only choice he felt he had left available to him was to pack a bag and walk, his home on his back, for his survival; to save his life. On the way, he hoped to reignite that dim flame inside him until it burned bright and he had fire in his eyes and a spring in his step once more. He had rediscovered his sense of self, hope, happiness and place in the world.

When I met Chris, I was very content in my life, carving out a future for myself in the way I'd wanted to for a long time. I was choosing to leave behind the career I'd built, the stability I knew and much of the identity I'd created ever since leaving home at eighteen. Giving it all up to join him was a huge leap of faith, a plunge into the unknown and a massive gamble. For me, this wasn't a choice made out of necessity or desperation, it wasn't survival, it was about trusting my gut and rolling the dice in order to be with the man I loved and pursue the kind of experiences I'd dreamed of – a life of wild adventure outdoors with new and unexpected experiences every day.

I broke the news to my family and friends over the phone. Both my parents were taken aback, as this was certainly not the path they had envisaged for me. My mum admitted she had already been on the brink of sitting me down to have a serious heart to heart about where I was going in life. She had always expected me to travel and see the world, but had certainly not expected my life to take a turn in the direction it now was. In her eyes, camping out in all weathers was not a life she would choose, but she reminded herself I was in my mid-thirties now and this was my life to live, not hers – she just hoped I knew what I was doing! Nevertheless, as my mum, she decided she would be flexible and accept my life choices.

As for my dad, he was well aware of my adventurous spirit,

so, in one sense, he said it came as no great surprise that I would make this kind of impulsive choice. He'd always said he could visualize me throwing caution to the wind and rolling the dice. However, both my parents had championed my pursuit of a successful career, always supporting and encouraging me along the way, and I think he found the notion of me packing it all in to live in a tent with a homeless, penniless nomad I'd only just met difficult to digest. At this point, neither of my parents had Facebook to follow the walk or knew anything about Chris.

My friends were less surprised, however – I was always regaling them with ridiculous tales from my travels and they knew my spontaneous, adventurous side well. I'm sure deep down some of them had a few reservations, but they were never voiced. Mainly, my friends were just excited to see how my new life played out and they were really happy for me that I'd met Chris.

There was one thing I wasn't willing to sacrifice as I started this new life, however. If you'd asked me what I wanted most in the world, deep down, above all else, having children was top of my list. I'd known that since my early twenties and, on some level, it even played a role in why I wanted to leave teaching.

So, back in the cabin, before I committed to joining him, I'd asked Chris outright: 'Do you think you'd ever want more children?' I was thirty-four and this was non-negotiable for me. I wasn't going to tiptoe around it. I wasn't about to waste my time with someone who didn't want the same things. He told me that, after Caitlin had left home, he was certain he'd never go down that road again. But now he'd begun to feel differently. With the right person, in the right relationship, one built on real love and shared parenting responsibilities, rather than struggling as a single father as he had with Caitlin, Chris said he'd love nothing more than to have a child together. I didn't know how we'd make it happen within the current framework, but knowing it could happen was enough.

I had been living out of my backpack for most of the past year, jetting between Malta and other travel destinations before lockdown. In that sense, other than ongoing work commitments, there were no loose ends I was leaving behind that I needed to sort out, no notice to give or bills to deal with. I still had some savings left from my work with Oak National Academy during lockdown, so I was able to invest in some new camping gear for the walk and see us through when it came to buying food, for the time being. I'd already moved out of my flat in London the previous summer, so all of my belongings were already in storage at my mum's in Malvern, taking up most of the spare room and the garage, and she'd said she was happy to keep them there for now.

That day, we walked from Whitehills down to the bottom of the sea cliffs outside the town of Macduff. We pitched the tent behind the walls of a disused Art-Deco lido, originally built in 1931, now looking rather sorry for itself, with quite an eerie feel. Before settling into the tent that night, I walked to the water's edge to look at the sea. I had to pinch myself that this was really my life now. The enormity of it felt both exhilarating and daunting, as if I were heading out into the open sea before me without a compass. Everything I thought I knew about life was about to change. Being a person of no fixed abode, for who knew how long – certainly a matter of years rather than weeks or months. It was a lot to take in, but I also felt a bubbling excitement about the experiences that lay ahead.

That night, to help take my mind off the cold, I decided to provide some evening entertainment – gone were the days of TV! So I regaled Chris with the tale of how the character Macduff came to slay one of my all-time favourite literary villains, Macbeth. 'Turn, hell-hound, turn!' I boomed.

'Bloody hell! There go my evenings of peace and quiet!' he laughed.

Given I'd only just started on the walk, I wasn't yet thinking about home comforts I might miss – Netflix, a hot bubble bath, the ability to buy and cook any food I fancied – I just wanted to experience life really outside of my comfort zone and see to what extent I could manage without all the luxuries we take for granted. I wanted to challenge myself to find out what I was truly capable of. It was only November, but the temperature at night on the east coast of Scotland was already in the minuses, and I was freezing! Chris had overseen a ruthless cull of the contents of my backpack before we'd set off, as he knew I would underestimate the long-term toll of carrying any gear that wasn't absolutely essential. I was like the Michelin woman, layered up in every item of clothing I had with me to the point of barely being able to move. Chris's one-man tent was now home to all three of us, so we were as squashed as sardines, but with this level of cold I was very grateful for the extra body heat. Jet included! When stretched out, she very nearly took up the same amount of space as another human.

The next morning, we packed up the tent in driving rain and battering wind, heaved on our backpacks and headed straight up a cliff. Shielding my face from the storm, my boots sinking in the squelching mud, the entire morning was spent fighting winds that kept trying to topple us as we zigzagged up and down cliffs towards Gardenstown. We trudged over boggy ground, scrambled up narrow ravines, crossed burns and paused in hidden coves. The sea cliffs were ruggedly dramatic, far more so than I'd expected, and at one point I stopped midway through a steep scramble to admire the untamed beauty of this coastline and lost my focus; my foot slipped and I soon found myself doing the splits down a wet, muddy bank. I laughed as I watched Chris and Jet tackle it all like a pair of pros, and we decided that his other female companion was far more graceful! Nevertheless, hard going as it was, it was invigorating to walk so exposed to the elements in such wild weather, and, with a smile on my face and humour as my ally, I plodded on.

I was quietly relieved to reach Gardenstown, a tiny, picturesque village where fishing cottages line up right against the sea. With the rain finally subsiding, we stopped to devour a couple of steak pies we had kindly been given by the owner of a local pub the day before. It felt strange to accept the charity of others – something I'd never done before and certainly never expected to do. I felt guilty, in a way, that people might now feel compelled to offer things to both of us, rather than just to Chris. I knew it would take some getting used to. But I also knew that Chris never asked for anything – he accepted food, gifts or help only when freely offered. And, from the little I'd seen so far, it was clear people genuinely wanted to help. They lit up with joy at being able to support the journey and feel part of it in some small way. It was a warming feeling to be on the receiving end of that generosity, and at this point I had no idea just how central the kindness of strangers would become to our story.

The sandy beach, framed by cliffs in rich autumn hues of russet and green, provided the perfect pit stop to refuel, rest and give Jet a playful break before heading towards Pennan, hoping to reach camp before dark.

However, this stretch of Aberdeenshire's coastal trail mostly followed a road that was quite set back from the coast. Right from his first steps in 2017, Chris had adopted a coast-walking philosophy of 'if you're going to do something, do it properly' and had stuck absolutely doggedly to the coastline even when it was completely unpathed and fraught with challenging obstacles (the reason Scotland's west coast and islands alone had taken him so long!). Now, his philosophy had become mine.

WILDERNESS MUM

That afternoon, I found myself going head-to-head with his choice of unpathed route. Whenever we reached a barbed-wire fence, we would have to coordinate: Chris would jump over first, then I'd lift and hand over all 25 kilos of Jet, so he could lower her safely. I would then either crawl sideways through tiny gaps – I quickly learned going feet rather than head first was definitely the best way forward if I wanted to avoid ripping my hair out – or Chris would hold his bag over the spikes so I could scale without the risk of shredding my nether regions! It was an art we soon mastered, although it quickly became clear that my gym leggings were not going to last the week. We also had to scale several gates and forge our own path tracing the cliff edge. I was fully on board with Chris's mindset; not only did it make the journey all the more exhilarating but I admired his integrity and determination to stick to his guns and never cut corners or take the easy option of the road unless absolutely necessary. When it came to coast-walking, he was a purist, and now, so was I.

That night, we reached the bay before Pennan just in time for sunset and quickly set up camp. It had been a long day and, as I sat outside, I welcomed the calm, clear sky, a single pink stripe tingeing the horizon. We heated up some army rations we'd been given and ate inside the tent to shelter from the biting cold, which had set in early. I didn't have any camping cooking equipment to bring with me and there wasn't enough for the two of us, so I ate my Bolognese out of Chris's camping coffee mug. That night, I was so cold that I just couldn't get off to sleep; I simply didn't have warm enough gear and felt frozen solid.

At one o'clock in the morning, we were both rudely awoken by the sound of tent flaps shaking violently and the fact that the tent had flooded! Our one-man tent had been in constant use for a long time by this point – it wasn't designed to withstand the relentless battering of wind, day after day, and over time it had begun to deteriorate. We were also so squashed in, we'd had no choice but to lie right up against the tent lining, which meant the two skins of the tent were essentially fused together, enabling the water to flood in. Our sleeping bags were swimming in a pool of water and all our kit was soaked. Worse still, the icy water was now seeping into our sleeping bags where we lay cocooned. The tent flaps were crusted with ice and we were being shaken so violently I genuinely felt concerned the poles wouldn't hold and we were going to take off and be carried out to sea! 'Don't worry,' Chris said calmly. 'This tent has withstood much stronger than this up in Shetland. She'll hold.'

I began to realize just how clueless I'd been about what I was letting myself in for. All I could do was trust Chris's instincts that we would make it through the night without sailing off into the North Sea, and trust in myself that I could do this. It was becoming clear that I was getting a real taste of what the elements had in store for me; Scotland clearly enjoyed reminding me who was boss! My first two nights had been a crash course in wild camping in a Scottish winter. I'd catapulted myself straight from all the comforts of a warm house with central heating into a Scottish winter on the east coast, and it was going to test me like nothing I'd ever experienced before – and winter had only just begun. Could I withstand this level of hardship day after day, night after night? Did I really have what it took? There were no answers in the storm – no hint of what tomorrow might hurl my way, no guarantee it would all be worth it, just the relentless hammering of rain and wind. It felt like nature itself was daring me to quit, but there was no way I was going to let it get the better of me, especially so soon.

10

Getting in Step

We ventured out of the tent at 6 a.m. and, although it was still raining, the sky had calmed and shafts of light began to punch through the clouds, illuminating the huge puddles.

Just as I was contemplating what on earth we were going to do about our soggy situation, two ladies who'd been following Chris's journey on Facebook pulled up in their car. Knowing we'd been weathering the storm in a tent all night, they'd got up early to try to meet us along the coast armed with woolly jumpers to help keep us warm and dry. They'd got a rough idea of where we might be from a video Chris had posted during the night – I couldn't believe people had dragged themselves out of bed this early to come and check we were okay. We said a big thank you to the two ladies, Ann and Elaine, along with Elaine's little chihuahua, Rosie. The warmth of the woolly jumpers was such a relief and they'd even brought a towel with which to rub down Jet, and some hot soup that they gave us before offering to let us sit in the car to help warm up.

We were told the local farmer, Bill, owned the nearby cottages, which he rented out, and before we knew it, there he was. He took one look at the state of us and offered us the use of one of the cottages to shower and dry off. By the time we emerged, another lady had already arrived and loaded our Bergens (backpacks developed by the British military, named after Bergen in Norway, that servicemen use to carry essential gear and supplies) into the back of her truck.

'You're coming with me – you can't stay out in this!' she said. 'It's absolutely freezing and you're drowned rats, the pair of you. We've got a caravan on our driveway and it's all ready to go. You can stay there for a few nights and enjoy a dry bed and some good home-cooked food.'

Her name was Di, she was ex-navy and she wasn't taking no for an answer! It was only 9 a.m. and already the morning had been an eye-opening introduction to this sort of incredible kindness from strangers. I was blown away. Di and her husband, Mike, and their children, Josie and Archer, welcomed us into their caravan for the next few nights. They invited us to join them for dinner in their home, wash and dry our kit, shower and enjoy the luxury of a warm bed in the caravan to ride out the spell of stormy weather. Then they'd drop us off at our next start point so we could carry on walking, and pick us up each night.

In order to maintain the walk's outdoor pursuit, and to raise awareness for the plight of homeless people, Chris made a point of never accepting a room in a house no matter how many times people offered. He'd accept any manner of outdoor-style accommodation offered – sheds, barns, garages, polytunnels, caravans – but never a house. In fact, it was one of the non-negotiables for us moving forward together. I was more than willing to find out how many strange and surprising outdoor spots I'd rack up as places to lay my head!

Staying at Di's, it became very apparent that we could no longer continue in the one-man tent. Chris had absolutely no money but refused to ever ask for anything. In his mind, it had been his choice to embark on this journey, so he didn't feel right asking for any kind of help to fund it, meaning there was no GoFundMe page or suchlike. He felt very strongly about this and remained absolutely steadfast no matter how many people tried to persuade him otherwise. I admired and agreed with his principles, but I did have some savings from my previous job and, for as long as they would last, I was happy to use them, so I splashed out on a new two-man MSR tent.

After thanking Di and family for their amazing hospitality, we pressed on with the walk. The plan was for Di to bring the new tent to us after it was delivered to their house. As we pushed on along the cliffs and through the last of the quaint little fishing villages, I thought about how much I'd enjoyed this stretch of Aberdeenshire coast. The four villages we passed through, Gardenstown, Crovie, Pennan and Rosehearty, had so much individual charm and history, each embodying the timeless rhythm of traditional life by the sea.

By the time we reached Rattray Head Lighthouse a few days later, we still only had the one-man tent. When we awoke, a sandstorm had rolled in. We tried to walk along the beach but fierce gusts whipped sand into our eyes, stinging our skin and making it hard to see. We were very conscious of Jet, lower to the ground, who looked particularly uncomfortable – if only we'd had a pair of Muttley-style sand goggles for her! But alas, it was impossible to move on. All we could do was spend the day hunkered down in the tent, waiting for the winds to ease. Given it was now December, I suggested we hang the battery-operated fairy lights we'd been given to bring a touch of Christmas magic to our tent and lighten the mood. It was no easy thing for the three of us to sit so cramped in that tiny tent all day, so by mid-afternoon, Chris and I took it in turn to brace the gusts and stretch our legs while the other stayed in the tent to keep Jet company.

I jogged up and down the sand dunes, watching the waves smash high against the lighthouse, and ran towards the retreating sea, the waves chasing me back, threatening to soak my feet. I turned and watched in awe as the moody theatre of the North Sea vented its anger. Despite it being a challenging day, I felt so alive embracing the raw energy of the coast that it has actually become a cherished memory for me. After all, this was a big part of what I wanted from this adventure – the unvarnished reality of living in the wild, learning to withstand the elements and harness them as Chris had. The real, unfiltered experience, complete with all of its hardships.

By now, after just over a week of walking, I could sense that, while Chris was excited to have me join him, he was also struggling with the shift in dynamic. I think the biggest change for him was simply the added noise of another person. For years, it had just been Chris and Jet, and for the past two and a half, they'd been walking through the remote wilds of Scotland, where peace, silence and solitude had shaped their entire experience. Now, the presence of another voice disrupted that calm, and it was understandably a bit disorientating for him. Chris also had a very set routine which I was now a part of: we'd get up early, make a coffee and bowl of porridge on the gas stove, assess the weather and the maps to check the route for the day, pack up as quickly as we could, particularly to save Jet from getting cold while she waited, and get on with walking. I was very keen to learn, but at this point was probably a bit more gung-ho and nonchalant about just how much needed to be taken into account while walking: constant risk assessments, scanning ahead, scouting out alternative routes, reading incoming weather, assessing the landscape for driftwood or materials that could be foraged for a fire. After years of practice, all of this was daily habit for Chris. I'd sensed slight hints of frustration in those moments where we'd had different views about which route to take, where to pitch the tent, what to cook or how we'd divide the daily tasks that needed to be carried out.

People so often assume that walking was the hardest part of the journey. And while trekking all day was exhausting, for most people that's when they'd go home, have a hot shower, cook food in a functioning oven and get a good night's sleep. But, for us, the real work began once we stopped. We had to find food and water, pitch the tent, feed and warm Jet (we would stock up on food for her whenever we found a shop, much like we did our own, and carry it). We'd forage for driftwood, get the fire going, prep food and cook, all of which amounted to hours. And we weren't just doing this for a few days or even a few weeks, having to cope temporarily, knowing we'd return to the warmth and familiarity of a home – we were doing this day in, day out, for the long haul. The permanence of this for us meant no let-up. No matter how drained we were, we'd always take time to update social media to keep fundraising – usually hiking up hills just to find a signal.

It was hard to stay in regular touch with friends and family as the signal was often intermittent and our battery power was very limited, especially after we'd got our social-media posts out, but they were very understanding and knew we'd get in touch when we could. I was always slightly concerned about my mum's health, but she was adamant that neither my brother nor I should ever sacrifice our own lives to care for her, and at this point any deterioration was still a long way off. She was managing, and I would check in whenever I could. I also set both my parents up on Facebook so they could follow the journey. This really helped give them peace of mind as they could watch from afar and get an idea of where I was and what was happening even when I wasn't able to explicitly tell them myself. It also really helped to sway their opinions about my decision to join the walk. Reading the comments from followers who mentioned time and time again how much this walk was helping them through a personally difficult time made them realize there was far more to this than me just running off with a homeless man in a tent – people were drawing a lot of strength and inspiration from what we were doing and there was a much bigger picture here than simply two people wanting a taste of a life less ordinary.

Compromise wasn't something Chris was used to, nor did he particularly enjoy it. It was a huge change for him. This walk had been his solitary journey, shaped entirely by his own choices; as he saw it, for the first time in his life, by listening to his own intuition and not feeling clouded or influenced by the opinions of others, he had found his feet and made a success of it against all the odds. He had become used to doing things solely his way, used to the predictability of his own company and used to relying on no one but himself with no one to answer to but his always obliging, agreeable and devoted Jet.

Then, suddenly, I was there. This new variable in the harmonious balance he had created. A woman with a strong personality and a voice of her own, who wanted to feel heard and involved in her new life. I knew I was stepping into something that had already been in motion for years and I was very aware I was the newcomer, the outsider, joining *his* adventure. I didn't want to disrupt that healing sense of peace he had found but, at the same time, I wanted to feel like it was a partnership now, a joint endeavour. It was very tricky to navigate. Chris and Jet were the experts and I was the apprentice. I realized that finding my place here wasn't just about being able to carry heavy weight, walk all day and survive in a tent at night, it was about gradually becoming an equal and being seen as one, in an already well-oiled and tightly knit team. The physical demands of joining in winter were challenging enough, but it was made all the more so by the fact that we were both finding our feet in a very new relationship under the most unguarded, stripped-back and intense of circumstances. It was a lot of pressure on a nascent relationship. I needed to lean on him but I also wanted to stand on my own two feet. I needed to learn but also prove that I was capable. I needed to follow but also hoped I would eventually share in being able to lead the way myself.

Yes, it was his walk, but, step by step, I needed him to see that it had become mine too.

We awoke the next day to surprisingly calm skies and the most beautiful sunrise. Looking at this white lighthouse that yesterday had stood so resilient against the elements, with waves smashing high against its walls, it was hard to believe it now looked so peaceful, bathed in the pastel pink of dawn.

Over the next two days, with a night sleeping on wooden benches in a very rocky boat in Peterhead harbour, we made our way to New Slains Castle, at which point our new tent finally arrived! The atmosphere couldn't have been more fitting. The sun began its descent, soon morphing into a huge yellow orb illuminating the ghostly ruins of the castle. As we drew ever closer, the castle became a dramatic silhouette, a reminder of the eerie, supernatural stories it held within its crumbling walls, providing inspiration for Bram Stoker's novels, including *Dracula*.

I was so excited to pitch within its walls and have the castle grounds all to ourselves to explore at night, surrounded by the dramatic crashing of white waves against the sheer cliffs. That night, we explored the derelict labyrinth of corridors, then climbed to the top floor in the dark and stood under the stars, the low moon mainly hidden but occasionally sailing through grey misty clouds. We peered out of one of the long, slit windows, watching the sea roar below. It felt like we were standing on the edge of the world within this spooky relic.

There was no doubt about it, my first week had been a real baptism of fire. It had felt like some sort of cruel initiation ceremony such as I'd seen done to the newest rugby recruits at university; only in my case masterminded by the Scottish weather. As though it were slapping me on the back and sending me on my way with a 'Welcome to your new life – good luck!' I knew I could call it quits at any time if I wanted to, but that wasn't in my nature. I had made a commitment to Chris and to the walk, but most importantly to myself. This was my new reality, and the future was both thrilling and nerve-wracking. I realized that this wasn't just a walk – it was a leap of faith into the unknown and I had dived in head first. But, if these first experiences were anything to go by, I was in for one hell of an adventure.

11

Lockdown in the Woods

We spent a few nights camped up in the grounds of New Slains Castle, only to discover a second Covid lockdown was being imposed! We found out thanks to a follower who'd come up to see us the night before at the tent. They turned up again the next morning with news of the latest lockdown announcement, which would come into full force on Boxing Day. Chris had spent the last lockdown, between mid-March and July, marooned with Jet on the uninhabited island of Hildasay, off the west coast of Shetland. Being essentially homeless meant that, when the lockdown was imposed, he'd had nowhere to return to, so a fisherman he'd met on Shetland, called Victor, offered to take him and Jet to Hildasay on his fishing boat to wait it out. Victor would return when weather allowed to drop off food and fresh water, and in the meantime Chris learned to catch crab and lobster from the sea and to survive off the land.

Despite his reservations that being stuck in one place for a prolonged period of time again might bring old ghosts back to haunt him, it turned out to be a transformational experience for him. He'd spent his days foraging for seafood, watching wildlife (sheep, rabbits and birds – he always describes Hildasay in spring as being like a bird sanctuary), making fires and cooking outdoors (he made four outdoor ovens in the corners of the island to cater for all wind directions), and revelling in the beautiful sunsets while Jet raced around. He also worked out every day using rocks as weights and even did extra challenges to help boost his fundraising, such as tying a rope around his waist and lugging 50-litre barrels of water behind him as he ran around the island for as long as it took to reach a certain target. There was even an occasion when a helicopter did a fly-by and landed on the island to present him with a special badge in honour of his efforts.

On Hildasay, he came to realize that the walk wasn't just a temporary plaster over his wounds; he really had found a renewed sense of happiness, purpose and pride within himself. As we were to have a second lockdown, I was in absolute agreement that we should stay living outdoors, as he had done on Hildasay – and so we went about finding a way to deal with this lockdown in the wild.

We pored over the maps and decided that a patch of woodland only a few hundred yards from the coastline between Gourdon and Johnshaven would be our best bet to set up a lockdown camp. The two villages meant we had access to supplies just a few miles' walk away, the woodland would provide plenty of fallen logs for fires to keep us warm and there was a phone signal.

Up in Scotland, the lockdown came into force from midnight on Boxing Day, meaning we had a few days to find our spot, set up camp and get organized for the foreseeable future. Before it came into force, we decided to spend Christmas Eve sleeping rough on the streets of Aberdeen to help raise awareness for the homeless. As we nestled into our sleeping bags for a night under the ornate historical landmark of Mercat Cross in

Castlegate Square, I knew it was going to be a long, cold night ahead, but joining Chris in this endeavour was important to me because I understood the significance it held for him. I shared his deep desire to do what I could to raise awareness for those who face such hardship on a daily basis, often for years, feeling like they have no way out. I was lucky enough to have a very sheltered upbringing and, while I'd seen extreme poverty and harsh realities on my travels, the reality of homelessness in the UK, particularly at night-time when the streets are dark, empty and lonely, was a world I fortunately had never experienced. Doing this was a window into that world for me and allowed me to shine a light on homelessness in a way that might help.

I'd never spent Christmas away from home before. That night was a stark contrast to the warmth of a Christmas Eve around a fire, the twinkling lights of a tree guarding presents, and there was no shaking off how vulnerable I felt lying there. My dad had initially been upset with me for deciding not to go home and be with my mum over Christmas, given her circumstances, and it had been a difficult choice, but I knew my mum had other family members to share the day with and I felt like, having just joined the walk, I needed to be all in. Throughout the night, Chris posted on his Facebook page, about our experience as well as homelessness statistics, particularly relating to veterans. With his growing presence on social media, he had a powerful platform from which to do good in the world.

The next morning, we dragged our stiff, thawing bodies back down to the coast, where we were met with the slow unfurling of a blackberry dawn. I stood and gazed at it in awe for what felt like hours; I had never seen such an intense sunrise before. The purple turned crimson and softened to a warm pink-orange that sprawled behind the dappled clouds. It felt as if the sky was handing us a hot chocolate with marshmallows to warm us up after a night on the cold, hard concrete of the Granite City. To this day, it remains the best sunrise I have ever seen in my life, and it wasn't in Bali or the Maldives or a Caribbean Island – it was in Aberdeen, of all places. It was the perfect way to welcome Christmas Day, and the best Christmas present I could have received.

By the time we got back to the woods, we were absolutely exhausted. It was too late in the day to attempt a bushcraft Christmas dinner, so we put it on hold for a few days. Chris had learned a lot about cooking outside over the years, so I couldn't wait to learn from him as we knocked up our Wilderness Christmas Dinner Extravaganza! Two children from a local family had even dropped off painted clay ornaments they had made to help decorate the Christmas tree we'd found for extra festive spirit.

We spent the next two days lugging supplies down to the woods, constructing a spit using fallen logs and branches tied together with twine, as well as preparing underground ovens. By the time it was dark on the second day, we had a roast chicken cooked on a spit alongside a honey-glazed ham, roast potatoes and roasted vegetables, all cooked in a Dakota oven. (These are underground cooking fires with a second hole for airflow; they work well in windy conditions, use less wood thanks to efficient burning, produce less smoke and are less visible than above-ground wood fires.) It definitely took a lot of time and effort to set up, and the food got cold within seconds, but as we sat by the fire, tucking into our hard-earned meal, I swear no Christmas dinner had ever tasted so good! For afters, I decorated Chris's beard with baubles for a touch of extra festive spirit and made him play my own take on Snakes and Ladders, which I'd made from a cut-up piece of roll mat scribbled on with biro. It was my first Christmas on the walk, my first Christmas dinner cooked on a fire outdoors and my first Christmas with Chris and Jet. It was such an eye-opener into how dramatically different my life now was, but I couldn't have asked for a better day!

My home now a tent, I found myself confronting a raw, unrelenting cold unlike anything I'd ever experienced. It was the coldest winter in Aberdeenshire in twenty-five years, with temperatures plummeting to -17°C by February and Storm Darcy bringing an extra blast of intense cold and snow our way. Keeping warm became a daily ritual, one that required hours of work and planning. We both agreed it was essential to stay busy, both to keep warm physically and to lift our spirits mentally. Mornings were mostly spent gathering firewood. We only ever used fallen wood, of which there was plenty, given the time of year, but collecting enough to cook and keep warm into the night took a lot of work. We had to collect enough of each type – kindling, mid-sized sticks, and logs for the fire to take hold and to keep blazing well into the night. Chris also trekked miles to go and haul heavy bags of coal down the track to our camp from the roadside, where a lovely lady called Sarah would drop them in a black bin for us to burn. A daily fire had essentially become our lifeline and it was fascinating for me to learn from someone who had spent years perfecting the art of harnessing fire in all weathers. Chris taught me how to make fires in wet weather, which logs were too wet to use, techniques for getting it started and how best to dry damp logs quickly so that they could be used when needed. These were the kind of survival skills I'd been excited to learn, and our little woodland was becoming my outdoor classroom as well as my new home.

We also found plenty of other ways to keep ourselves busy, such as sprinting around a field with Jet and doing exercise drills, though they inevitably ended with me losing a sit-up challenge, much to Chris's delight. To keep things fun, I created the Lockdown Lotto – a game to inject some creativity into our days. I tore up scraps of paper, scribbled down a mix of completely random challenges and stuffed them into a Tupperware tub. Each morning, we'd take turns plunging in like a pick 'n' mix, the results ranging, for example, from *'Create an effigy of the other person using only natural materials'* to *'Sculpt Jet out of anything you can find'*, *'Build an obstacle course'* and *'Perform a dance-off by the fire'*.

I completely gave up on wearing make-up; I would sometimes wash my hair in the sea and, against my better judgement, even let Chris cut it with a pair of craft scissors. Given that I had no mirror, all I could do was sit there helplessly as the power went to his head – I could just tell he was itching to hack away and snip me into something resembling an electrified squirrel! After this, I decided to experiment – I'd heard that, if you leave hair unwashed long enough, it eventually cleans itself. I'd always had very fine hair which got greasy quickly, and, to avoid looking like I'd stuck my head in a chip pan, it ideally needed washing at least every other day. I figured this was my opportunity to finally test the theory. I gave it five months and can testify that, for me at least, it didn't work!

There was a small convenience store in the local village where we could buy supplies and a Co-op further along the coast in Inverbervie. We were also incredibly lucky to have the support of Diana, a kind-hearted woman from Inverbervie who ran a food bank. Every week, she put together a big basket of supplies to help sustain us, and it was so cold that any meat was easy for us to store for a few days without a fridge. Breakfast was always porridge with some dried nuts or fruit if we had any left, and bacon cooked over the fire, for a treat! Hanging an iron pot over an A-frame, we would mainly cook hearty stews each night. I would often sit there in the afternoon for an hour or so chopping vegetables as my hands went numb, usually carrots, parsnips, potatoes and broccoli (or whatever was on offer), which would go in the pot along with some stock, boiled water and chunks of meat if we had any. That seemed to warm our bones and fill us up most nights better than anything else. I'd have loved to have learned more about foraging in the woods while we were there, but it's very season dependent; there was next to no wild food available, given it was mid-winter, particularly with the extreme cold blast we were experiencing, and certainly not enough to sustain us.

There was a lovely retired dinner lady in Johnshaven who would also leave home-made soup and cake for us, and occasionally locals would come down to drop off the odd bottle of beer. A man we became friendly with, Dan, an American who had moved to the area and was now teaching outdoor pursuits at a local school, was also a huge help. More than once, he showed up with fillets of salmon and litres of bottled water for us. As a thank you, Chris gave him one of his treasured buffs – versatile head and neck warmers – printed with 'Jet' and a few paw prints. I could see Dan was genuinely taken aback by the gesture and it was clearly a gift he would treasure. By this point, my savings were almost gone, so we had very little to live off. However, the local community really rallied together to help us over that period. There were certainly times when we felt we could murder an Indian takeaway washed down with a nice bottle of red, but we couldn't complain – we were grateful to be able to eat each day, and for us that was enough.

By mid-January, I found myself balancing two realities in a way that felt increasingly impossible. I was still tied into a year-long contract with Oak Academy, following up on the educational videos I'd created during the first lockdown. This meant tweaking recordings based on feedback, making professional development videos for new teachers, and showing up for meetings – all while living in the wild.

One particular evening, I found myself on a Zoom call at 5 p.m., using my phone's 4G for internet, sitting in complete darkness, head torch strapped on, and bundled in every layer I had. My hands and toes were numb, but there I was, trying to hold focus in an hour-long meeting, with everyone else safe and warm in their living rooms, chuckling at the sight of me camped out in the woods. It was surreal, like I was straddling two completely different worlds; a strange in-between space that wasn't quite my old world but not fully my new one. I also had online training dates set up and was still pushing ahead with the Global Citizenship textbook I'd been working on intermittently over the past few months. But the more I tried to keep up, the more I realized this split life wasn't sustainable.

When I first joined the walk, I thought I would be able to juggle this work to see it through, maintain my career connections and support us financially, but it became clear that this walk was all-consuming and demanded my full focus. There was no way to flit between it and my professional commitments, and with Chris by my side I knew where my heart lay – something had to give. I finished my textbook, wrapped up my videos, and honoured as many commitments as I could. After some hard thinking, I called my manager to explain the extent to which my reality had changed. The walk needed my all. Letting go of those last professional ties felt dauntingly final, but I knew that, if I was going to complete the walk with Chris, I had to be all in. I'd already sacrificed so much to leave my old life behind. It was hard to do, but not once did I think I was making a mistake; I was dedicated to this path.

To keep warm we also dived into a new project: building a shelter using a method called cob walling, a technique dating back to the Iron Age. First, we scouted the woods for logs sturdy enough to withstand the elements, then dragged them back to camp and stacked them. Between each layer, we packed thick clumps of mud, using it as a binding agent to create walls that felt both strong and secure. The mud was icy cold, and my hands would go numb as I packed it down, pressing it between the logs until the structure took shape. Inside, we dug a firepit, so we'd have a place to cook out of the rain when storms swept through. For storage, we built a small, covered unit at the back of the shelter to keep our food protected and accessible.

Finally, we stretched a massive tarp that we'd borrowed from a local fireman over the shelter to create a makeshift roof. When we lit a fire inside, we could fold back part of the tarp to let the smoke out, while still keeping the majority of the shelter warm and protected. Little by little, the shelter became our winter home, a place that offered some reprieve from the elements outdoors.

During the day, we'd only really use it as a refuge we could stand up in during bad weather, otherwise we would be out and about in the woods or by the coast. It was at night when we used the shelter most. We'd sit around the firepit playing repeated games of handball or makeshift board games I invented. More often than not, we'd sing while Chris played a guitar that a local school teacher had kindly lent him, sometimes belting out eighties classics until the early hours with not a soul within earshot to hear the racket! It was incredibly freeing.

We completed the shelter just in time for Valentine's Day, after a month of non-stop work. As I contemplated the finished result, I was so proud of our efforts. The shelter felt like more than just a bit of extra space in which to keep dry: it was our haven, a testament to our teamwork, resourcefulness and creative spirit. That night, as if on cue, it began to snow for the first time that winter. As snowfall drifted slowly through the dark, the shelter lit up by the warm glow of the outdoor fire and candles nestled in ivy-draped logs, our woodland home looked so magical. It was one of my favourite memories from that time – a romantic, snow-dusted escape in our little pocket of the woods.

12

By Some Fiendish Stroke of Luck

The cliff edges steepened as we trekked the last few miles towards Old Slains Castle, and I really started to struggle with the weight of my Bergen. So much so that eventually we had to stop so Chris could carry it on his front, along with his own on his back. I was mortified. This was our first leg of the walk now lockdown had been lifted, and I felt I'd failed at the first test, despite my efforts to keep fit. I was furious at myself for burdening Chris with my extra weight. He was a gentleman about it, but I vowed it wouldn't happen again. If that meant fitness drills by the tent, so be it.

By now, it was the start of April 2021. We had hoped to ease back into the walk against a backdrop of warm spring sunshine, but Scotland had other ideas. Relentlessly strong winds made the narrow cliffside stretches especially treacherous. With the weight of my Bergen on for the first time in months, I found myself wobbling at times, focusing hard on each step.

By the time we set up camp in the bay beneath the ruined remains of Old Slains Castle, I was shattered, though I suspected Chris was even more so.

The next morning was Easter Sunday. It was snowing and so blustery that we grabbed our gear and climbed to the top of the cliffs in search of shelter – at least a wall to block the wind while we cooked breakfast. Next to the ruins, we stumbled upon a derelict house. Chris had found plenty of these along the journey, but, for me, it was a first. We climbed in through a broken window, and inside it felt eerily apocalyptic – dusty books by the fireplace, a teapot still on the side, a pan left on the stove, as though someone had just left in a hurry. I explored the place with a real thrill and it soon became the setting for our Easter Sunday feast – porridge, dried fruit and that all-important coffee!

The next day, the winds were wilder still, with bursts of hail hammering down. I ventured out regardless to explore Old Slains Castle, destroyed in 1594 by King James VI after its owner was implicated in a plot to secure Spanish military support for an uprising against the Protestant king. Meanwhile, Chris tested the conditions at the clifftops and made the call: it was too dangerous to continue along the exposed paths. 'I haven't got this far by taking unnecessary chances,' he said.

We were forced to take an inland route into Collieston, where we pitched up by the harbour cliffs and locals soon brought supplies and checked if we needed anything. That night, we were eventually persuaded to seek respite from the blizzards and sleep in a motorhome on a couple's driveway. The kindness of Scottish hospitality continued to bowl me over. The next day, we left our bags at base to walk back and cover the missed section of the coast.

Before we left, Chris, having already endured multiple snowy winters on the walk, gave me a bit of a talking-to about safety. We had no crampons and we'd be walking on the coastal side of a barbed-wire fence, with no more than two metres between us and a sheer drop into the sea. He wasn't worried about Jet;

after everything she and Chris had been through together, she was practically a winter-adapted mountain goat. Me, on the other hand? I was still more of an unknown quantity.

Chris found it hard to shoulder that extra weight of responsibility for me. I often felt he was overprotective and assured him I'd be fine, there was nothing to worry about. Knee-deep in snow at times, we moved carefully but quickly between erratic blizzards, the waves smashing the cliffs far beneath us in thunderous roars.

Mindful of the huge drop, I stepped into Chris's footprints to make walking safer and fall into a rhythm. It couldn't have been more than a few minutes later when my attention – if only for a second – faltered. And that's when I slipped. Suddenly my world tilted as I fell sideways, my heart in my mouth. Without thinking, my arms flailed as I attempted to reach out for the barbed-wire fence and missed.

So this is how I meet my end.

As I continued to fall, the smooth fabric of my waterproof trousers acted as a sledge and I started to gain momentum! I let out a sharp cry, which grabbed Chris's attention; he turned and looked at me with desperate horror, knowing that I was out of his reach. But, by some fiendish stroke of luck, the ground beneath me levelled out slightly before it suddenly steepened into a sheer drop to the sea below, and I ground to a halt. Chris dived forwards, grabbing my hands, dug his boots deep into the snow and pulled me to safety. We sat together, Chris's arms wrapped tight around me. It had all happened so quickly! Just like that, I had very narrowly missed sliding right off the edge of a sea cliff.

'Blimey, babe, I'm going to have to tie you to me by rope from now on!' he said, chuckling nervously. 'Come on, let's sit down by the fence and take five.'

Chris seemed quite annoyed with me, which was probably

because he felt he would be responsible if anything were to happen to me. As we continued walking, he made me walk in front so he could see me. 'I think I'd rather have thrown myself off that cliff after you than have to tell your parents,' he shouted against the wind. 'Now, please, don't ever make me face that prospect again!'

We both laughed. It was my first close encounter on the walk. We may not have been skiing through the Arctic or canoeing down the Amazon, but, at the constant mercy of the elements, there was a definite danger in walking so close to the cliff's edge.

Every year on the walk, Chris made himself a promise that, no matter where he was, the first day the sun had enough warmth to actually feel it on his skin after months of brutal winter would be a rest day. A little reward for making it through another winter. The first year I joined him was no exception. As we walked from Newtonhill to Dunnottar Castle, the sun finally emerged from behind the clouds and I will never forget the feeling of that first warm day for as long as I live. Of being able to lie down outside without being buried in a sleeping bag, with no urgency to pack up and move just to keep warm. Together, we made a pact that we would continue this tradition for the rest of our lives. For us, this was the first true day of spring.

Being able to take our time in those early spring days made me reflect on the truism that a journey is so much more than just the destination. Yes, we had a finish line to aim for, with borders and key cities as milestones along the way. But I realized that focusing too much on pushing forward can rush a journey that's really about the day-to-day experience. In many ways, we already embraced this mindset. Each morning, we'd set off with a rough idea of where we wanted to end up, but that goal was never fixed – we let it shift. We lingered when a place felt right, rested when we needed to and adjusted depending on supplies. Sometimes, I felt the urge to push harder, to go further, knowing my body had settled back into the rhythm of walking. But then I'd ask myself – why?

In the end, it wasn't really about getting somewhere. Rushing to the end was pointless – neither of us were in this for breaking records, and rushing wouldn't help us raise more money for SSAFA. It was about being where we were – exploring the landscape, enjoying each other's company, meeting new people, getting the word out there for the charity. Those were the moments that stuck. That's what made the journey memorable.

13

Shellshock

The street was heaving with people. We stopped in our tracks, totally taken aback. We had forgotten that it was Bank Holiday Monday and that bars and pubs were open for business after lockdown for the first time. People were desperate for a big night out after months indoors, and they'd gathered in their dozens on the pavements and in the road to make sure they got one. Had we known this was what venturing into Dundee would be like – our next big leg, not long after we'd spent time camping in an absolute gem of a spot tucked into a bay right beneath Dunnottar Castle – I think we might have tried to find a way around it.

This was the first time in about six months I'd seen this many people in one place, and for Chris it was the first time in years. As we pushed our way down the street, I glanced over at him and saw how bewildered he looked and how much he wanted to get out of there. After so long in the wilderness, the sudden chaos of the city hit Chris hard – it was such a stark contrast to the remote life we'd been living. Meanwhile, poor Jet was jumping out of her skin every time a lorry thundered past.

WILDERNESS MUM

Dundee was a city I knew well from my university days at nearby St Andrews. Here I was, back in a place I'd spent time partying in my late teens and early twenties, my first years away from home, and now returning with a man to whom I was deeply committed. Memories of nights out at Fat Sam's nightclub, packed onto a bus full of St Andrews students, hoping but often failing to make it back at the end of the night, came flooding back. Then there was Radio 1's Big Weekend, where we blagged backstage passes thanks to our extra-curricular gigs at Star FM, St Andrews' student radio. And, in one of my more questionable life choices, I once spent a night at Gala Bingo with my flatmate just before graduation – our attempt at some *Gavin and Stacey*-style comedy gold. 'Down on your knees, forty-three!'

By contrast, Dundee was a living nightmare for Chris. Too many people, too much noise and chaos. In fact, it was only a few weeks later, when he showed me photographs of what he'd looked like before he started the walk, that I truly appreciated the impact that being back in a city had had on him. I couldn't believe it was the same man in the photograph; he looked so gaunt and withdrawn – almost skeletal, with no life behind his eyes. It was plainly evident just how far he'd come since he'd escaped his old life and embraced wilderness living – the man standing before me now couldn't be more different.

Dundee forced me and Chris to make a decision: instead of crossing road bridges, we'd walk the full length of the Tay Estuary through Perth, and later do the same at Stirling. Walking the estuaries was going above and beyond, but, in our minds, following the coastline meant sticking beside the sea until it became a river. And if we were doing that, we might as well walk the entire length of these estuaries, bagging ourselves some time in more populated areas to help spread the word about SSAFA. It added hundreds of miles and weeks of extra walking, but we were determined not to cut any corners. So off we went, following the tidal riverbanks of the silvery Tay.

By now it was May – and unfortunately for us it turned out to be one of the wettest on record. Honestly, for those first three weeks, I think it poured almost every single day. Between having no way to dry out our clothes and pitching and putting away the tent in pouring rain for days and weeks on end, we were having to work harder than ever to keep our spirits up.

By the time we reached the Bridge of Earn after coming through Perth, we and all of our kit were completely soaked through. We were so grateful to meet a couple called Heather and Reid, who ran the 14th Perthshire Scout Group and kindly put us up in their scout hut. To our delight, they also opened up both the store cupboard and the kitchen, giving us a chance to dry off, warm up and entertain ourselves for the evening. First, we attempted a game of tennis against the wall, though with only one racquet we had to improvise, taking turns using a saucepan lid instead. Then Chris had another bright idea – he thought it might be fun to teach me how to box. True to form, I went all in and Chris ended up sporting a black eye!

The timing was terrible, because the next day we had filming scheduled with ITV's *This Morning* show. Jet was set to appear on a segment called 'F-u-r-i-e-n-d-s' with the show's resident vet, Dr Scott Miller, recognizing her extraordinary contribution and loyalty in supporting Chris on the walk, and in particular during the lockdowns. They managed to conceal Chris's shiner by cleverly filming him from one side – probably to avoid an influx of messages from concerned viewers wondering what on earth I was doing to him in the tent each night! Dr Scott was clearly taken with Jet and her story, and before leaving he gave us his number and told us, 'If you ever need me, just get in touch.' At the time we thought nothing of it – little did we know that the day would come when we'd take him up on his offer.

Scotland's Outdoor Access Code meant we'd faced very few restrictions when it came to wild camping, but as we began to move through more built-up areas, things were beginning to shift. Locked gates, fenced-off land and invisible boundary lines started creeping into our route, something Chris hadn't dealt with for years on the remote west coast and islands. It wasn't a major issue yet, but it was becoming clear that navigating through these areas was going to take a little more thought.

As we neared Newport-on-Tay, we needed to get back onto the coast to find a camp spot for the night. Spotting a wall, we climbed over, only to land in a huge, gated property with a winding driveway leading to a mansion. Aware we were on private property, we saw cars in the drive and decided to ring the doorbell, ready to explain ourselves and ask permission to slip through quietly. No one answered. After waiting a few minutes, we figured the owners were either out or otherwise engaged, so we went for it and started making our way across the grounds towards the coast. Clearly, someone had seen us on CCTV. Moments later, we heard voices and engines starting. Suddenly, a pair of Land Rovers began patrolling the grounds. When the track ended, people got out and began pursuing us on foot.

We looked at each other and ran. What followed was like something out of a comedy film, the two of us desperately trying to move stealthily fast through the trees, encumbered by our massive backpacks, pausing to duck down and hide quietly every now and then, listening for how close they might be. We were definitely at a disadvantage when it came to outrunning them! In the end, the voices died down and we managed to hop over a wall, diving into woodland along the coast. Out of sight, we found a perfect sheltered spot among the trees to pitch up for the night. It was a real taster of the fact that one of the trickiest parts of the journey wasn't just the weather, exhaustion, daily chores or sourcing supplies: it was land access.

As we completed the estuary, we joined the Fife Coastal Path. For Chris, having already walked for nearly four years by this stage, crossing county borders didn't mean much any more. But, for me, it came with a real sense of achievement. Heading towards the Tentsmuir National Nature Reserve, we spotted a sign attached to a fence post inviting us to pop by and see the local lighthouse up close, and even grab some freshly laid eggs and a drink. It was such a sweet gesture; how could we possibly resist?

Later that day, a bloke called James came to find us, offering to carry our bags for the rest of the day's walk – a luxury we weren't about to turn down! He even gave us supplies for a fish and potato stew, which we cooked that evening on the gas stove, having pitched up beside an old icehouse dating back to around 1852. It earned its name from its original purpose, storing ice collected from local ponds to preserve freshly caught salmon before it was shipped south. The ice was wrapped in heather or straw to insulate it, creating a basic but effective deep-freeze system. Now, though, it had a new purpose – it was home to a colony of Natterer's bats.

I was excited to reach St Andrews, a very picturesque coastal town about 30 miles north-east of Edinburgh: home of golf, haven of history and, above all, the site of my student years. I couldn't wait to give Chris the grand tour of what we affectionately called 'The Bubble' and show off all my old stomping grounds. As a student, St Andrews was a world of its own – tiny, with only three main streets, meaning you couldn't walk an inch without bumping into someone you knew for a chat. It also boasted what I'm fairly sure is the most expensive Tesco in the country and some brilliantly unique traditions, including Raisin Weekend, a sort of wild annual initiation ceremony in November where 'academic parents' took their adopted freshers under their wing, dressed them up in ridiculous outfits, plied them with far too much alcohol and then unleashed them into the town for a weekend of chaos, all culminating in a massive shaving-foam fight in St Salvator's Quad.

Then there was the May Dip: fires down by the beach on Castle Sands, followed by a dawn swim in the North Sea on the first day of the month. In my final year, I was determined to go the whole hog, swimming all the way out to the end of the pier and back. It was absolutely freezing, but I saw it through, with my friends ready with my towel to help dry me off when I emerged. Then, at graduation, I rounded it off with the traditional pier jump, because I simply couldn't wave goodbye to my student years here without that final icy plunge! The place was packed with memories, and the friends I made there nearly twenty years ago remained some of my closest. This would mark my first return since graduating in 2009, and I couldn't wait to take a trip down memory lane with Chris by my side.

We wild-camped on West Sands the first night, then were swept up by rangers the next day, telling us we'd have to move as the beach was owned by the St Andrews Links Trust. However, given what we were doing, we could pitch up in their garden hut, with the added bonus of being able to charge our battery packs! We spent the next two days touring the town and, I must say, it felt surreal to be back – not as a student, but as a trail-worn, wild-camping wanderer, with my bearded, kilted boyfriend in hole-ridden wetsuit boots and our beloved adventure dog alongside me.

Back in my uni days, my five-year degree was spent forging

a path towards the future – looking forward, planning, wondering where life would take me and gearing up for the job market. I never expected that, twelve years after graduating, I'd be returning on foot, halfway through a six-year walk around the UK coastline. If I'd told my younger self that, I think I'd have choked on my pint in The Central.

University is a time of major transition, whoever you are – the bridge between adolescence and becoming a self-sufficient adult in the 'real world'. Passing through St Andrews again made me reflect on transitions I hadn't anticipated. Some were practical: adapting to life in a tent, learning to live with only what I could carry, and waking up each day knowing we'd be on the move again. But others ran much deeper. Perhaps the most unexpected was what this journey was really transitioning into for me. When I set off, I had romanticized the raw, remote, rugged wilderness, and imagined this walk as a solitary, untamed adventure, shaped by the elements, the landscapes and the challenges of the wild. Yes, I'd had a good taste of that, but what I was discovering now was a different kind of purity, one not just found in nature, but in people. I began to realize that this journey wasn't just about the walking or the charity, it was about who we were meeting along the way. It was about the incredible unexpected kindness of strangers, the moments of human connection, the way people's generosity shaped our experience just as much as the land beneath our feet, and the fact that all of this goodwill was a constant reminder to maintain faith in the world.

Despite my high hopes, Chris did not enjoy the experience of being in St Andrews. To him, a place full of posh golfers and cashmere-clad university students was not his idea of a great day out. It felt a world apart from the one he knew, and he was craving being back in the wilderness.

It really hit me then how vastly different our educational

backgrounds were – we really were from two different worlds. Chris had been hit hard by his parents' break-up, he was very disengaged at school and never felt interested academically. He saw no purpose in learning things he thought he'd never use and, as a result, was placed in the bottom sets for everything, a path that eventually forced him to join the armed forces at sixteen – still just a boy. By eighteen, he was already in the Paras, training for combat.

I, on the other hand, had grown up loving school and, at sixteen, had earned ten straight As at GCSE, was taking on A levels and preparing for university applications. There was never any doubt that I was heading for higher education, with the aim of getting a good job – that was just intrinsic to my upbringing. Although my parents divorced shortly after I turned eighteen, I had grown up in a stable family home with plenty of guidance, and was always conscious of how hard my parents had worked and everything they'd sacrificed for my education. At eighteen, I was attending lectures, writing essays and partying, while Chris was parachuting out of aircraft, handling specialized weaponry and being deployed on dangerous missions overseas.

He simply couldn't relate to my university experience in the slightest. Our upbringings, educations and life trajectories had been polar opposites. And yet, here we were. Somehow, despite everything, our paths had crossed, and that seemed to make it all the more remarkable.

I did wonder at times whether our very different backgrounds would present themselves as an issue if we ever had children, but whenever we'd sat up late in the tent and talked about starting a family, our goals, dreams and values always felt very aligned. We both had visions of raising a child in a way that prioritized togetherness as a family as well as access to nature, adventure and experiences in the great outdoors. We also felt we really complemented each other well in terms of the different things each of us could bring to the table when it came to parenting. Whenever I saw Chris around children, it always made me smile. They were drawn to his warm and childlike playful energy; he had a commanding presence about him which made them listen, but he was also daring, compassionate and caring. I felt like he'd be a great combination of firm, fair and fun. I think what I loved most was that I felt he would be very hands-on; I saw how much he would get stuck into play, join in wholeheartedly and become a part of a child's world on their level.

I was very committed to Chris, and after six months in each other's company 24/7, the fact that we hadn't knocked each other out with a cooking pot proved that our relationship had strong legs! I'd often look at Chris and have a secret chuckle thinking that my future children might be fathered by this wild and untamed Viking-like figure, and, while it wasn't on the cards yet, I began to feel excited about the prospect of us one day starting a family together.

The rest of the 117-mile Fife Coastal Path was beautiful, winding through charming fishing villages like Crail, Pittenweem and Anstruther. I couldn't believe that, despite all my years living in Fife during uni, I had hardly explored any of it.

We camped up in various caves filled with ancient Pictish carvings, spent a night on a boat in Anstruther's harbour, slept on the floor of a sailing club and even tackled the Elie Chain Walk – a thrilling scramble along the cliffs, with metal chains to grip for safety. Making our way around the Firth of Forth, the landscape shifted again. Each morning, we unzipped the tent to superb views of the three iconic industrial bridges – the Forth Bridge, Forth Road Bridge and Queensferry Crossing – and before long we found ourselves camped on a beach with the lights of Edinburgh twinkling across the water.

WILDERNESS MUM

I could tell that Chris had been gearing up for this moment for a while. That night, after dinner, he stood up from the beach, waded fully dressed into the sea up to his waist and threw his arms triumphantly into the air. As I watched him, I cried. I could feel the weight of it. The magnitude of what this meant to him. Although we weren't quite at the border, reaching Edinburgh meant that Scotland – his biggest test up until that point in the walk – was finally in the bag.

I realized that none of us, myself included, would ever truly understand what it had taken for him to get here. For almost four years, he had stared at the map, wondering if he'd make it this far. Wondering if he had what it took to conquer the brutal west coast, the wild islands, the harshest of winters. Wondering if he would ever achieve what so many had said was impossible. Sticking to the coastline as no one else had before, including all the islands – as far as we knew, Chris had walked more of the UK coastline than anyone in history. We were nowhere near finished, but as I watched him, I saw a man standing there, euphoric, full of self-belief and hard-won achievement, with the confidence to know that he *would* finish this walk. I felt overwhelmingly proud of him.

Yet, at the same time, and this might sound strange, I knew that when we finally reached the finish line, it would be an extraordinary achievement for me, but a part of me would always wonder what it would feel like to have walked every single step of the way as Chris had done.

14

Piped Over the Border: Leaving Scotland

With Edinburgh conquered, we were on our final stretch of Scottish coastline and the reality of leaving was beginning to sink in. We were determined to savour every last moment. Thankfully, the North Berwickshire coastline did not disappoint!

As we moved south, we found ourselves slowing down, admiring every golden bay, hidden cove and dramatic clifftop view. It was now June, and, with the sun shining, the coastline felt vibrant and alive. Splashes of purple viper's bugloss flowers stood tall against the cliffs, their bright stems adding bursts of colour to the landscape.

It had now been seven months since I'd joined the walk, eight since I'd seen my mum, and over a year since I'd seen any close friends due to lockdown. Scotland was a long way for my mum to travel, my dad was living halfway around the world and my friends were all still largely in and around London. I knew I'd see more of them once we made it to England and were geographically closer. I'd ring friends now and then, while walking, for a catch-up, and we'd always have a good laugh as I told stories about my new life in the wild with my kilted

An emotional last day after ten years spent teaching in east London.
It felt like such a huge decision, but adventure was calling.

Trekking Mardi Himal in Nepal. I couldn't help but feel dwarfed by
these mighty peaks but, gazing down over that thick blanket of cloud,
it seemed like I was standing on top of the world.

Landing deep in the Colombian jungle. No baggage reclaim here –
just a horse hauling your luggage across a remote airstrip. My kind of place!

Watching the waves crash against the cliffs at the foot of the Whaligoe Steps.
I had no idea that my future was sitting right in front of me.

Our first date at the bothy in Eathie. Chris likes to title this picture 'Beauty and the Beast' – me being the beast! Did I say his humour was one of the things I love most about him?

Hiking around Band-e-Amir National Park, Afghanistan – one of my riskier trips, but there is so much beauty to be found there.

Very early on in the walk with Chris, I learned the harsh reality of what I'd signed up to. Only a few hours after this photo was taken, our tent would be flooded in the middle of a huge storm!

A freezing-cold Christmas Eve spent sleeping on the streets of Aberdeen, trying to raise awareness for the homeless.

Our home for the whole of the second Covid lockdown: the tent and a shelter we built from fallen logs in our woodland camp on the Aberdeenshire coast.

We spent a month building our shelter – extra space and warmth during a biting winter. A firepit for cooking, food stored in boxes stacked at the back and ivy-draped logs lit with candles. Home sweet home!

Walking through blizzards to fetch water. What I had once taken completely for granted now became a time-consuming, essential task for survival. Our days revolved around chores like this, but it also felt rewarding to work so physically hard for things.

Finally we were on the move again – after three and a half months spent freezing in one place, we were unleashed, moving forward and so ready for spring! I loved this spot: walking over the Needle's Eye on the clifftops of Arbroath, having camped just below the night before.

Wind, rain, sun or snow, all daily plans were made over our morning coffee. There was something really satisfying about enjoying a coffee from the tent, feeling so much a part of the landscape.

From the top of a hill in North Berwick, we could see England for the first time on the walk. A huge moment for us and a perfect camp spot for the night, waking up to wild ponies outside the tent.

Left: Pitched on a clifftop promontory at Cove with five-star views. It amazed me how quickly I adapted to tent life and came to see our little orange dome as home.

Below: The Three Musketeers: me, Jet and Chris, looking over to our next stretch of coastline. Although Jet appears to be distracted – she probably smelled a rabbit!

Above: The banner held by a cheering crowd of well-wishers who had gathered on the Humber Estuary as we walked towards Hull. The support on this journey was incredible, filling me with pride, warmth and so much gratitude.

After weeks sleeping on the ground due to a punctured roll mat, our 'hay-bale hotel' with two horses for company felt like pure luxury. It was here, on the day after my thirty-fifth birthday, that I found out I was pregnant.

coast-walker. Friends that used to be colleagues would fill me in on tales from the classroom and it astounded me how much of a world apart all that now felt.

Having a good laugh and a gossip with my friends over a glass of wine was what I missed the most – seeing their faces, experiencing their warmth, understanding and humour, hanging out in person rather than long distance over the phone. However, one of my closest friends, Verity, had fortuitously moved to Northumberland with her boyfriend during lockdown and was still living there. She was also about to have a baby. We'd be passing through that coastline very soon, and I was so excited at the prospect of seeing her in person at long last.

It was a hot stretch for Jet, so we made sure to stop often, dousing her with water to keep her cool. For a dog who spent all her time by the sea, she unfortunately refused to go in it (that's hounds for you!), but she let us soak her down before stretching out on the sand, completely content, basking in the warmth after another long, unforgiving winter.

We didn't know exactly how old Jet was; we guessed about nine by now. In the three and a half years she'd been with Chris, she'd walked thousands of miles along some of the wildest, most remote stretches of coastline, places where the notion of a path was non-existent. She'd sniffed out deer tracks on mountainsides, jumped countless fences and leapt across miles of peat bog. No mean feat for any dog, let alone one with an unknown history of hardship behind her. But Jet was made for this life. She had thrived here in Scotland, with the freedom to roam, the space to explore and the constant attention that Chris was able to give to her. There's no doubt she was leading the ultimate dog's life.

That said, after so long in the wild, where she was so clearly most at home, the growing number of towns and cities was starting to wear on her. She was also, inevitably, beginning to slow down with age; we were conscious that the summer heat might take its toll and we wanted to make sure she enjoyed the rest of this walk as much as she had up until now. I could see the growing concern for her in Chris, and for a few weeks we'd been making contingency plans, sketching designs for a buggy we could build to tow her if need be. We'd recently received a small payout for our time filming a documentary for the BBC, and we used some of it to order a buggy we could customize.

Yes, it was going to make things harder for us in places. There would be steep cliffs we couldn't tow it over, and stretches where it would have to be transported further down the coast. But if it made things easier for her, it was more than worth it. We very much doubted she would take to it straight away; after all, all she'd known was walking behind Chris. Nevertheless, we were excited to make it her own. We hoped that, once she realized it gave her a comfy ride when she wanted to rest, she'd come to love it. She'd given so much to this walk and she deserved to finish it.

One thing I can say with absolute certainty is that, when you spend every second of every day in the closest company of your dog – living together, walking together, sleeping cuddled-up together, facing every challenge side by side – that connection deepens into something beyond words. For the past seven months, I had been an observer of the unbreakable bond between Chris and Jet, a relationship so profound it almost felt telepathic. And just as Jet had been by his side through every hardship, every winter storm, every moment of doubt, she had also been there for me. Through every moment, every thought, every feeling, she was there. By now, I had walked thousands of miles with her, learning her quirks, understanding her moods, feeling her steady, loyal presence beside me. I had proven to her that I was here to stay and I knew that she now trusted and loved me, as I did her.

As we prepared to leave behind the wild open freedom of Scotland, I felt an ache in my chest, knowing that this chapter of our lives together would one day be something we'd look back on, rather than be living. And that thought made me want to hold onto every single moment while I still could.

Walking along Yellowcraig Beach felt almost surreal, like a UK version of the Hamptons, lined with millionaire mansions, most of them seemingly empty. Near the car park, the beach was crowded, but as we walked further, rounding the corner out of sight, it became completely deserted. We camped there, soaking in uninterrupted views of Fidra Island, Craigleith, the Lamb and Bass Rock, all part of a dramatic volcanic fault-line.

Bass Rock, a towering volcanic crag, has had many lives – first a seventh-century Christian retreat, later a fortified castle and then a brutal island prison, Scotland's very own Alcatraz. Now, it belongs solely to the wild, hailed by Sir David Attenborough as one of the twelve wildlife wonders of the world. Home to the largest colony of northern gannets on the planet, over 75,000 pairs nest here, turning the rock into a ghostly white monolith – stained from centuries of accumulated bird poo! We watched thousands of gannets wheel and dive with astonishing precision, plummeting into the sea like missiles.

I was also excited to be camping opposite Fidra, said to be the inspiration for Robert Louis Stevenson's *Treasure Island*. That evening, we waded out for a moonlit paddle, the cool water soothing our feet, seaweed massaging our soles as we gazed across at the silhouette of the island – not a bad evening's entertainment, certainly one to give Netflix a run for its money!

Talking of money, we were now living on an extremely tight budget. Foraging in the way Chris had learned to sustain himself previously wasn't so easy now that the landscape was no longer as wild. We certainly couldn't drink out of mountain burns (streams) using life straws any more, due to the run-off of chemicals and animal waste produced by farmland. We were having to buy and carry all of our water; now that it was summer, we needed around 15 litres for all three of us, which was an extra cost, not to mention huge extra weight! We were also moving on too quickly to get to know the land well enough to find out where its edible treasures lay. However, even though Chris was now sick to the back teeth of shellfish and could no longer stand the sight or smell of them, we occasionally pried limpets or whelks off the rocks to boil with some stock and rice, and edible seaweed from the shore to cook with a pasta sauce.

I'd recently been paid a few hundred pounds for finishing the textbook project in lockdown, but, other than that, it was the kindness of strangers that sustained us. Every so often, people would come out to find us on the coast path and hand us a bank note, insisting that the money was for us to keep going, rather than a donation for the charity. We often woke up to messages from people offering to shout us lunch in a cafe or a bacon roll for breakfast. People would often come and find us in the tent in the evening with a hot meal or leave a carrier bag of goodies outside in the night for us to find in the morning. The kindness of strangers on the walk was absolutely phenomenal and we always said they were the ones putting fuel in the engine to keep us going.

The next evening, we decided to go the extra mile or two and climb to the top of North Berwick Law to camp for the night. When it came to trekking all the way up a hill like this, the reward needed to be worth the additional effort, and in this case it certainly was! From the top, we had a breathtaking 360-degree view of the coastline, the islands dotting the horizon, and the sun casting golden light over the Firth of Forth.

In the morning, we pulled open the tent flaps at 4 a.m. to an incredible sunrise, with wild ponies right on our doorstep – most definitely a five-star view!

WILDERNESS MUM

After visiting a school the next day to give a talk in assembly about our walk, we pushed on past Seacliff Harbour, the smallest working harbour in the UK, with just one boat moored inside. Blasted out of the rock in 1890 by the local estate owner using a steam engine and compressed air, with an entrance of just two metres wide, it sits tucked into the coastline like a hidden secret. There, we met Tommy, a local farmer whose family had worked this land since 1834. Overlooking the harbour, he treated us to a lobster lunch on the rocks, sharing stories of the area and passing on a few tips for navigating the upcoming farmland along the coast.

For me, this was one of the most stunning stretches to date, with bay after bay of yellow sands and clear turquoise waters amid all sorts of dramatic rock formations and towering sea cliffs. We had an eventful afternoon once the tide came in and cut us off from the beach, and the coastal path became too overgrown or ran dangerously close to the cliff edge. With no other option, we forged our way through wilder terrain, scrambling up cliffs, pushing through dense vegetation, grabbing onto whatever we could (which, more often than not, was just nettles!), ducking under electric fences and clambering over wooden ones. Eventually we emerged at yet another unforgettable wild camp beneath the crumbling remains of Tantallon Castle, perched dramatically on the cliff edge.

With no one else around, we spent the evening sunbathing before I plunged into the sea for a naked wild swim. It was icy, exhilarating and exactly what I needed after almost four weeks of walking without a rest day. Given I'd lived and worked in London, wild swimming had been a real rarity in my life pre-walk. For Chris, it had become a prominent feature of his lifestyle, always bathing in freshwater lochs and mountain burns on the west coast. Here on the east coast, we could only use the sea, but I embraced it alongside him whenever we found ourselves completely alone. It was a way to freshen up, soothe tired muscles, feel even more connected with the landscapes we passed through and, most importantly for us, a way to wash. The sea was our bathtub and we took advantage of the opportunity whenever we could. It felt like an act of freedom, one I knew would soon be off the table. England was drawing closer and, with it, busier coastlines, fewer places to disappear into the wilderness and much stricter rules when it came to exercising our freedoms in nature. We were both emotional and deeply apprehensive about crossing the border into England.

Under the Countryside and Rights of Way Act, which came into force in 2000, just 10 per cent of England's land is legally accessible to the public via designated rights of way, and even then, only for walking, not for camping. Hundreds of years of private property laws have shaped a strict cultural code that places heavy restrictions on people's ability to access nature. The vast majority of England remains completely unknown to those who live there, not because it is remote, but because we are prohibited from stepping foot on it. By law of trespass, we are excluded from 92 per cent of the land and 97 per cent of its waterways.[1]

By contrast, Scotland had given us something priceless: the ability to really live within the landscape, not just observe it from a distance. The Scottish Outdoor Access Code is built on the principle that rights come with responsibilities, allowing people to experience nature in a way that fosters respect and care. In the UK, this right of access is unique to Scotland and therefore incredibly special. I strongly believe that, when access to the land is restricted, people lose their connection to it. If we can't touch it, smell it, hear it, and enjoy and experience it fully, how can we expect people to care about it enough to protect it? Going into England felt like stepping into the home

1 Nick Hayes, *The Book of Trespass* (Bloomsbury, 2020).

of an overly controlling parent with too many rules and restrictions and no can-dos. I'd grown up in England and had never thought about any of this before, but my new way of life had opened my eyes to how little access we have to our own land.

With the border on our horizon, we were about to lose our right to roam, to sleep under the stars, to camp and to make a fire to keep warm and cook our food. The magic we had experienced in Scotland – deer and wild ponies grazing outside our tent, wild pitches perched above sea cliffs, sunrises we woke to with the sea at our feet – was all about to be rebranded as trespass. Ahead of us lay an invisible border, marked by nothing more than a sign, but the moment we crossed it, a core part of our existence would suddenly become illegal. Under English law, simply for living outdoors, we were about to become criminals.

This wasn't just a logistical challenge; it felt like an attack on something fundamental to who we were. I could feel a quiet rebellion stirring in me, because this went so much deeper than camping. Access to the land should be a human right, tied as closely to our identity as our social, economic and cultural freedoms. And yet, in England, that right was being taken away from us.

We were scared of what this meant. There was no way we could afford accommodation or campsites, nor did we want to – we weren't hikers looking for a holiday, and being penned in a field sandwiched between a load of other tents was not our thing at all. Wild camping wasn't just our way of sleeping; it was a necessity and a huge part of what made our lifestyle so enjoyable. But in England, we would be forced into the shadows. In my mind, I imagined us returning to the experiences Chris had told me about from when he first started this walk: creeping into private woodland under the cover of darkness, sprinting across golf courses at 4 a.m., dodging farmers and landowners, knowing that at any moment we could be caught and moved on.

It dawned on me that, if I were ever convicted of trespassing, given the laws in England, I would have a criminal record which would stop me from being able to teach again due to the necessary DBS checks. Chris and I certainly never moved with any intention of breaking the law; it was just a means of sheer survival for us, to enable us to continue with the walk and raise money for SSAFA – to me, what felt criminal was the fact that I could lose my entire hard-earned career just for doing so!

The true wildness of our journey was coming to an end, and with it, a part of us. For now, though, we were still here, still wild, still free, and we intended to make the most of it. One of the most unforgettable wild camps for me on this journey came just before the border, not far from the tiny hamlet of Cove, where a beautifully quaint little harbour sits, only accessible through a small tunnel dug into the cliffs by locals in the 1700s. After a major uphill scramble on our hands and knees, we pitched the tent on a small patch of grass on a clifftop promontory, perched high above the sea, with panoramic views of wave-sculpted rock formations below.

From our spot, we could see the harbour tucked beneath wild, weathered cliffs, surrounded by natural arches, sea stacks and old smugglers' caves. When the tide went out, it revealed a vast layer of volcanic rock, transforming the view entirely. It felt like a whole new landscape had been unveiled, one we hadn't even known was there. That's one of the things I loved most about walking the coastline: it was always shifting, forever different. Even within a few hours, the tide reshapes everything, revealing stories written in stone that you'd never notice if you didn't take the time to look.

On the morning of the border crossing, we stopped about half a mile short of the border to sit on the cliff path and take it all in. We were very emotional; Scotland had left its mark on each of us in such profound ways. For Chris, it had been a slow and steady path back to himself. From the depths of despair, to pride, purpose and happiness, this land, with the help of Jet, had quietly stitched him back together. For Jet, it had been a transformation too. When she first joined Chris, she was skinny and unsure; now, she was strong, her body rippled with muscle, her posture was regal and proud, her trust restored.

For me, Scotland had given me my own little family for the first time in my life. We met in Scotland as strangers and were leaving deeply and forever connected by everything we'd been through together. But it was more than that. It had become a love story with the land itself, and with the people here who had opened their hearts to us in so many unexpected and generous ways.

Perhaps even more profoundly, Scotland had given me a truly unique gift: real freedom. For eight months, I had lived wild and untethered. It was much more than just greater independence and unshackling from the 'real world' for a spell; it was about experiencing what it truly means to feel free. The freedom to move at walking pace, to sleep under stars, to live without walls or noise or constant pressure. The freedom to simply live in the moment all day, every day. It felt so precious, something people in our Western world rarely ever get to taste. And I felt truly privileged to have known what it felt like. Deep down, I knew we'd go in search of it again.

When the moment came, we were bagpiped over the border by a man named Jamie, who had travelled down from Edinburgh in full kilted attire in order to give us a proper Scottish send-off. We couldn't believe it when a crowd of people turned up to welcome us into England, some having travelled from as far south as Newcastle to be there. The rain fell, of course – wouldn't have been right without it – but spirits were high. There was no fanfare from the coast path itself, just a modest sign next to a wooden fence, but in our hearts, it really marked the end of an era.

The moment was made even more monumental by the news that the fundraising for SSAFA had reached more than £200,000, double the amount Chris had initially intended. That was a moment of pure powerful personal triumph for all of us, knowing everything it had taken to get here and how much it meant to have our efforts rewarded by way of helping others.

Crossing into England, Chris turned to me. 'Look at the Scottish side, all wild and uncut, and then the English side, all neatly mown, leading straight into a caravan park!' He laughed. 'Buckle up, Kate. This is going to be interesting.'

I grinned. 'I wouldn't have it any other way.'

15

The Birth of a New Plan

Verity burst into tears the second she saw me, and gave me the biggest hug, which I returned with equal ferocity. She was one of my best friends, whom I'd known since my uni days and whom I was so happy to be seeing now that Chris and I had made it along the coast into Northumberland. Looking back, it was extremely kind of her to even entertain the idea of having us and Jet to stay – she'd given birth to her daughter, Tabitha, only three weeks earlier! But she and her partner, Sam, were delighted for us to pitch in their back garden for a few days. Chris and I would walk during the day, then we'd return in the evenings so Verity and I could spend time catching up. It was during one of our long chats that Verity, cradling tiny Tabitha, turned to me and said, 'Mate, you should have one!'

I laughed. 'It might have to wait a while.'

I hate the notion of the biological clock – it can weigh so heavily on women, shaping decisions that should be free from pressure. But, for me, there was no denying its presence. Now in my mid-thirties, the truth was I carried the weight of it with me everywhere. Besides, even if we started trying now, there was no guarantee anything would happen straight away. I'd known plenty of couples who had struggled to conceive. Fertility issues were far more common than I'd ever realized. I'd been diagnosed with polycystic ovaries when I was nineteen, and ever since, I'd carried a quiet fear that it might affect my ability to have children. It had been one of my biggest, most constant underlying worries.

Yet Verity's words stuck with me. Seeing her nursing her child also stirred something in me I hadn't expected, and I started thinking about my own desire to have children and how that might fit into this new lifestyle of mine.

There is an underlying assumption, which even I had held for most of my life, that motherhood comes after the wild years – after the big, crazy adventures, when life becomes stable and sensible enough to make it feasible. As someone whose life revolved around adventure, the thought of having a child inevitably came with deep-seated fears around sacrifice. How much of this would I have to give up? I'd only just got started. I didn't want to feel like I had to choose between travelling the world and motherhood, or that having a baby would mean the walk would have to be over for me.

Yet, the more I thought about it, the more I realized there's never a perfect time. No one ever feels fully ready, emotionally or financially. I began to think, if I'd handled everything this lifestyle had thrown at me so far, maybe, just maybe, I could handle this too. What if I didn't wait? What if I could combine motherhood and the big adventure?

In so many ways, it was ludicrous to even entertain the idea. From the outside, our circumstances were not remotely conducive to bringing a child into the world. We were living in a tent, walking the coastline, with no fixed income, no permanent home, carrying everything we owned on our backs. We didn't know where we'd end up next. Bringing a child into that scenario was, by most definitions, unthinkable. And yet, despite our lifestyle, I found myself conjuring up a kind of logic. Chris and I had discussed that, once the walk ended, we'd go on to do something even more extreme – trekking across Kyrgyzstan, perhaps, or dragging sleds across Antarctica. Doing either would be far more complicated with a baby than what we were doing now. For one thing, we were still in the UK. Still on home turf. We had friends nearby, familiarity, and a support network built from the support of strangers. That invisible safety net made me feel that, in some crazy way, it might actually be doable and perhaps even easier.

By now, the landscape had shifted and so had our rhythm. In Northumberland, once-mighty strongholds cling to the coast and wide, sweeping beaches stretch for miles. The change in law knocked our confidence, and we were unusually hesitant, second-guessing ourselves constantly. We held back from wild camping, and I wasn't sure how things were going to work, especially as the first few days had us trudging through pouring rain. But, once again, we were met with incredible kindness. Strangers offered us shelter in anything that kept us off the radar but still technically 'outside': a log cabin, a static caravan, a seventies van parked on a driveway or a patch of grass in a back garden.

Soon enough, we came to Lindisfarne, also known as Holy Island. Twice a day it gets completely cut off from the mainland by the rising tide, and the stillness that follows is almost spiritual. Luckily, the skies had cleared, the sun was shining and we were able to enjoy Lindisfarne in all its glory: windswept dunes, pristine beaches, wildflowers nodding in the breeze, rich wildlife and medieval ruins. We were even treated to a private tour of the castle rooftop, normally off-limits to visitors, which felt like a real privilege. For us, it was an unusually classy way to take in the view.

For me, the real magic was getting there and back: squelching barefoot for 3 miles through the tidal mudflats along the Pilgrim's Way, an ancient route walked by Christian pilgrims since AD 635, when King Oswald gifted the island to St Aidan to build a monastery. As we walked, the haunting song of hundreds of seals echoed around us, and the moody skies created shimmering, silvery-blue reflections on the water. Jet looked so beautiful in that light; I snapped one of my favourite photos of her there.

We followed the stilted poles rising from the sands, guiding people in safe passage just as they have for over 1,300 years. A few even had rickety, roofless wooden boxes perched on top: a stark reminder of how quickly the tides can turn. *That'll make for an interesting scramble if we get caught out,* I thought.

All the pilgrims who must have crossed here over the centuries, barefoot and hopeful, probably just as mucky as we were, all in search of something sacred: I felt a sense of kinship in that. Our journey might have looked different, but it struck me as a kind of pilgrimage too. And, on a lighter note, after so much time spent walking in boots, plodding barefoot through that cold, dark, viscous gloop that oozed between my toes felt oddly fun and refreshing – a medieval-style foot spa for tired feet!

It was while we were pitched up at Verity's that I brought up the topic of us starting a family, and Chris and I talked about it over the next few nights in the tent. I'd always imagined myself getting married before having children; I was quite traditional in that sense. Chris had also voiced that he liked the idea of us getting married one day, but, timing-wise, it didn't feel important or necessary to us at this point. I think both of us knew that life doesn't wait until it's perfectly lined up or for things to happen in the ideal order. We were like-minded when it came to thinking that, if we'd made it this far, walking for years, living with so little, then, if the time was right, we'd find a way to make it work. We'd built so much trust on this journey, in each other, in the path, in the unknown, that the concept 'where there's a will, there's a way' had never felt truer.

So, if we were ever going to roll the dice, maybe this was the moment. In the end, we decided to start trying and see. Just quietly. Just to see what happened.

After saying goodbye to Verity, Sam and Tabitha, we carried on through Northumberland. Rounding Budle Bay, Bamburgh Castle came into view – and what a sight it was. Arguably England's finest coastal castle, it stands bold and theatrical on a massive outcrop of basalt rock overlooking the North Sea. Its history dates back to the first Anglo-Saxon king, Ida the Flamebearer, who built a wooden stockade here in AD 547 to serve as the capital of Northumbria. In an incredible twist of fate, we ended up sleeping inside its grounds. Will Armstrong, whose family have owned the castle for generations, invited us to stay the night. We bedded down in a historically accurate replica of a Viking/Anglo-Saxon tent, complete with animal furs and a view fit for warrior kings – an experience I'll never forget.

By the time we reached Amble, I knew we had to face our fear around wild camping in England. We were so grateful for the kind offers, but organizing them had become a mission, draining our time, energy and ever-dwindling phone battery life. More than that, we missed the freedom. We missed the tent. For Chris, who'd lived under canvas for nearly four years, it was more than just shelter; he felt more at home in a tent than in any house. And even for me, much to my surprise, I'd grown comfortable in the cramped confines of our little orange MSR.

It had become a cocoon, a safe haven. My home. And I wanted it back.

I knew Chris's hesitancy wasn't really about him. He was being protective; he didn't want me to have to deal with the stress of being moved on after a long day, or to face one of those awkward altercations with someone hell-bent on laying down the law. But I could feel the need for change building in me. We weren't being true to ourselves or to the walk.

So, I tackled it head-on. 'Chris, we can't keep doing it like this. Wild camping is what we do. It's how this journey has always been done and it's how we have to keep doing it. We just need to bite the bullet and go for it.'

That night, on a beach near Amble, we pitched up. We scrawled, 'Walking the UK Coastline for SSAFA' in big marker-pen letters on both sides of the tent and held our breath.

But we didn't need to. That night, and for the rest of our Northumberland experience, we were met with nothing but warmth and kindness. We both woke up with a sense of quiet triumph.

'Okay, then. Business as usual,' I said.

Chris and Jet both gave me a sleepy morning grin.

By now, July had finally come into its own and the weather was baking hot. We were waking with the sun around 3.30 a.m., packing up quickly and setting off early to avoid walking in the heat of the day with Jet. I'd never really been a morning person, but now I was waking up naturally, no alarm needed, in suspiciously high spirits, drawn out of sleep by the promise of another fiery sunrise.

Meanwhile, Chris would still be buried deep in his sleeping bag as I serenaded him with songs about his morning grumpiness or, if I was feeling particularly lively, I'd belt out a full Spice Girls number just to torture him even more. His muffled voice would emerge from the sleeping bag: 'Oh, here she is –

someone bring out the Awake Medal!' Jet would greet me with a big toothy grin, as if she found it funny too – two girls in on it together!

Even by 7 a.m. it was already too hot for Jet, so we'd settle on a beach, rig up some kind of shade and wait it out until the cooler hours returned. We often dug her a huge sand pit to lie in – her own made-to-measure exfoliating sand spa.

At times, I could sense Chris getting frustrated with me when it came to Jet. I'd naturally pick up the pace when walking and he kept having to remind me to slow right down for her now that age was holding her back. She still refused to go anywhere near her bespoke trailer, so, for now, it was being passed along the coast by kind followers who were keeping it safe for us until Jet changed her mind.

The days felt endless. Up at 4 a.m., walking for hours, constantly exposed to the sun. Any scrap of shade we found went straight to Jet, and the long summer evenings stretched out late, too. It was tiring, but thankfully Northumberland's relatively flat coastline was on our side.

It was around this time that a lady called Judith messaged, asking if we'd like a tour of a tall ship in Blyth. Never one to turn down an adventure, I replied, 'Yes, please,' having no idea it would lead to one of the most memorable nights of the whole section.

That evening, we slept aboard the *Williams II*, a 106-year-old replica of the original vessel once captained by Blyth-born Captain William Smith, the man who very few know first discovered Antarctica! The journey was intended as a global trading voyage, initially setting sail for the Chilean port of Valparaíso back in 1818 to deliver cargo from England and India. On his way round Cape Horn, battling some of the most treacherous seas in the world, he veered off course in a desperate bid to outrun the fierce storms, and in doing so accidentally discovered the first land in Antarctica, now known as the South Shetland Islands, further south than any recorded land at the time. His discovery was monumental, yet he was never credited with his find. He remained an unsung explorer who eventually died a pauper in an almshouse in London. A replica of the ship was brought over from Denmark to finally give him his rightful place in history and now it's the beating heart of the Blyth Tall Ship project, a local charity that supports heritage boatbuilding.

That night, we also chatted with two brilliant women, Janice and Astrid, who were part of the Williams Gansey Project, a knitting project which had a unique tie to our nautical accommodation. The gansey – also sometimes called the guernsey – was the traditional jumper worn by fishermen from the fifteenth to nineteenth centuries – warm, water-repellent, hard-wearing, often hand-knitted by the communities themselves and likely worn by the original crew on Smith's historic expedition.

In 2016, Janice and Astrid discovered there was no specific pattern for Blyth, so they created one from scratch for the *Williams II* crew. Their design combined traditional symbols – ropes, ladders, staithes – with modern touches like the Blyth Tall Ship logo and the Northumberland flag. Each jumper was knitted by a local volunteer, complete with a tag bearing the knitter's name so the sailor could connect with the person who made it. Little did we know that Janice and Astrid would go on to create something very special for us a little further down the line.

We bivvied out on deck beneath a clear sky – no tent, no shelter, just sleeping bags and stars, with Jet cuddled in between us. It was such a unique place to lay our heads, and a first for me; not just being on the deck of a tall ship, but in all my adventures I'd never simply laid down and slept under the open sky. It was the perfect night for it as well – warm, still and peaceful, surrounded by creaking ropes and billowing sails. I felt like a sailor in an old adventure story, bedding down beneath the stars, only now with a dog I adored and the man I loved beside me, and a quiet, hopeful thought taking root inside me.

16

Urban Maul

As we moved further south into the more urban, industrialized areas of Newcastle, Sunderland, Hartlepool and Middlesbrough, we made a point of highlighting some of the charities doing amazing work along the way. In Sunderland, we visited Veterans in Crisis, which at the time supported over 400 veterans, offering them somewhere to sleep, wash clothes and cook if needed. They also provided a range of wellbeing activities, including boxing, walking and paddleboarding, as well as help with housing, computer literacy and employment.

The North-East has some of the highest homelessness rates in England outside of London, though the figures available only reflect the people who actually present to local authorities. The real number is far higher. That reality hit home when we spent a night volunteering at The People's Kitchen in Newcastle, where a queue stretched down the street and 250 meals were served that evening alone.

What shocked me most was how young many of the destitute people were. It echoed statistics showing that 44 per cent of those who access homelessness services in England are between eighteen and twenty-four, with many facing complex challenges that overlap, namely addiction combined with mental-health issues. Evidently, accessing help for both is extremely difficult. In the five council areas around Newcastle, just before the pandemic, around seventy-five single people were temporarily housed in B&Bs. By January 2021, that number had jumped to 926. We were also told that, when people are finally rehoused, they often arrive to an empty shell – no furniture, no bedding, nothing. The People's Kitchen provides not just meals and clothes, but new bedding, donated furniture and even pictures for the walls.

As we continued south, walking through the busy, built-up stretches of the North-East, I began to really struggle with the change I saw in Chris. It wasn't sudden, it had been creeping in slowly for months, but now it was starting to wear on us both.

After years of remote isolation, the transition back into civilization, the noise, the density, the grey sprawl was difficult for him to process. There was an ironic tragedy in it. By sheer determination, he'd made it this far, only to find that, in doing so, he'd left behind what he loved most about the journey: the wild, the quiet, the beautiful places.

Now, we were walking through major cities and built-up areas, navigating busy roads through housing estates, power stations and dockyards. For Chris, it wasn't just a change of scenery but rather how impersonal places now felt to him. For the first time in his life, he'd finally found the perfect balance between wilderness and people; for years now, in the small communities he came across, people had been so kind and welcoming, always taking the time to stop and say hello, not just to him but to each other. He had fallen in love with the strong sense of community where people really looked out for their friends and neighbours.

Don't get me wrong; we were still receiving lots of support and kindness from people who knew who we were and what we were doing, but, for those that didn't, we were lucky if a handful of people even looked up, let alone said hello. For Chris, this was a world he had once fought to escape. He often said he would rather live in a cave alone than be in a world which was so centred around money, self-obsession and material things, a world where human kindness takes second place to one's success. It was a constant reminder to him that freedom was worth far more than what the majority chose to chase. I could see that he was no longer enjoying what he had once loved so much, and it made me so sad for him.

Being around him like this was hard, too. When we met, I'd been drawn to his positive energy, his drive, his focus, his fun-loving, uplifting spirit. But being away from the wild had sapped his soul a little and no amount of bright skies or coastal views seemed to fully bring him back. I tried to inject fun and lightness into our days; sometimes it worked momentarily, but I could feel the weight he was carrying.

His frustration was simmering beneath the surface and it was only made heavier by his growing concern for Jet. He was protective of her in a way that came from somewhere deep, as if she were his child, and I could sense that protectiveness was starting to turn into fear. I had never seen Jet in her heyday on this walk. I'd seen plenty of videos of her zooming rocket-like around the isles with boundless spring and energy, but I'd never seen it with my own eyes. So I wasn't able to see the same level of change in her now as Chris did, and I don't think I realized just how agonizing it was for him. The fact of her getting older and her body beginning to shut down really scared him, and it was only set to get worse.

Chris had always insisted that the walk wasn't a plaster for old wounds, that it had genuinely healed him and brought him back to himself. I really believed that too, from looking at photos of him at the start of the walk compared to him now. It tore me up to see what he had been reduced to back then. The man I knew was now strong inside and out – full of self-pride, conviction and positivity about life and the future. I knew this walk had done something truly powerful. He spoke about the idea that mental health has no face, but it had been written all over his.

Because of that, I couldn't help but begin to worry. I felt he was strong enough now to overcome the change in people and place that bothered him, but I wasn't sure he'd overcome his feelings around Jet's decline. I worried that the man who had re-emerged from the wild might begin to disappear again. If there was anything that was going to set Chris back, it would be the loss of Jet. His anxiety, which he largely kept hidden, would manifest itself in irritability, which at times became the one source of conflict between us and one I had to tread very carefully around. I tried my utmost to be as understanding and supportive as I could, but I also felt out of my depth, scared that some of the old demons he'd put to rest might start to rear their ugly heads again.

We breathed easier once we hit Redcar on the Yorkshire coast and fell back into our usual rhythm again, lighter and happier. Determined to get back to what we loved most about this journey, we made a pact to wild camp the entire stretch. After weeks of pitching in back gardens, sheds and garages, we were craving that feeling of waking up outdoors properly, with the sea breeze on our faces and a morning coffee on our little gas stove outside the tent flap. We also knew it would be much more comfortable terrain for Jet, which gave us huge peace of mind.

Yorkshire had always been a special place for me. I was born in Suffolk but moved up north when I was seven and spent the rest of my childhood there until I was eighteen. I had so many good memories of growing up in Yorkshire, yet apart from a childhood trip to Whitby, I'd never really explored its coast. I was excited to see what it had to offer!

We were treated to a beautiful view coming into Skinningrove, complete with a rainbow arching over the sea. That evening, a welcoming party of locals came down to the beach to say hello and, with true northern hospitality, the chef from the local cafe trekked down in the rain to hand-deliver us a hot meal right to our tent: chicken Parmigiana, his speciality, followed by sticky toffee pudding for dessert. It was absolutely delicious after a long sweaty day in the heat, and the personal effort made it all the more special.

Unfortunately, the night that followed was far less hospitable. We found ourselves in the middle of a full-blown sand-flea invasion: fat, juicy, translucent critters that dart, leap and get everywhere. I could feel them crawling all over me in the dark and I found one in my armpit, one in my hair and another floating in my coffee the next morning. In a desperate attempt to keep them out, we had to close every air vent in the tent, turning it into one clammy, sweaty, wet fiasco. The whole thing felt like a throwback to the midges on the west coast of Scotland and a reminder of why, despite the hardships of the cold, we actually found summer the hardest season for walking.

From Skinningrove, we headed through dense fern and wildflowers in vivid shades of pink and purple, winding our way through a mountainous landscape scattered with fallen boulders. It was absolutely stunning; Jet's white coat stood out beautifully against the riot of colour, and both Chris and I relished the added challenge of a few proper climbs. By the time we reached Boulby, we were walking along one of the highest cliffs in England, soaring 203 metres above the sea. Right beneath us ran a vast network of underground mining tunnels leading to the UK's deepest underground mine, where the road salt that grits our icy roads during winter is produced. A striking metal sculpture marked the spot, honouring the generations of miners who had worked below.

Staithes was full of charm, with its colourful, red-roofed houses stacked along the cliffs and cobbled streets leading to the harbour. It's also steeped in seafaring history: it was there that a young Captain James Cook first learned his trade as a seaman, before setting sail years later from Whitby on his famous voyages of exploration. We were on the Cleveland Way, and the picturesque coastal towns of Robin Hood's Bay, Whitby and Ravenscar, amid beautiful coast, made it a truly enjoyable coast to walk. The steep ravine of Hayburn Wyke turned out to be one of my favourite wild-camp spots, leading to a beautiful, big-pebbled beach tucked between green cliffs, with a waterfall cascading down to meet the sea. We pitched our tent right there by the water and woke the next morning to a breathtaking pastel sunrise, soft pinks and oranges washing over the sky like watercolour. I was so glad we were sticking to our pact to camp without restriction.

At Filey, we unknowingly pitched on a piece of aviation history. The next morning, a local told us that the crumbling concrete slipway next to our tent had once been the launch site for some of Britain's earliest recorded flights. In the early 1900s, a Yorkshireman named Robert Trammer had built a hangar above our pitch and made his first flight there in 1910. It was a complete coincidence that we chose this spot, but it reminded me how much fascinating history there is to be found on every inch of our coast and how easy it can be to just wander right past, never the wiser.

We continued through the wild, overgrown fields and along to the RSPB reserve at Bempton Cliffs, home to an incredible variety of birdlife. We were unbelievably lucky to spot a black-browed albatross, an incredibly rare visitor to British shores that had wandered off course during its North Atlantic migration and ended up right here on the cliffs at Flamborough. An RSPB volunteer pointed it out, and we watched it nestled calmly among the gannets through a zoom lens – a once-in-a-lifetime sighting on these shores!

Pressing on towards Withernsea, the cliffs began to tell a different story. Coastal erosion was stark. Garden fences and even homes teetered scarily close to the edge. Entire villages, almost thirty of them, had been lost to the North Sea. Names like Auburn, Owthorne, Withow, Ravenspurn, some only remembered through medieval tax records or stories passed down in writing. Ravenspurn, the last to vanish in the 1800s, was where Henry IV landed in 1399 to seize the throne from Richard II; it's a place mentioned by Shakespeare in three of his plays. Now, they all lie beneath the waves – houses, farms, churches and centuries of life, swallowed by a merciless sea.

As we continued, the route brought more challenges: skirting round a stretch at risk from undetonated explosives, wading through waist-high weeds, crawling under brambles and trees, grabbing onto fences to pull ourselves through (our shoes were completely wrapped in spiderwebs after!) and getting permission to scale private clifftop land to avoid the swamped beach at high tide – a good reminder that sometimes the only way forward is just to ask.

Our kit wasn't faring well. We were sewing up rips in our clothes daily and our roll mat had punctured yet again, meaning we'd had a run of nights sleeping directly on the hard ground, which was agony for our backs. So, when a woman named Sarah messaged via Chris's Facebook page to offer the use of a shed in her paddock by the coast, we jumped at it. Anything for a slightly comfier night's sleep. We found ourselves staying in a tiny, corrugated-metal shed, bedded down on waist-high stacks of hay bales, tucked in beside our two new 'neigh'bours – Toby and Brook, a pair of beautiful horses we quickly won over with apples and Polo mints. At one point in the night, I genuinely thought we might have to bunk in with them – the rain was hammering down and the roof of our hay-bale hotel had sprung more than one leak. I kept waking up to dodge drips and to shift Jet to keep her dry, while Chris slid off the lopsided haystacks in his sleep. Oh, and the place was absolutely crawling with spiders! We had to laugh!

The next morning, Sarah turned up with the local farmer and a forklift tractor to add more hay bales and level out our sleeping spot. She and her daughter Beth were both total diamonds. They picked us up and dropped us off from the start and end points of each day's walk, brought hearty, home-cooked dinners to our stable every evening and let us use their outdoor tap to refill water, saving us the backbreaking task of lugging an extra 15 litres each day in the summer heat.

Then I discovered that somehow, in the midst of all this, Chris had managed to secretly plot a birthday surprise for me! I turned thirty-five on 21 August, and he was determined that I should celebrate in style. That evening, we dined al fresco in the paddock under a canopy of fairy lights, with roses, home-made spaghetti Bolognese, Prosecco and birthday cake, all courtesy of one of his lovely supporters, Michelle, who had driven up from Hull to set it all up with him while I was whisked off on the pretext of grooming the horses. Michelle had gone above and beyond to help Chris make the evening special for me, and I was blown away by their efforts.

Little did I know that this wasn't the only surprise in store.

17

Haystack Hotel

We woke the next morning, sluggish, stiff and soaked through. I peeled myself up off my haystack mattress and laughed. To spend even one night sleeping on wonky stacks of hay in a tiny, leaking, spider-strewn shed would be most people's idea of hell, and yet here we were on our fourth night, just so grateful to be lying on something other than the solid ground – our roll mat replacement still hadn't arrived. I lapped up the absurdity of it. We had slept in some truly random places on the walk, but our haystack hotel was fast becoming a favourite.

After a slap-up 'breakfast in bed' of leftover birthday cake, my mind turned to the fact that my period was around three weeks late. My periods had always been slightly irregular, so I hadn't thought much of it. I could usually count on one a month, but never ever to the exact date. Friends had regulated their periods with varying methods of contraception, but I'd never wanted to go down that road. I think it was partly due to my fears around infertility – I didn't want to upset my natural hormone balance. It felt important for me to keep an eye on what my body and my cycles were doing of their own accord without being affected by any contraceptive drugs. This had always made things a bit trickier on the walk, as I never knew exactly when my period was going to rock up; but that had always been the way, so I was used to rolling with the reality of its spontaneous arrival.

Chris and I had only been trying to conceive for around a month – whenever we could muster the energy for it after a long, hot day! I felt certain the delay was just down to my period being irregular as always, and I didn't have any symptoms. But just to answer that little niggle in the back of my mind, I had bought a pregnancy test a few days prior from a pharmacy in Hornsea. To take the test, I squatted on top of the hay bales and peed into one of our titanium cooking pots, doing my best to aim over the end of the stick. 'You're washing that up!' Chris joked to me. Then I handed it to him and we both sat in silence, waiting for the verdict.

For those three minutes, time stood still. I didn't want to get my hopes up. Every second that ticked by felt so loaded, packed with uncertainty, lingering possibility and anticipation, all giving way to hope. The small plastic stick seemed to wield an obscene amount of power, and I realized I had absolutely no control over it. Yes, trying to conceive had been a choice, but the outcome of that choice was not in my hands. It felt like I was at the mercy of a power bigger than myself, deciding my entire future on the flip of a coin.

Chris looked up at me. 'Sorry, mate, not this time.' It was our first test and we'd only just started trying, so I don't think Chris thought anything of it – there was plenty of time and plenty more attempts to be had! Deep down, I felt a pang of disappointment, but laughed it off and grabbed my coat ready to get going that day on our stretch to Holmpton.

All of a sudden, Chris whipped around. 'Hang on, wait – you're not going to believe this – you are, you're pregnant!' He'd taken a second look at the test to double-check, on the off chance, before heading out the door. 'It's positive!'

'Chris – give over! That is not a funny wind-up!'

'No, I'm serious! Look – there's two lines! You're pregnant! We're going to have a baby!'

I stared back at him in disbelief. 'Are you joking? Really, I'm pregnant? Check it again.'

'Yes, two lines – definitely two lines,' said Chris.

'Are you sure? Because you did manage to read it wrong once already!'

'Yeah, I looked too early – turns out I may need a bit of help to count to three minutes, after all!'

While Chris jokingly congratulated himself on his pedigree sperm, I grabbed the test off him and stared at it, stunned into silence – a rare occurrence for me. I was in total shock. I couldn't believe it could have happened this quickly. After all those niggling infertility worries for so many years, how was it possible I could be pregnant within the first month of trying? I honestly couldn't believe the test was right. That day, as we passed through Withernsea, I bought five more tests and took them wherever I could – the public toilets, a cafe toilet, the lighthouse toilet and behind a few bushes. All of them were positive.

By the time we returned to the hay bales that night, we both knew it was for real. The results of six pregnancy tests felt pretty conclusive! Chris and I embraced in love, happiness and excitement. I could see his eyes welling up. And, after everything he'd gone through, I was excited for him to have this fresh start at parenthood and to be a part of making sure it was different for him this time around.

The following day, we reached the very unique heritage coast of Spurn Point, home to one of the world's most rapidly evolving coastlines. On certain high tides, Spurn is cut off from the rest of the Holderness coast and becomes the UK's newest tidal island. We had to take turns to do the eight-mile round loop so that one of us could stay with Jet – dogs were not permitted due to the abundance of birdlife. Chris ran to get back as quickly as possible for Jet, as she was so anxious whenever he left her side, and then it was my turn to do this section on my own. I was grateful for the time alone as it gave me the chance to really digest my news, and amid such special surroundings.

I was stunned, excited, elated and apprehensive all at once. I honestly thought that, by the time we conceived, we'd be much further on in the walk or very nearly at the end. At this point, we were still so far from Llangennith, Wales, our destination, that it felt highly unlikely we'd make it to the finish line before the baby came.

As I reached the very end of the narrow shingle spit, the southernmost point of the Holderness coast that curves into the Humber Estuary, I stopped for a while. Although Spurn looks like a permanent feature on the map, it has actually disappeared and then reappeared many times since the last Ice Age, every 250 years or so.

Spurn was a place I never knew existed in the UK. Not only did I find myself once again in a truly unique landscape on home shores, but the fascinating geography and history here summed up so much of what I loved about the walk. It felt so poignant for me to be in that particular spot at that moment. In this place of ever-changing coast, I too was about to experience the biggest change of my life.

I felt a real urge to wade into the water. As I stood there, barefoot on the shingle, water lapping around my ankles, the sun on my face, I thought about my situation. I knew that if I'd said to Chris there and then that I wanted to stop walking to focus on having our baby while he carried on, that's what we would have done. Ultimately, it was my choice. Yes, I felt a sense of trepidation. How could I not? It was big news to swallow.

Yet the trepidation I felt was more about how my own life would change and how I would change, rather than how I'd cope. I had no idea what to expect, but, in my mind, there was no reason why I couldn't just carry on as usual. Not once did it occur to me that I wouldn't manage or couldn't do it. I knew myself and I wasn't going to let anyone tell me I couldn't, because I knew I could. I think, after living so simply outside for so long, I'd come to believe that a true sense of security comes from the inside. It's our self-belief which gives us the confidence and the strength to know that we're capable of big things. Chris had come to think in exactly the same way. We trusted in ourselves and in each other and we believed we could make it work. Never could I have imagined that this would be the way I would experience my first pregnancy and bring my very first child into the world. I just took a really deep breath, smiled, and said to myself, 'Right. A baby on the walk it is!'

More than anything, I was excited. This was something I'd wanted for so long and now it was actually happening. I was so excited to be a mum. I was also excited to continue on the walk with this new dynamic in play and see how far my mind and body could take me with this. I was excited to show that life doesn't always have to fit the mould when it comes to pregnancy and I was excited to carry my baby this way. After all, I resolved, what better way could I choose to be pregnant? I was outside all day, sleeping in the fresh air, active every day, and I could rest or nap whenever I needed with no external pressures creating any stress for me. This walk had already turned into the most incredible adventure and now an arguably even more amazing one was afoot within it. From now on, the walk would never be the same again. Each step, each day, I would be growing a baby inside me, giving it a whole new level of personal meaning.

The next day, it was time to leave the shed. Our new roll mat had finally arrived courtesy of Damien, who we'd met back in Cayton Bay. Like Chris, he was a former Para, and had incidentally been part of a rescue mission in Iraq involving Chris's younger brother, Mark. Damien had come out to see us with his family and had told us of his struggles since leaving the forces. He'd been shot in the head while on a mission in the Middle East; he told us he was with two others at the time: one got shot in the leg and the other – the only one unwounded – was left in such shock that, when he administered the morphine, he held the pen the wrong way round and accidentally jabbed himself with it instead of the others! He then had to load his injured mates onto the vehicle and drive back to base completely off his face! Damien was so grateful for our part in raising funds for SSAFA that he kindly volunteered to replace our roll mat, and we were incredibly grateful in return.

I felt emotional leaving. It had been the longest we'd stayed anywhere since our woodland lockdown, and our haystack hotel would always hold a special meaning for me as the place where I learned I was becoming a mother for the first time.

As we came around the Humber Estuary, after a night inside a bird-watching hut, we came into Hull. I decided this would be a good point to see a doctor to confirm the pregnancy and get some advice, given my situation, so I visited a walk-in centre. I'd very kindly been given a lift there by one of our supporters, a man called Paul. He offered to wait outside to take me back to the coast to resume walking after my appointment and I was therefore conscious I didn't want to be too long. I was both extremely nervous and excited as I entered the centre. I knew

I would have to take another test to confirm the pregnancy, but being at the doctor's felt far more defining, a formal validation of sorts that this was real. The doctor confirmed the pregnancy to me in a private room and, while it certainly felt scary to know my life was going to change completely, I breathed a deep sigh of relief that the happiness I'd felt over the past few days hadn't been false hope. The doctor had a kind manner and listened with interest as I explained my circumstances, before relaying my options to me.

I was told that no one would treat me unless I stayed within a thirty-mile radius of a regional GP practice, midwifery centre and hospital in order to qualify for maternity care. In short, I had three options: to stop the walk entirely and settle somewhere for the duration of the pregnancy; to continue and run the risk of not receiving any maternity care, and just head to the nearest hospital when I was ready to give birth; or, lastly, register somewhere I could return to as and when needed for necessary appointments, and preferably not disclose that I wouldn't be in the area for the time periods in between. I sat and listened politely, but, beneath the surface, I was staggered by what I was hearing.

How on earth, in this day and age, in an 'advanced' country by world standards, when more and more people travel frequently and are opting for full-time van life, would I not be able to access maternity care just because I lived a nomadic life on foot? Looking back, I should have sought a second opinion straight away, but even going to this appointment had meant arranging for a follower to drive us forty minutes inland, wait for us to finish, then drive us back again to the coast. It wasn't that easy. I already knew that society makes it hard to live a non-conventional life, particularly one that is nomadic – we'd come to learn that the lack of a fixed address makes it incredibly difficult to open a bank account or access online banking services, register with a GP or pay tax or phone bills, and we couldn't afford to pay for any kind of PO-box service. It definitely felt like, if you didn't have a front door or a postcode, you were almost outcast from society, yet you were still somehow expected to participate in a system with very limited means to do so. This now took on a whole new dimension when it came to raising children, particularly for a mother who wanted to maintain her level of movement and adventurous lifestyle. Pregnancy is associated with stillness and rest; motherhood with settling, stability in one place and self-sacrifice. I felt trapped within a box of expectations where the walls were closing in under the pressure of opinions and societal norms about how it should be done. It seemed like I was being handed a script to follow and God forbid I dare to deviate from it, as that would surely put my child at risk or make me a bad mother! It certainly felt difficult both practically and emotionally when faced with so much pushback, and I knew I would need a lot of courage and conviction in what I was doing to stay my course.

But I had gone to a professional to seek the facts and, though I found it hard to believe, I trusted in the advice I was given and took it at face value. As a result, I felt I had no choice but to register back in Malvern, at Royal Worcester Hospital, using my mum's address, and somehow find a way to get back there when needed. However, that was a major logistical headache, as Malvern is located in the Midlands near the border with Wales, while we were walking on the other side of the country, on the east coast – a good four-hour drive away, not to mention we were solely on foot! Yes, this was a setback, but I was determined to make it work, because completing the walk with Chris was my life now and I wanted it to be my unborn baby's life too.

18

Early Days

Despite the setback, there was still no question of me leaving the walk. We would just have to find a way to ensure I could return to Worcester to access the maternity care that I needed, when I needed it. There was plenty I could do on the walk in the meantime to ensure I remained fit and healthy throughout the pregnancy, so I went to a local pharmacy and stocked up on enough folic acid to see me through the first trimester.

It was at this point that I began to notice a shift in Chris – his protective instincts towards me now that I was carrying his child heightened. After navigating our way around the tricky industrial area of Immingham Plant, we finally arrived at Grimsby Docks, only to find ourselves stopped in our tracks by a series of locked gates. As I stood peering through one of them, hoping that this wouldn't mean walking back on ourselves, we stumbled upon a dock worker who not only kindly opened the gates for us but, after we'd told him about our mission, quickly disappeared inside a cabin and returned with an invitation to take us to the top of the Grimsby Dock Tower for a private viewing! I couldn't believe our luck! The tower is not open to the public any more, so the opportunity to be taken to the top would be a real treat. Years earlier, I'd applied to take a tour to the top of Big Ben but was turned down due to impending restoration work. This felt like the perfect consolation prize. Built in 1852 with over a million bricks, the tower, 94 metres high, was once a hydraulic accumulator for dock machinery, inspired aesthetically by Siena's Torre del Mangia. It had survived a lot, including an earthquake in 1931 measuring 6.1 on the Richter scale and discussions to demolish it during the Second World War when it was used as a beacon by the German Luftwaffe to attack Liverpool. Now, there's even a Lego replica in its honour at Legoland, Windsor.

Inside, the tower was dark and derelict – light slicing through narrow slits, scaffolding spiralling upward into a seemingly never-ending abyss – the thought of climbing it was exhilarating! Chris and I donned hi-vis vests, gloves and hard hats, taking turns to climb while the other stayed below with Jet. I went first. He seemed very worried about me going up while pregnant, but I reassured him: I was only a few weeks along, feeling fine physically and wasn't about to miss such a rare opportunity just because I was with child. The ascent involved a tight and dizzying spiral staircase followed by ten tight and wildly different ladders. At the top, I reached two viewing decks: one broad, with sweeping views of the Humber Estuary and docks, the other much narrower, home to the tower's very own nesting peregrine falcon, and the icing on the cake – a close-up of the striking octagonal glass dome at the very top. Standing there, with the world at my feet, it felt like such a privilege to explore this place that was now off limits to the rest of the world. It was made all the more meaningful by the fact that I had family history rooted in the docks below; I thought of my nanna, who was raised here, and her father, my great-grandad, who had worked on these docks and received an MBE for services to the fishing industry. One-off experiences like these had become part and parcel of the walk, and I loved the spontaneity and variety of them. Standing on the roof, I felt reassured that I didn't need to cut out the more daring pursuits just because I was now pregnant; I just needed to weigh up the risks more carefully.

I was very conscious that I wanted to eat as healthily as possible too, even though I experienced a loss of appetite those first few months. Dinner would usually consist of soup or some kind of fish or meat with vegetables, always with a side of spinach and an orange for dessert. I didn't experience an aversion to any foods, had no obscure sense of smell or any particular cravings. I suppose, if I did have any cravings, it wasn't coal or ice, coffee grounds or toothpaste, or anything else similarly weird – it would have been oranges!

It also made it easier that I wasn't experiencing any of those first-trimester symptoms that plague so many women. I had one friend back in London who was three months ahead of me in her pregnancy and she'd suffered so badly from morning sickness that she'd ended up phoning her midwifery team several times in tears, desperate to hear some kind of assurance that the phase would soon be over. Thankfully I had no morning sickness, no breast soreness, no strange metallic taste in my mouth, no aches and pains, no discomfort whatsoever, in fact. I wasn't able to maintain regular contact with friends to exchange pregnancy tips from those who had been there before me, but it was fun to check in every now and then with the one mate who was three months ahead of me to see how her bump was progressing. We spoke a lot, closer to my due date, so I could gain some insight based on what her birth experience had been like.

The only symptom I felt was tiredness, but, on that front, I was in a pretty good position. I wasn't having to make it through a working day; we were in the early stages of autumn now, which meant the weather was generally still good enough for me to be able to pause whenever I felt overwhelmingly tired, pull out the sleeping bag, lay it out and take a nap. We could also choose to call it a day whenever I needed, pitch up the tent and, once we'd cooked, I could get an early night. The fact that we had no strict schedule to stick to really worked in my favour. The tiredness did become slightly more of an issue in areas that made it harder for us to wild camp: we'd accept kind offers of alternative accommodation and I felt more pressure to stay up and chat as a way of showing my gratitude.

By now, we were in Lincolnshire, where the coastline was flat and it made for easy walking. However, it did feel strange to be separated from the sea by miles of tidal mudflats as far as the eye could see. At one point, after walking through Donna Nook, home to the largest seal colony in the UK (although we were too early to see the thousands that come to breed here each year), we were invited to stay in a shepherd's hut in the back garden of a lovely couple, Amanda and Mark. At this point, no one knew I was expecting, not even close family, as we'd decided to keep the news to ourselves until after the first scan.

Amanda and Mark were incredible to us, dropping us off on the coast and picking us up each day, inviting us to share hearty home-cooked meals with them in the evening and even using the opening of their new cafe enterprise to raise £450 for our SSAFA cause. However, I found myself really struggling with the tiredness through dinner each night and, one evening, I fell asleep as soon as we got back from walking and slept through the dinner period entirely. Chris was left to apologize on my behalf and make up an excuse for my absence.

It was while we were here that we decided to return to Worcestershire to register at my mum's local GP, so I'd be eligible for midwifery care and hospital scans. When Chris's stepmother had tragically passed away in 2018, he'd had to hitchhike all the way from Uist to Brighton and back again to attend her funeral. A man called Steve ended up giving him a lift all the way from Brighton to the Isle of Skye and the pair had chatted en route. Chris's story had a real impact on Steve, who was struggling with his own mental health at the time. When they parted company, Steve had told Chris that, if ever he needed him, in whatever capacity, he would be there. So, when Chris called Steve to explain our situation, he assured us that, wherever we happened to find ourselves on the east coast, he would happily come and pick us up to take us back to any necessary appointments. That was no small gesture, given he lived in Birmingham! It was evident Chris had found as true a friend as any in Steve, and now I was very grateful for his friendship, too.

So, we did a quick twenty-four-hour round trip all the way there and back, just to register with the local GP near Malvern, so I could be linked up with the Sunshine Children's Centre in Malvern for midwifery care and be booked in at Royal Worcester Hospital for my first dating scan. At this point, we estimated I was about eight weeks pregnant.

I found the precarious nature of those early weeks hard. I am not a natural worrier or easily paranoid, so it surprised me that I sometimes found myself in the tent at night quietly wondering, hoping that all was well. I found my mind battling, fully aware how common miscarriage was by now, but also telling myself not to stress, to keep positive and that everything would be fine. We weren't in a position to pay for any early private scans to check how things were progressing. For twelve whole weeks, I was completely in the dark. All I knew was that I was pregnant, but there was no belly growing yet, no kicks or movements to feel, just this very elusive notion of the beginnings of a baby growing inside and no way to know if everything was okay. In many ways, the wait felt like an eternity. All I could do was place trust and faith in my body and hope for the best.

This is where the nature of what we were doing really helped. Being on the move every day, walking, discovering new surroundings worked wonders to take my mind off all that. I found that, as I walked every day, with every place being so varied, I was able to really absorb myself in the moment rather than dwell on what was happening with my body and the health of the baby at this early stage. I was able to get lost in the day-to-day and let nature take its course.

By the time we walked through Skegness and reached the Wash, I was beginning to wonder why I was experiencing so few symptoms. It may well have just been luck, but I did wonder whether the fact that I was living in constant fresh air, day and night, walking each day, was helping. I felt like it was probably more than mere coincidence. Exercise and fresh air can improve prenatal health by reducing stress, improving mood and sleep and potentially easing some of the early symptoms such as morning sickness and back pain. Outdoor exercise seemed to be particularly beneficial as the endorphins it releases boost mood and reduce stress. Sleep disturbance is common in pregnancy, and walking, coupled with all the natural light and fresh air, is said to help regulate sleep patterns. There are also a number of studies which show that spending time outside helps boost the immune system, which also helps alleviate symptoms felt during early pregnancy. I was obviously taking all of this to the extreme end of the spectrum, but I felt great for it, so I could only conclude that there must be truth in the science – it was certainly working for me!

It was here that I suddenly felt the shift in season. It was now late September and, as we camped on the banks of the River Haven, the temperature dropped and there was a definite chill in the air. That night, Mother Nature welcomed the autumn equinox with a vibrant sunset that gave rise to a luminous pink-red orb that looked more like the sun than the moon. We watched for hours as it evolved into a full, glowing harvest moon, casting stunning reflections on the water. I knew we'd seen out the last of the warm weather and this was the beginning of some seriously cold nights to come. It dawned on me that the majority of my pregnancy would be walking and wild camping through the colder, darker half of the year. By the time spring arrived, I'd be almost ready to give birth. I knew how cold it could get in the tent and I did wonder whether I was going to feel the cold more and whether I'd need to take extra measures to ensure the baby inside me was kept warm.

It was on this stretch that I also thought a lot about our shared and individual experiences. Of course, any two people on a journey are always going to have different realities, different perceptions, different thoughts and feelings. Yes, Chris and I would continue to walk the same path and navigate parenthood together, but, now that I was pregnant, our paths felt like they were diverging somewhat. There was no getting around the fact that my experience of this journey was about to be wrapped up in becoming a mum for the first time, and it felt so deeply personal.

19

Cold That Numbs Your Bones

It felt like we were on fast-forward on a video, scuttling back and forth across the sand like little crabs. Working feverishly, Dan and I rolled the measuring wheel across the golden expanse, then used rakes to scoop out the detail we wanted to stand out. Chris was an eager spectator, sitting by the tent with Jet to ensure she rested after that day's walk.

All of a sudden, Chris leapt from his seat and came sprinting over. 'Guys, if you don't hurry up, you're gonna lose the light. The sun is going down!' With that, he grabbed the rake off me and proceeded to frantically rake like never before! He and Dan between them finished the job just in the nick of time. Then Chris, Jet and I lay inside the design, while Dan got the drone up to photograph us.

Anyone passing must've wondered what the hell we were doing, but to us it was just another part of this wild journey we were on together, albeit a very special part. Dan was a friend Chris had made on the west coast of Scotland who worked as a sand and landscape artist. As soon as we hit the vast sandy beach of Hunstanton on the Norfolk coast, we knew we'd found the perfect spot for him to come and help us make some sand art to commemorate our happy news. We were coast walkers, after all – what better way to announce the pregnancy than with a creative piece of sand art, right by the sea. Together, we sketched a design and, with Dan's mathematical skill, we worked out the ratios to make it on a much larger scale in the sand. We could only work at low tide and, to make matters harder, there was a double tide here, which meant it was a race against time to get it all measured, sketched out in the sand, shaded and photographed, before the tides came in and washed it all away!

It was really hard to imagine what the final result was going to look like – we'd never done any sand art before, certainly not on this scale – but the fruits of our labours were worth it! The result looked even better than I'd hoped. A huge circle framed a large heart in the centre, within which were four sets of footprints in order of size: Chris's, mine, Jet's paws and, finally, a pair of baby feet, all surrounded by a vast stretch of sand, the incoming tide and the thin, meandering lines of the surrounding tidal rivers, with the backdrop of a sunset. It was such an imaginative and bespoke piece of art, designed and made by us, which made it so much more special than anything we could have ever bought. Yes, it would disappear thanks to nature, but in a way, given that we lived by the rhythm of the sea, its fleeting nature made it all the more precious. We had the photo we would share with friends and family when the time was right. We forever owed Dan a debt of gratitude for helping us create such a wonderful memory and keepsake to show our child when they were older.

As we pushed on through Norfolk, we came to the beautiful sands of Holkham Beach, where Jet and I played together, then lay down on the sand for a cuddle. I could sense she missed her freedom, just as Chris did. Now we were further south, there were often signs forbidding dogs from being on beaches between May and October. She had to be on a lead nearly all the time and I just knew she longed for the days of being able to roam free to her heart's content, as she had in Scotland. The fact that she was clearly slowing down was a huge worry. We didn't really talk about it – I never wanted to upset Chris, nor him me, and we never wanted Jet to sense our concern – but making sure she rested enough each day became paramount. There was an extra kinship between Jet and I; we both needed the journey to slow down now for different reasons.

By the time we reached Dunwich Heath in Suffolk, it was time to set off to Worcester for the 12-week dating scan. Despite needing to wake at 4 a.m. to pack up the tent in the hammering rain, we couldn't wait to see our baby on the ultrasound for the very first time and just kept grinning at each other. We were so excited, in fact, that as we hauled our Bergens across a mile or so of sand dunes to locate Steve – who had woken up himself at 2 a.m. to drive us – we recorded a short video as a keepsake to show the baby when he or she was older. Clad in our soaked green ponchos and head torches, we explained where we were, how excited we were to see them and how we were getting to the hospital.

I was full of nervous anticipation too, wanting to know that all was well after a painfully long wait. As I sat in the waiting room among all the other mums-to-be, most of whom were much further along, I looked at their body shapes and found it so surreal that my body was going to change that much in the next six months – and that I was going to be walking the coast and living in a tent while it did! I guess this would have been a good time to stop and question what I had coming, but I never did.

It was 20 October 2021 and we discovered that I was 13 weeks and 5 days pregnant, so the baby's due date was 23

April – St George's Day. Given our little adventurer would be carried and born on the English coast, I liked the fact that he or she was scheduled to be born on the day celebrating the patron saint of England. We paid £5 for the scan photo printouts and I tucked them safely into a little zip pouch I carried along with me, where I kept my emergency sewing kit and my prenatal vitamins. My 20-week scan was booked in for seven weeks later, on 6 December.

Now I knew we'd made it to this stage, I felt I could relax a bit more and worry less about the chances of miscarrying. What's more, the tiredness had gone and I was able to really begin to enjoy and embrace being pregnant. This was an experience I'd waited for my whole adult life and I was excited and grateful to enjoy it in this really unique way, living outdoors on the coast.

That afternoon, still near Worcester, I broke the news to my mum. I knew, deep down, she would certainly and understandably have a million questions and reservations about how we were going to do this, but she did an excellent job of keeping them at bay for now, to show she was happy for us. 'Congratulations!' she beamed. Now that I'd let the cat out of the bag with her, it was only right to tell my dad. We called him via Zoom, as he lives in the Middle East. As I shared the news, he said, 'What?!' and collapsed back in his chair. He was in complete shock, as though he'd just found out he'd lost his entire life savings! I knew full well that Dad's reaction didn't mean he wasn't happy for me – I knew he'd be thrilled to welcome his second grandchild (my brother and his wife already had a little girl, then aged two, living in Belgium) – it was more that he could not get his head around me having a baby on the walk and he had no idea how the hell we were going to do it.

It was only after she'd properly absorbed the news that my

mum began to voice her concerns about how we would manage if I chose to carry on with the walk, both from a practical and financial standpoint, as neither Chris nor I was earning an income. She certainly didn't view my pregnancy as a very practical scenario.

'How on earth are you going to manage?' she fretted.

'Don't worry, Mum, it'll be fine!' I assured her.

She couldn't believe I was this confident about it. She told me she knew I would manage one way or another, but that I was being far too optimistic, given my circumstances. She expected to find me coming to live with her for at least several months pre- and post-birth. Despite her doubts and concerns, I knew she was always there for me if I needed her, so we hugged goodbye and, with that, headed back with Steve to Suffolk.

Now, I was into my second trimester and winter was in full swing. We decided it would be wise for me to stop carrying my heavy backpack – it weighed 20 kilos and was the equivalent of carting around a medium-sized microwave oven for five hours a day. Once again, the kindness of strangers saved me. Followers of Chris's along the Suffolk coastline got in touch and offered to pick up my bags. Each night, we'd spend time arranging for a nearby follower to come and meet us in the morning, near to wherever we'd camped, pick up my bag, keep hold of it for us for the day and then drop it back to us wherever we stopped. They'd always offer to take Chris's bag too, which gave him some welcome respite from carrying such a huge weight each and every day for so many years. We still always carried the tent and one sleeping bag for emergency shelter if horrendous weather came in suddenly, but the lack of a backpack certainly offered some temporary relief for his back and shoulders. It did make for a lot of extra logistics to arrange each night, which was tiring, but given our circumstances it was the best we could hope for and we were incredibly grateful. Often, whoever helped that day knew of a friend slightly further along the coast who could help us out the next day, so the baton of bag-carrying support was passed along through word of mouth.

As winter set in, the cold became an extra challenge to contend with. To help keep us warm, we'd often make our go-to winter dinner: a one-pot stew, made with chunks of meat combined with vegetables and potatoes, cooked in stock. Our chores outside of the walking had always been a 50:50 effort and I wanted to maintain that, so I'd sit outside the tent with Chris until about 5.30 p.m. peeling vegetables by head torch in the dark to prepare our food in the evening. However, once the sun went down, I began to really feel the cold, and he could see it. This was when being in England, where we weren't allowed to have a fire, became a real problem. I found myself yearning for the days when we were in Scotland.

From this point on, for the rest of my pregnancy, Chris would usher me inside the tent with orders to get warm inside my sleeping bag with Jet while he finished the chores. He'd pass my food to me to eat in the tent, then he'd take on all clearing-up duties, including washing our pots as best he could. We were in a two-man tent and I had the body heat of Chris and Jet in there, but I found I definitely needed a hot-water bottle to keep me warm enough throughout the night. It was now mid-November and starting to get really cold, particularly in the evenings. Once the sun had gone down, it became the kind of cold that makes your fingers and toes numb and seeps into your bones no matter how many layers you're wearing.

The coast was synonymous with wind, but now winter had set in that wind was harsh and biting. Hail showers became more frequent and often painful to the point of feeling like being hit by driving nails. This was my second winter on the walk, so I was hardened to it – and we were further south than the year before, which helped – but seeing it through in a tent night after night while pregnant was seriously tough. I soon found I needed two hot-water bottles to get me through, which was a big drain on our camping gas stock because we had to heat enough water for both. Chris would save any leftover water boiled during cooking to fill at least one of them for me. When there was none of that, we had to use our drinking water instead.

As for my clothes, my hiking trousers were too small now, but I was managing by using my bum bag to keep them held up. I was also struggling to zip up my down jacket. This was an absolute necessity over winter, so I began to research maternity options to be able to extend the front. It was during this time that I experienced the most challenging physical aspects of my pregnancy: my nipples were in excruciating pain all the time from the cold. It transpired that I had Raynaud's syndrome, which is caused by a temporary interruption to normal blood flow in the small blood vessels. It usually affects body parts like the fingers, toes, nose, lips and ears, turning them white; however, for pregnant and breastfeeding women, it can also affect the nipples. The pain was often unbearable and always worse in the cold, despite my layers and down jacket. I found myself walking with my hands over my breasts, rubbing them, constantly trying to warm them up, which must have raised a few eyebrows along the coast path! I tried everything from cutting up squares of fleece and blanket to place inside my bra to shoving heat patches next to them. When nothing worked and the pain became too severe to continue, I'd have to find somewhere to go inside, if possible, for half an hour or so, just to give me some respite. This continued right the way through winter.

Interestingly, Jet, who had always slept either wedged between us or at the bottom of Chris's sleeping bag during winter, was now sleeping on top of me each night. This was such a major shift in behaviour for her, we almost couldn't believe it. Chris would often joke he'd been betrayed by his one and only! She either lay alongside me, tucked up together in my sleeping bag, sometimes even nose to nose (which was slightly too close for comfort, as I'm not sure whose breath was worse – hers or Chris's!), or further down the bottom, with her head resting on my tummy. I don't know whether or not she knew I was pregnant in the early days, whether she knew before even I did, but she was certainly aware now and the changes in her behaviour were very evident.

Not only had her sleep habits changed, but she would also spend more time by my side, like a bodyguard, and was increasingly affectionate. Whether it was out of protection for the baby or simply a display of allegiance and solidarity, her maternal, or perhaps just her fellow female instinct was kicking in. It felt like it was her way of telling us that she knew, that she was happy for us, and that she would protect us. It really comforted me that she clearly felt a connection to the baby, even at this stage, and made me feel much less concerned about whether she would accept the newest member of our little family.

By now, we had our teeth well and truly stuck into Essex. The coastline is the second longest in England after Cornwall, clocking in at over 350 miles – the equivalent distance of London to Germany! Essex also holds claim to thirty-five islands, more than any other county in England, most of which lie within its five estuaries, and some of which are cut off from the mainland twice a day by the tides. Those five estuaries seemed to make up most of what felt like never-ending miles for us as we plodded along raised mudbanks next to vast expanses of saltmarsh and mudflats. The path was narrow and sloped, which often meant walking with the lower foot on a downhill angle. I couldn't believe how remote it felt out here in this county to the east of London; so much so that we struggled more with phone signal out here than anywhere else we'd walked to date.

It was also strange to be in such close proximity to the capital. Reminders of major industries would appear – trawlers, oil refineries, defence fortresses and huge shipping warehouses. It had been only two years since I'd left London, where I'd worked and lived for a decade, but it felt like a world away now!

As we prepared for my 20-week scan, Chris and I were divided when it came to finding out the gender. I was adamant we should keep it a surprise, but Chris was itching to know. His argument was that we didn't have the time or battery power on the walk to waste researching names for two genders when we could halve our work! We even debated the prospect of him finding out at the scan and then keeping it a secret from me until the birth. However, for me, waiting until your baby is born to know whether it's a boy or a girl is the ultimate surprise in life and I wanted that; sure, it felt like a long time to wait, but, in my eyes, the wait would make that moment all the more beautiful. Also, neither of us felt he could keep the secret, so we passed on that idea!

The scan meant another trip back to Royal Worcester Hospital. The logistics of having to divert back to the other side of the country for my maternity care was definitely inconvenient; it meant a lot of organization, and the back and forth created a lack of consistency when it came to the walk, which we found difficult, mainly because consistency was important when it came to donations. However, it was around this time that I received a message from one of our Facebook followers, who happened to be a midwife, alerting me to the fact that I was, in fact, entitled to receive maternity care on the move. She told me it should definitely be possible for my notes to be accessible across multiple NHS trusts, but even if that proved problematic, as long as I kept my notes with me, I should be able to explain my situation and book appointments and scans in different locations as I walked. I was so relieved to hear this and wished I'd sought out this information much earlier. It was a real lesson in advocating for myself and trusting my instincts when something didn't feel right.

From then on, I decided to change my approach when it came to my maternity care; as long as I could, I'd organize it on the go.

20

You Can't Buy These Experiences, You Have to Walk for Them

I'd come to expect bad weather in Scotland, so it was a shock to find ourselves caught between two severe, almost back-to-back storms on our return to Essex after the 20-week scan. Storm Arwen struck towards the end of November while we were walking Mersea Island – it turned out to be one of the most powerful and destructive storms of the past decade, with a red weather warning, and we took a real Nordic battering pushing through the fiercely blustering winds and driving cold rain. To make matters worse, we really struggled to find a spot to pitch up that night, as nearly every piece of land we found seemed to be off limits. It wasn't until 9.30 p.m. that we finally managed to pitch our tent in the dark. It had been a real slog of a day but, thankfully, the tent survived a torrent of hailstones during the night. The next morning, we woke up to calm skies and golden clouds, the sun illuminating all the pastel-coloured beach huts!

Then, about twelve days later, Storm Barra hit and we were faced again with the daunting task of finding a spot to pitch the tent where we could take shelter overnight. Luckily, we had so many people following the walk on our social media and looking out for us that a man called Mick and his wife, Vicki, came to our aid and offered to let us pitch in their back garden.

As we got ourselves settled, Mick grabbed us some spare pillows and the difference was unbelievable: I'd got so used to simply using the dry bags in which our clothes were kept that a real pillow felt like pure luxury!

Mick and Vicki bent over backwards for us during our stay, dropping us off and picking us up each day so we could continue the walk, and cooking us delicious meals. We'd often return at night to find Mick had been to the local butcher and, with the help of his Australian lodger, he would barbecue steaks or lamb chops and serve them up with new potatoes and delicious salads, with a good bottle of red for the drinkers. We were dining like royalty and it was such a welcome break from what we could manage on the gas stove, given we could no longer cook on a fire because of the regulations. Mick and Vicki were unbelievably kind to us; he even drove us at 4 a.m. to make a brief television appearance in the hope it would bring in more donations for SSAFA.

It was nearly Christmas 2021, and I was a year and a month into the walk. In one sense, it felt utterly crazy and surreal that this was my life now. Nothing could have prepared me for the consistent cold nights for months on end, yet it had surprised me how quickly I'd adapted to a lifestyle that was so far removed from the one I'd always had. My house was now a two-man tent and I moved through the days, weeks, months and years on foot, always waking up somewhere new. There was no doubt that the past year had tested me physically, emotionally and mentally more than any other time in my life, and when you spend 24/7 with someone, confined in a tent at night, you definitely contemplate smothering them in their sleeping bag at times! But I wouldn't have changed our life for the world. I had learned so much about myself and gained so many unique, exceptional experiences and memories that no amount of money could ever buy.

Earlier in the journey, we'd met someone called Brian, another stranger at first who we now count as a treasured friend, who said to me, 'You can't buy these experiences, you have to walk for them.' His words rang so true. Entering my second year on the walk, knowing I was about to achieve my dream of being a mum, I was so excited for what was to come.

As Christmas neared, there was a surge of Covid cases in and around London, and it had become an almost impossible struggle to find anywhere in Essex to pitch the tent. We didn't want to encroach on people's personal space and their family celebrations over the festive period by being in their back garden, but we wanted to keep up our own tradition of being outside at Christmas. This simply wasn't possible along the Essex coastline, because everywhere was either too industrial or was privately owned land. Woodland spaces were often gated and chained with padlocks at night, and the nature reserves were off limits for camping. The campsites that did exist were also shut during winter, and we certainly didn't want to spend Christmas pitched in a dank, dark, concrete tunnel behind Tilbury Docks.

So, we took up an offer to return to a woodland in Northumberland where we had spent a few nights in a teepee during the summer. The set-up was the passion project of a man named Mark Tuff, who has turned a patch of woodland in the grounds of Howick Estate near Alnwick into a forest school known as Clarty Commandos. Mark had set up a volunteer-run, alternative provision outdoor education project there that helps children and young adults with special educational needs, as well as those who suffer from stress and anxiety and struggle in mainstream schools.

I loved the concept of forest schools, which centres around a very child-led, hands-on approach to outdoor learning and holistic development in nature. I knew they were very prevalent across Scandinavia, particularly in the early years before children begin formal education, aged six or seven, much later than here in the UK. Although it wasn't an approach I'd been able to get to grips with in inner-city London, I was now a big advocate for this type of education, especially since my experiences on the walk had given me such a deep connection to nature, and I felt this was very much the kind of learning experience I wanted for my baby one day.

Mark is another example of someone we first encountered as a stranger who we now count as a friend. In return for staying, we helped him clear up the damage caused by Storm Arwen ripping through his woodland. It was the least we could do. Mark got his chainsaw out to remove the fallen trees that blocked the entrance to the outside toilet, while we got to work on clearing out the teepee. It had only just survived the storm, so while Chris did all the heavy lifting to remove debris, reinforce some of the beams and make the log burner usable in order to make it safe to stay in, I got to grips with the interior, adorning it with festive fairy lights and a few candles to make it cosy. That night, we gathered firewood, breaking it up into different sizes to burn in order to cook our dinner. It had been so long since we'd been able to have a fire freely outside and it was a long-awaited relief to have access to that necessity once again!

We salvaged a fallen Norwegian fir for our Christmas tree and I began to make handcrafted decorations from fir cones and twigs to hang on it. I'd always loved getting creative when it came to adding special touches, and felt even more spurred on given a baby was growing inside me – an extra desire to make the day special and say a little 'Happy Christmas' to our unborn adventurer. We'd loved our previous woodland Christmas so much that we wanted to recreate the experience and make it even better now that we had another year's wisdom of living outdoors under our belts. We were determined to take the bushcraft cooking up a notch and Mark had given us the perfect set-up to go all out.

At some point, the walk would end, and we had yet to decide what life might look like after it. Also, we were so committed to our mission of living outside and fundraising for SSAFA that enjoying home comforts indoors, even if it was Christmas, felt like cheating. Why would people donate to the cause if they saw us choosing the easier option?

We spent all of Christmas Eve designing and preparing our outdoor ovens, including the A-frame for roasting a chicken on a spit over the fire, and several outdoor ovens to cook the trimmings. We were determined to perfect our roast potatoes this year, and being in one space for a few days meant we had time to get that bit more technical with our oven handiwork. That night, we seasoned and skewered the chicken so it was ready to go as soon as the fire was hot enough the next day.

It was that afternoon that I began to feel really worried that I hadn't experienced any movements from the baby. I was now five and a half months and had yet to feel a thing. It dawned on me that we were in the middle of nowhere over the festive period, with less access to public transport and medical care, and suddenly I was taken over by a surge of panic. An hour or so later, a local taxi driver rocked up with some supplies for Mark. I'd been unable to shake my worry and Chris insisted it was better for me to get checked out sooner rather than later, for my own peace of mind, so that I could enjoy Christmas. It would also be easier on Christmas Eve than Christmas Day.

The taxi driver took me to Alnwick Infirmary and waited while I went in. It turned out that the baby was absolutely fine, but the fact that I had an anterior placenta was blocking my ability to feel the baby's movements. I felt silly for letting paranoia get the better of me and guilty for taking a taxi when we couldn't afford it. I was also sure the driver was desperate to get back to his family on Christmas Eve rather than cart me around. But I knew I'd never forgive myself if the worst had happened and I'd ignored the warning signs. When we returned, the driver absolutely insisted there was no charge. His kindness brought me to tears and I hugged him in a way I'd hug a friend I hadn't seen in years. To have peace of mind regarding my baby was the one and only gift I needed, and he gave that to me; it was an act of kindness I shall never forget.

Two days later, I felt my first kick.

21

The Good Doctor

As soon as we woke on Christmas morning, I got to work peeling the vegetables while Chris put the finishing touches to the meat and got the fire going. We were able to have a coal fire, which burned longer than wood. Chris had devised a series of interlinking ovens, which I must say were remarkable! The heat from one underground oven funnelled heat up into another two, meaning we could roast vegetables and potatoes at the same time. Chris had spent years meticulously studying the way fires and heat behave. I'd seen how good he was at this, but this was on a different level. If a zombie apocalypse were to happen, I was with the right man!

I laid the table and decorated the tree with my handmade woodland decorations. Mark and his son, Harvey, also came to spend some of Christmas Day with us, cooking up their own feast on the camp's firepit. Between us, we shared their steaks, pigs in blankets, halloumi wrapped in Parma ham, as well as our traditional roast with all the trimmings. It was like a special bushcraft episode of *Come Dine with Me!*

On Boxing Day, my dad and his wife, Val, arrived to visit for a few days, and for the first time gained a proper insight into how hard we had to work to sustain ourselves living outdoors. The temperature was below freezing and Chris was barely able to leave the woods as he needed to spend the entire day chopping wood for the log burner in the teepee to keep us warm enough at night and into the next day. Dad and Val saw how precious the daylight hours were for us and that, if we went anywhere, we needed to return before nightfall so we could get organized for the evening while there was still light. While they were going back to a B&B with a log fire and central heating, we had to work for our heat.

Over the next few days, it also hammered with rain. I was frequently getting up in the night now to go to the toilet, but as I peered outside, I decided I didn't feel like getting soaked on a trip to the compost toilet. I peed in a pot instead and put it down by the side of our sleeping area, ready to dispose of when I woke up. It was so dark in the teepee that, when Chris woke up and got out of the sleeping bag, he stepped right in it!

But staying warm wasn't the only worry on our minds. During the festive period, I'd been stroking Jet when I noticed a lump around her tummy area. This wasn't the first lump she'd had since I'd known her; she'd had one removed during lockdown, but we had clocked it early and it had been so tiny that the vet had assured us we needn't worry. I told Chris immediately about this latest one and, given she was that bit older now and noticeably slowing down, we decided to take up the offer from *This Morning*'s Dr Scott Miller, who had given Chris his number when he'd met him in Scotland. Coincidentally, he had been meaning to ring us in the hope of filming an episode about Jet for his Australian YouTube series, *Bondi Vet*, so we agreed to go ahead.

We returned to Essex in early January and met up with Dr Scott on Canvey Island. In front of the cameras, he did an assessment of Jet and discovered the one lump I'd felt was actually one of six lying deeper beneath the skin. It was such a devastating moment and I honestly felt like our world had shattered. I looked at Chris. His eyes welled up as he stood in silence, rooted to the spot, and I knew he was trying desperately to hold it together but was breaking into a million pieces. Scott offered to operate on her the next morning to remove the tumours, completely free of charge.

He warned us that it was major surgery and, although he would do everything he could, there was no guarantee she would make it through. To think that we could suddenly lose Jet within a matter of hours was unfathomable and crushing. We couldn't get our heads around it and spent the rest of the day on autopilot, holding back tears while trying to be strong for Jet, so that she didn't pick up on our worry.

The next morning, we woke at the crack of dawn to take Jet to her surgery in Isleworth, in a hire car provided by Dr Scott. He kindly let us both into the operating room so we could stay with her right until her eyes closed as the anaesthetic took hold. There was some good news before the op: blood tests had revealed that, even though she was around nine now, she had the heart, liver and kidneys of a four-year-old. Her outdoor life had made her strong inside and out, and we hoped that it would be enough to save her.

The wait was excruciating. We were so wracked with panic that we couldn't even leave the hire car. I was also terrified as to what it would do to Chris if she didn't pull through. Her surgery took double the time expected, but by 2 p.m. it was finally over and, thankfully, had gone as well as it could have done. There will never be words to explain our gratitude to Dr Scott; the fact that he took such swift action after the diagnosis and treated her with such care and dedication made all the difference. She had survived and that was everything. Now, we needed to prioritize her recovery. Jet had looked after me all those cold winter nights in the tent; now it was my turn to give her every bit of care and comfort she needed. I called my mum and she immediately agreed we could go there, the walk on hold for as long as Jet needed to be fighting fit again.

Jet received round-the-clock care as we cleaned and dressed her wounds every day. My mum even gave up her bedroom upstairs with the en-suite bathroom for Chris and Jet to use. I slept in the study. I was getting up incessantly throughout the night to use the toilet and Jet needed undisturbed rest rather than me waking her up.

During that time, Jet received such an outpouring of love from people all over the UK who had fallen in love with her while following our journey. People of all ages sent us artwork inspired by her – hundreds of creations in the form of drawings, clay, stone-art, poetry, weavings, paintings, needlework, bead-work – even cake decor! It really was a testament to what Jet had come to mean to so many on our journey; to us, it felt like she really had won the hearts of the nation.

Meanwhile, I walked along the Malvern Hills every day and followed an antenatal exercise programme online. I was also contacted by two ladies from Worcestershire-based charity Becoming Families, which supports local families throughout the critical 1,001 days from pregnancy through to two years old, offering education, support and wellbeing services. One was a midwife named Helen and the other a perinatal wellbeing specialist named Jo. They were conscious that, due to my situation, I'd been unable to attend any antenatal classes and offered to come and share some of the information they deliver in their classes to me in the comfort of my mum's living room while Jet recovered!

Helen and Jo felt that my outdoor lifestyle would be brilliant for attachment and would lay really strong foundations for neurodevelopment and growth. In their eyes, my choices were what they referred to as a 'salutogenic approach', putting my physical and mental wellbeing at the heart of my daily life, which they told me optimizes the health of the unborn baby inside the womb and during his or her early life.

When it came to my determination to carry on the walk post-birth, their views were that living in the great outdoors without the distraction and noise of modern living would enable me to be totally present, to hone into my baby's way of communicating and to rely on my intuition in a way that was far more reliable than opening up a laptop to ask Google.

One afternoon, I was downstairs in my mum's kitchen when I heard a disturbing shout from Chris. I immediately panicked, thinking something was wrong. I rushed to the staircase only to see Jet standing up next to him, where she belonged. She had jumped off the bed and was standing strong for the first time since her operation. There had been moments in the past few weeks when I'd wondered if I'd ever see the two of them standing next to each other again, and I can't begin to tell you how happy it made me. After such an agonizing time, we knew she was going to be okay.

I gave her a gentle hug and broke down in tears. For me, she had become a fellow female best friend, but so much more than that – she had been my strength and solace throughout it all. She was the source of so much joy, but also the easiest to turn to whenever things got a little bit tough. To see her standing again, it felt like the three and a half Musketeers were back together, as they should be. There was no doubt Jet was a warrior; over the coming weeks she continued to recover quicker than any of us expected. We should have known our girl wasn't about to be taken down that easily!

After a month and a video call with Dr Scott, we were given the green light to get going again, taking it slowly for Jet. Given she was used to life outside, on the walk, it was deemed best for her to return to what she knew and loved.

*

With a week to go until the end of February, we were back where we left off on Canvey Island. I was now seven and a half months pregnant. As we found our stride again, we worked our way round London Gateway Port and Tilbury Docks, contending with power station after power station and graffiti-filled tunnels, broken up with the odd historical fort, before finally reaching Kent. Known as the Garden of England, Kent meant more green space and a welcome change from all the concrete.

When it came to maternity clothes, I hadn't bought anything new. My mum and I had sewn a large purple patch into the side of the Lycra thermal top I always wore, so that it stretched far enough around my tummy. A lovely lady on the Essex coast had sewn an elastic band into my hiking trousers to give them enough stretch. When it became evident those weren't going to hold, a follower very kindly got in touch with a small company that makes maternity hiking trousers, and was gifted a pair to give me. Those, alongside a hand-me-down pair of maternity leggings I'd been given by a friend, would see me through until the end.

We didn't have a concrete plan quite yet with regards to the birth, but it was on our list to work out very quickly. Now that I was in my final trimester, my maternity appointments were more frequent, every three weeks, but from this point they would all take place on the move. By 32 weeks, as we came along the River Medway, sleep deprivation really kicked in. It felt like the baby slept all day and partied all night! I was also now getting up to go to the toilet an average of nine times a night. I had given up trying to haul myself off the roll mat and out of the tent every time, so we made our peace with sacrificing one of our cooking pots so I could squat over that, do what was needed and empty it out of the tent flap. I just had to make sure I didn't empty it right outside, so we wouldn't end up stepping in it before shoes were on when we got up in the morning! Finding enough public toilets during the day when we were in more built-up areas, to cater for my frequent need to go, also proved a major daily challenge.

We had no way of carrying one of those huge pregnancy pillows, so I'd brought a small cushion with me from my mum's to place between my knees to help me sleep more comfortably. It was thin, so didn't do a great job, but I certainly felt the difference without it. Even though the lack of sleep made me tired, I still felt that I really needed to walk during the day. I loved the daily walking. It made me feel rejuvenated, more energetic, eased the stiffness and definitely helped to keep my spirits high. It also meant I didn't have too much time to dwell on aches and pains or worry what labour would be like. I could just take the days as they came and really enjoy them.

I would be full-term in just five weeks, and it was time to make a definitive plan for the birth. I was well aware that birth plans can quickly go out of the window, but my hope was to have as natural a birth as I could: a water birth, as near to the coast as possible, and somewhere where I felt connected to nature. Environment had become increasingly important to me as the pregnancy progressed.

I'd received a message recommending an excellent home-birth midwifery team based around Dorchester in Dorset called the Cygnet Homebirth Team. I contacted them to explain my situation and my birth preference, and they were more than happy to accommodate me; I was able to register my personal details with them over the phone and then just needed to find a base in the area for the time covering the birth period. I would need to ensure I arrived by 37 weeks pregnant, the time from which I was full-term and could naturally go into labour at any point. Ideally, they wanted me to arrive slightly before then, as they needed to do their own blood tests to get up to speed with my specifics before I had any chance of going into labour. The ladies from Becoming Families, who we'd met while up in Malvern, had kindly offered us a birth pool that was no longer being used.

There were still lots of unknowns ahead, but the walk had shown me the power of community and the power of trusting in my instincts when it came to the path I'd chosen. It had given me a lot of faith in the goodwill of others and the universe as a whole. We never ever expected people to help us and we never relied on the goodwill of people, but they did rally round to offer help. Although we would accept it only if we truly needed it, it was incredibly heart-warming to know that people were behind us in such a big way.

It was while we were walking the Isle of Sheppey that we received a message from a family based on the Dorset coast, only five minutes from Ringstead Bay. Having heard our story, Dizzi and Ralph wanted to offer the use of their yurt, in which we could set up the birthing pool. After a video call, I was really sold on the idea. Dizzi and Ralph had two children of their own and seemed incredibly friendly, laid-back, family-orientated people, and the yurt right near the coast felt like a magical choice that so aligned with my ideal vision for giving birth. At this point, they were a good 200 miles further down the south coast from where we were.

When we got to the Kent coastal town of Margate, we headed to the hospital for a routine 34-week maternity check-up. A nurse insisted I get in a wheelchair so she could wheel me to the correct ward, as she deemed it way too far for me to walk at this stage. I couldn't help but laugh, given what I was doing every day! I said there was definitely no need and I did lots of walking, but she wouldn't take no for an answer. So, as I was wheeled through the hospital, I sat back and enjoyed being off my feet for a few minutes!

These on-the-go appointments were really eye-opening. Back in Worcester, all of my notes had been kept online using an app called Badger Net; apparently, there wasn't one universal pregnancy-notes system used across the country. On this side of the country, all notes were still handwritten and kept in a traditional filing system. I was given my notes on a Post-it to take away with me, ready to share with the next hospital!

But, wherever I went, the midwives were always really supportive of my pregnancy on the walk. 'Walking,' they would say, 'is brilliant for mum and baby; it lowers risk for developing gestational diabetes, cardiac disease, high blood pressure; it helps babies get into the best position for birth and makes you more likely to have a spontaneous labour, not to mention the benefits for your own mental wellbeing, which also means the baby's.' When I told them my plan was to continue walking with our baby post-birth, they thought it sounded amazing. 'What a life for that baby! Newborns just need to be close. Being held by you, being strapped to you, being carried, you can be totally responsive to their needs all the time – it's the ideal!' they'd say. I must say, it felt good to hear my own intuition about what I was doing corroborated by them so enthusiastically.

I was told at the Margate appointment that the baby was still breech. There was time for them to turn, but I knew there was a greater likelihood I could end up having a Caesarean section. Given how keen I was for a natural birth, I wanted to do whatever I could to help the baby flip, so, whenever I found a bench along the coast path, I would insist on stopping and hanging forwards off it, head to the floor, doing repeat forward-leaning inversions. Goodness only knows what passers-by must've thought, seeing a heavily pregnant woman hanging upside down off a bench on the clifftops! This was one of a number of techniques my midwives had told me to look up on a site called 'Spinning Babies'. I would also do what's called a 'breech tilt'. It's normally done with the aid of pillows, a sofa and an ironing board to lean against, but with no such luxury I did mine whenever I came to a hill. I'd lie with my head and shoulders on the ground and the rest of my body, feet at the top, against the incline of the hill, for as long as ten minutes, two or three times a day, the idea being that gravity would help lift the baby out of the pelvis, tuck its chin and hopefully somersault to rotate head down.

The day of that appointment marked another huge milestone for us: that afternoon, as we came around the Isle of Thanet to Ramsgate, we had finally conquered the east coast of England and were officially on the south coast. It was about time! We'd thought the east coast would be a doddle that we'd smash in a couple of months, but, with all the setbacks we'd faced, it had taken nine long months – almost the length of an entire pregnancy. I was about as ready now to meet the south coast as I was to meet my baby!

There was frost on the ground and big exhalations of icy condensation whenever we breathed out, walking from Sandwich to Deal and then into Dover. I felt huge at this point, lugging myself uphill over the iconic white cliffs, but it was a beautiful walk, especially when the sun came out and lit up the white of the cliffs against the turquoise hues of the sea. Dover was such a momentous point on the south coast, it felt like a real milestone to get there, and even more special to enjoy those views having hauled a bump the size of a honeydew melon to the top.

Beneath our feet, meanwhile, was an entire network of underground tunnels that had played a pivotal role in our nation's history. The tunnels had been excavated during the Napoleonic Wars to hold cannon guns, then were used as a hospital during the First World War, and, in the Second, the chambers became the operation centre for getting the troops out of Dunkirk.

I felt so grateful, standing there. I still felt strong and able to keep going, and I was determined to do just that for as long as it felt right. I could only hope that all this walking would work similar wonders when it came to being in labour!

It was a long day getting into Dover, as Jet's trailer, which we towed her in as much as possible now, had broken and it had been extremely awkward hard work hauling it over the clifftops, over the stiles and up and down all the steps. We were exhausted and still had no idea where we would sleep that night. Then we received a message from a couple, David and Corrie, who had organized for us to sleep within the grounds of Dover Castle! We were absolutely thrilled – we now had an evening destination in sight, albeit up another hill, and it brought back lovely memories of staying at Bamburgh and our spectacular evening within its 1,400-year-old grounds, perched on its rocky plateau, standing guard over the Northumberland coastline.

It was already night-time when we finally arrived, and we felt so lucky to have the empty grounds all to ourselves overnight. How many people are gifted an opportunity like that? After sharing ghost stories, we had some fun creating our own ghostly images, taking photos with our shadows against the castle walls, before standing on the castle ramparts marvelling at the twinkling lights of the town and Dover port below.

That night, we slept on the floor of a twelfth-century building right next to the Great Tower. We were also given a private tour of the tower, including an exhibition replicating what life would have been like back in Henry II's era. The king and queen's bedchambers were particularly impressive. As much as I wished I could sneak into one for the night, I was happy to make do with our roll mat on the floor. It was a small price to pay for the privilege of a night alone in one of the most iconic castles in Britain.

22

The Hope of a Sunrise

It was still dark outside when I decided to call it quits on trying to get any more sleep. I quietly zipped open the tent flap, removed the small cushion wedged between my knees and hauled myself out. Manoeuvring myself off the roll mat and out of the tent had become an art form in itself these days, especially since I felt like I had a bowling ball beginning to descend through my pelvis! I had managed almost my entire pregnancy to date wild camping in a tent and wouldn't have changed it, but there was no denying that the past month or so had become very uncomfortable.

We had made it to Hastings Country Park and, as I stood now gazing out to sea, I cradled my baby bump and hoped for a glorious sunrise. It was March, the year still sandwiched between late winter and early spring. The sea was coated in mist, the outer tent was damp and there was a definite chill in the air. The world was silent and still and, in that moment, I felt like I had it all to myself. However, a band of thick grey cloud sat heavy on the horizon, obscuring everything. No sunrise today, then. But all of a sudden, a vibrant pink orb rose out of the mist, painting the sky an incredible shade of pale pink before exploding into fiery orange. I had seen so many beautiful sunrises on this walk, but this one felt particularly special. This would be the last sunrise I would see before we pressed pause on our coast-walking mission to go and give birth to our baby.

Chris had called it, knowing I wouldn't. He could see I could no longer physically continue. The main issue was sleep, or complete lack of it. A few nights prior, I'd slept on a garage floor and actually cried when I woke up in the morning because it was so hard and uncomfortable – grass was one thing, but the solid concrete had been agony. Then, I'd happily upgraded to a sofa in one of the outbuildings of a campsite, only to spend most of the night looking at my enormous belly hanging over the edge of it. 'That's it,' he'd said. 'I can't watch you suffer any more. It's time to call it quits and get you something comfortable to sleep on until the baby comes. You're too bloody-minded for your own good. We're leaving for the yurt tomorrow.'

So, we'd be packing up and leaving as soon as he woke up. If I'd had my way, I'd probably have carried on walking right up until D-day. But Chris was keen to avoid a situation where my waters broke on the top of a cliff somewhere and he genuinely had to enact the YouTube baby-delivery crash course he'd been joking about!

The stunning sunrise felt like the universe was unwrapping its gift to me and my unborn baby, wishing us well for what was to come, knowing that, when I returned, I would be bringing him or her with me to witness its splendour unfold. It dawned on me that, the next time I stood on this spot, I would no longer be the same Kate that was standing here now but a different version of myself entirely. The next time I saw these clifftops, I would be holding a tiny baby in my arms. I would be a mum.

I looked down at my bump and thought about how unconventional our situation was. Chris and I had decided to have a baby with no house, no transport, no money and no jobs. Everything we had, we carried with us on our backs. We were on what would turn out to be a six-year walk around the entire UK coastline, raising money for charity. Despite this, it had still been a conscious decision.

In our society, having a baby under such circumstances is a very irregular choice and, as I had already begun to learn, the system certainly isn't geared up for it. I knew that, to many, our choice would be viewed as inconceivable, impossible, even seen by some as reckless and irresponsible. I also knew that our choice would make the experience of becoming new parents – and, in my case, a first-time one – much more challenging. Yet I had never felt so certain and steadfast in my conviction that we were doing the very best thing by our child, bringing them into the world this way: grounded simplicity with very few material possessions, rooted in the great outdoors. Ours was a world that prioritized slow, deep, meaningful connection with each other and with nature, and I couldn't wait for our child to be a part of that.

The past nine months had been eventful to say the least, but I was so proud of us for making it work. We'd had to navigate our way around a system of maternity care that wasn't well set up for our level of 'alternative', but we had made it to 36 weeks! Not only that – I'd had the most smooth-sailing pregnancy I could have hoped for and I was still feeling great, camping and plodding along the coast path, albeit much slower, much heavier, and carrying my cargo on my front now, rather than my back. I had grown this baby and kept them safe and healthy without a home, without central heating, without a comfortable bed, without any of the mod cons. We'd faced hundreds of questions, concerns, assumptions, protestations and projected limitations, and we'd never let them faze us.

When we announced the pregnancy on our social media,

people were thrilled for us. When I made it clear that my intentions were to carry on walking, most remained very supportive, but we did contend with some people voicing their doubts, concerns and criticism, particularly during my final trimester. The suggestions were that I should be resting and not pushing myself to these extremes, because it wasn't good for the baby. Some focused on the fact that I was still sleeping in a tent during winter and that could be harmful to the baby. Mostly, however, the comments revolved around our need to stop and get a house before the baby was born.

It was implied that I would need to stop the walk and either rent somewhere or go back to my mum's to have the baby and raise our newborn. Chris would also have to stop the walk for a few years, get a job and stick around until the child was old enough for him to resume where he'd left off; or I should look after our baby on my own in a house, while Chris carried on with the walk solo; we could reconvene with family life together once he'd made it to the finish line. To many, it seemed like there was no other fathomable option for us.

Once I voiced my intentions to carry on with the walk with our newborn in tow, again, most rallied behind us, but there were certainly many who voiced concerns, judgements, assumptions and preconceived notions that insisted what we were doing was not in our child's best interests. Apparently, the baby's immune system would not be strong enough to cope. The baby would be too cold. It was irresponsible to continue living this way now that we had a child, and we needed to stop, settle down, find a house, get jobs and ensure we could offer what society deems a stable and secure environment for a baby.

In the end, the phenomenal human kindness and support we received far outweighed those comments. Of course from family and friends, but most often from total strangers – those who were following our journey online, or those we crossed paths with on the way. It warmed my heart to know my child would be born into that kind of positivity, love and kindness outside of their immediate circle.

But there was no getting around it – we still had so far to go to complete the walk, around 2,000 miles. It was daunting. There were without question some monumental logistical challenges ahead of us: we still had the coastline of twelve more counties to walk, which included all of the South West Coast Path, as well as myriad islands, which we would now be doing with a newborn. And those were just the challenges we knew about, the ones we could foresee! I had no idea what it was going to look like or how the hell we were going to do it. I just had faith that it would all be okay.

To add to all that, I knew that, as my due date crept ever closer, and when the baby arrived, we were going to face an even bigger onslaught of 'How on earths'. I was also aware that I knew absolutely nothing about babies and wasn't that clued up about childbirth either. I thought back to the day after I'd discovered I was pregnant, standing with my feet in the water at Spurn Point. I had known next to nothing about pregnancy, but had followed my instincts regardless. I felt very much the same now; I was far from prepared for what came next with a newborn, but I just wanted to trust in my body and deal with the process one step at a time. Pretty much my only preparation for what lay ahead was the fact that I'd diligently spent the past two weeks staying up at night in the tent, listening to a hypnobirthing course with earphones in, while Chris slept or watched an episode of *Peep Show*, signal permitting! Other than that, I was about as unprepared as they come.

For now, I decided my ignorance was definitely bliss. If this walk had taught me anything so far, it was that, when faced with a mountain that feels too big, too scary, too hard to climb, the answer is always to take it one step at a time. So, I'd decided to only focus on the main task ahead: giving birth. I'd prepare myself as much as possible for that and cross all the other bridges when we came to them.

'What a beautiful sunrise!' remarked Chris as he emerged from the tent with Jet. 'You should have woken me earlier.'

'I know. Snooze, you lose! I was actually just enjoying the peace and quiet on my own for a minute, before you came and gate-crashed,' I joked. 'Just needed some time to digest the fact that, next time we pitch up here, our little team will no longer be three, but four.' We'd already agreed that we would restart the walk, after the baby was born, exactly where we'd left it.

Chris was nothing but positive. 'I know! Crazy, isn't it, but one thing I know is it'll be amazing! We're going to give this child the best life. But I'm sticking to my guns – we're getting you to that yurt.'

'Farewell, for now!' I exclaimed, waving at the place where the land meets the sea – the ever-changing coast, the place we had come to call home. I took Chris's hand in mine as we turned our backs on the vast blue sea, Jet loyally at our side. I squeezed his hand tightly. It was a big moment. When we returned here to resume the walk, it would be with our baby. I had no idea what lay around the corner and no idea what to expect. Relying on my intuition when taking risks and diving into the unknown had been life-defining for me. It had led me to my favourite, most memorable, transformational experiences in life. It had led me here.

All I could do now was trust my gut again.

23

A Small Tartan Pouch

The yurt in Dorset where I'd chosen to bring my baby into the world was perfect. I could just picture myself in the birth pool under the skylight, my baby born under the stars, surrounded by the magic of fairy lights and cosy colours. My first experiences as a mother would be here, and it made it feel sacred. All of my maternity appointments from now on would happen in Dorset, with the home-birth team coming out to visit me. The midwives were all excited by my choice to labour and birth in the beautiful setting of the yurt. My home-birth team saw it as a fundamental part of their role to support women in their birth choices, no matter how unusual they may be. My main midwife, Lyndsey, was fantastic, making me feel so comfortable that she became like a close friend I could confide in about anything.

While I was lying down on the bed in the yurt one day, she ran the tape measure over the length of my tummy to gain an idea of baby's growth and felt around to check baby's positioning (which had now turned – all that hanging upside down off a bench had worked!). 'I'm really in awe of the way you've managed to carry on this wild life while pregnant,' she said, 'not giving in to the toxic environment of all the social pressures to perform in one way or another as a "pregnant woman".'

I was still walking around 5 to 6 miles every day, mainly out of habit, but also to keep up what had felt so beneficial for me thus far. We didn't have a vehicle either, so to buy provisions from the local Co-op was a five-mile round trip. In between, I spent my time enjoying the better weather and the clear signs of spring now that the daffodils and bluebells were in bloom. I also spent hours making baby mobiles out of driftwood and sea glass collected from the surrounding beaches, doing origami and preparing a baby book.

A week before my due date, a group of local Dorset ladies, most of whom I'd never even met, whisked me off to the clifftops on the Isle of Portland for a surprise baby shower! They set up a gazebo adorned with bunting high up on the hill, with brilliant views over the coast, ready for an afternoon of baby-related fun. We spent the afternoon playing games, including attempting to guess what particular food might have made a stain on a nappy, and painting pottery, the idea being for each of us to paint designs onto mugs, plates and bowls which would then be glazed for Chris and I to have as a crockery set at some point in the future.

The women gave me such beautiful gifts – hand-knitted blankets, a leather-bound journal in which I could record my motherhood journey and a necklace made from sea glass collected from Ringstead Bay, the beach closest to where our baby would be born. I'd never expected to have a baby shower at all, given my circumstances and the fact that my friends and family were all so far away – I was extremely touched by the thoughtful effort. Little did I know, they were also in on a very big secret!

When I returned, I collapsed on the bed in the yurt, ready to call it a day and go to sleep. 'Kate, why don't we do something a little different and go and stay in the other woodland tonight, just to give us a change of scene? We could get a fire on, have dinner down there, it would be a nice change.'

I crawled under the covers, slumped on my left side and wedged my pillow between my knees. 'Oh, I really can't be bothered tonight, babe – all the excitement from the day has wiped me out! I'm gonna hit the sack and get an early night!'

'Are you sure? We could stay in the fairy-bender – we haven't stayed in there yet. I bet it's really special inside.' The fairy-bender was a rustic off-grid dwelling made entirely from hazel branches harvested from the surrounding woodland, intertwined and bent over to form a dome-like shape. It even had a stained-glass window reclaimed from a church. To make it, they'd enlisted the help of a master carpenter, and its construction had featured on an episode of *My Unique B&B*, aired on BBC.

'I'm sure – I just want to sleep. Night, night. See you in the morning.'

Chris stepped outside the yurt. I lay there thinking that he seemed a little disappointed – I hadn't seen him all day and it wasn't like me to turn down an opportunity to do something fun and different. Ten minutes later, I rolled over and heaved myself upright. *No, come on, you can sleep tomorrow; the woods might be fun; it'll be worth the effort!* I told myself. I emerged from the yurt and found Chris. 'Come on, then,' I said. 'I've managed to peel myself off the bed! Let's go for it. You only live once!'

With Jet beside us, we walked down the track and along the narrow woodland path lined with wild garlic and a carpet of bluebells. All of a sudden, Chris stopped me and suggested I put my hands over my eyes, to see if he could guide me the rest of the way as a bit of fun. When I opened them, there was a steel cooking plate hanging over a fire on which he was about to cook our evening meal, a bottle of alcohol-free bubbly, a vase of wildflowers on the picnic table and tea-light candles everywhere. It was really beautiful and I was so moved by his thoughtfulness and hours of effort that I had a tear in my eye. 'This is amazing – what a lovely thing to do! Thank you!' I said, giving him a big hug.

He insisted I sit and relax while he juggled cooking steaks, broccoli and new potatoes over the fire, timing it all perfectly so nothing was either burnt or cold when we came to eat it. After dinner, he called me over to him and, as we stood face to face, he said, 'I'm going to marry you one day, you know that.'

'I hope so!' I replied with a cheeky smile.

With that, he got down on one knee, pulled out a ring from a small tartan pouch and asked me to marry him. 'Marry me, Kate. I love you so much, I want to be with you for the rest of my life!'

I couldn't believe it – it was so unexpected! I'd had absolutely no idea that he had been planning any of this or even that it had been remotely on his mind! Given our conversations, the prospect of marriage had been way off in the distant future, *after* the walk, certainly not a consideration just now. As it turned out, he had been the key conspirator behind my baby shower, masterminding the whole thing and enlisting the help of these ladies to give him the time to set his proposal up. He had certainly nailed the surprise factor! In fact, he'd nailed the whole thing. 'Yes, yes, I'll marry you!' I replied, tears streaming down my cheeks. I looked down at Jet – she gave her nod of approval and looked up at Chris knowingly, as if to say, 'See – told you she'd say yes, Dad!'

Once I'd had time to digest the moment, I was able to take a proper look at the ring. When Chris had decided he wanted to pop the question, he got in touch with Kathleen, the lady in Shetland who'd knitted him the hat he'd given to me when we first met at the bottom of the Whaligoe Steps. He'd asked her if she had any of the Shetland wool left from the same batches she'd used to make that hat; she did, and used it to make three different hand-knitted engagement rings for him to choose from to give to me. The pouch he'd pulled the ring from was also made by Kathleen, using Chris's tartan kilt pattern, and she'd used the same batch of material to make the kilt for the bear she had sent as a gift for our baby! She had tied a red ribbon around it with a heart in the middle. Chris had then chosen to add the extra special touch of a piece of light-blue Dorset sea glass glued to the ring to act as his one-carat diamond! To me, the ring showed how much he really knew me. I'd always known I'd like a really unusual, one-of-a-kind ring if the time ever came. Honestly, I'd always assumed that, if he did do it, it would most likely be with a piece of tent rope! I didn't care about having a diamond or a platinum band, I just loved the fact that the ring was so personal and meaningful in a way that was so strongly linked to our story: to our journey, to our baby, to when we first met and also to some special people who had become a part of our story along the way. *And*, how many girls get *three* engagement rings?! Now, I could alternate for different moods and occasions!

That night, we stayed in the fairy-bender, which was a magical feast for the eyes and felt very romantic. Inside, it was adorned with sumptuous brightly coloured fabrics, as well as candles which Chris had positioned all around. We slept in a cosy little raised sleeping nook surrounded by fairy lights. It was everything I could have wanted in a proposal – not flashy or laden with extravagant expense, just full of thought, creative effort and personal touches.

I could never have imagined that, when I made that call to walk down those clifftop steps in the north of Scotland, I'd end up bumping into the man I would say yes to spending the rest of my life with! I would never have thought that, less than two years later, I'd end up with the most heartfelt, magical proposal in the woods, shortly before we were to welcome our little one into the world. It really made me think just how amazingly life can turn out and what unexpected surprises can lie just around the corner. Chris was my best friend, my partner in crime and my soulmate. We'd known so quickly that we were right for each other and we'd had so many epic adventures together already – I just knew that we had the best life ahead of us, and the icing on the cake was that our love was to be embodied in the form of our baby, who would soon be here to join us.

As I passed my due date, I felt absolutely enormous and uncomfortable to the point of almost needing to be airlifted out of bed in the mornings! Yet I was very relaxed about waiting for the baby to arrive in his or her own time, and there was no doubt I had become very invested in my birth preference – an intimate, peaceful, homely water birth in the comfort of the yurt. Then I had another scan at the hospital and was told the baby had a large head, broad shoulders and was weighing in at 9 lb 1 oz – a description which was frankly terrifying for a first-time mum hoping for a natural birth.

I was aware that home births could go wrong; I'd heard through a friend about shoulder dystocia, when the baby's head has been born but one of the shoulders becomes stuck behind the mother's pubic bone, delaying the birth of the body, which can lead to serious complications. It was suggested I be induced. While I knew that giving birth was one of those things you can't plan for, and that I should be open-minded and flexible, I was very anti-induction. More often than not, an induced birth leads to a Caesarean section, which I wanted to avoid at all costs, unless absolutely necessary.

The conversation at the hospital made birth feel very medical, clinical and quite anxiety-inducing, contradicting everything I'd been absorbing over the past months. These recent weeks in the tent, on top of the hypnobirthing course that I'd been listening to with earphones at night, I'd read countless positive birth stories online for inspiration and peace of mind. Once we'd arrived at the yurt, Dizzi had also lent me a video called *Birth Story* about Ina May Gaskin and her Farm Midwives – a group of women who had delivered babies without medical intervention on a hippy commune in 1970s rural Tennessee, in America. I made Chris sit up in the yurt with me at night as we watched this raw birth show, Chris shifting uncomfortably beside me as women were shown very graphically pushing out babies, their legs akimbo in the middle of a bus or caravan, in a very holistic manner, empowering women to give birth naturally (a far cry from his preferred *Peep Show*!). Dizzi also lent me her book called *Spiritual Midwifery*, which was a collection of birth stories by women who had given birth supported by her methods in this way.

I was determined to trust in the natural process of birth, and to trust what my body could do. I was fit and healthy, after all, because I had just walked from the Scottish Highlands to the south coast of England. My mind and body had got me this far – they would surely see me through what was coming.

24

Birth Part 1

We set up the yurt to prepare for the baby's arrival. Chris had secured a book deal to write his story of the walk, and the initial payment allowed us to buy all the essentials we needed, including a baby bath, nappies, wipes and a few clothes. Our approach to baby paraphernalia had to be minimalist, given we could only carry the absolute essentials when we set off again. So, no pram, no bassinet, no baby monitor and no bottle-feeding supplies, because I fully intended to breastfeed. My plan was to simply carry the baby in a sling and breastfeed on demand as we moved over the clifftops each day. Now that I was so close to the baby's arrival, a good friend tried to warn me various times about possible struggles with breastfeeding. I knew she absolutely had my best interests at heart, but at the time I just couldn't entertain it. I'd read a brief booklet about breastfeeding that was given to me by a midwife, which I'd carried in the side pouch of my backpack to read more thoroughly when the time came, but it felt like too much to worry about all the what-ifs with feeding just now. In my mind, I needed to focus entirely on the birth and I would cross other bridges if and when I came to them.

For the yurt, we were given a second-hand cot by Dr Scott Miller that he had used for his four children. It was one of many items we were gifted during those weeks of preparation – I was incredibly moved by the outpouring of love and support we received from people following our journey. Chris and I felt like Mr and Mrs Claus in a Christmas workshop – we needed an army of elves just to help unpack and organize it all! We were sent hand-knitted blankets, hats and cardigans, sleepsuits, all manner of slings, baby sleeping bags, cuddly toys, precious keepsakes, and boxes and boxes of hand-me-down clothes. Even though I was well prepared in many ways, there were some post-birth items for me I hadn't considered, such as breast pads, ice packs, perineal sprays and postpartum pants.

It was really touching. I'd always imagined that the love and support we needed would come from my close family and friends (and it did), but never in my life did I imagine so much of it would come from strangers. It was the first time we truly appreciated how many people were watching our story unfold and were willing us on, and I felt overwhelming gratitude for all the thoughtful gestures to welcome our child into the world. For all the negativity that exists in today's society, the walk was showing me that there was enough kindness in people to make up for it a hundredfold.

As the end of April loomed, I was 41 weeks pregnant and two weeks over my due date. My mum came down on a surprise visit to support us for a few days. First, we went to Lulworth Cove for a change of scenery. I hiked all the way around the clifftops there, but still no sign that baby was on his or her way. The next day, we headed to Studland Bay. Jet didn't seem in the mood for going far, so Chris and my mum stayed with her at the cafe while I went walking alone. When I still hadn't returned two hours later, they began to worry that I'd gone into labour on the beach and set off to look for me. When they found me, Chris ran up, clearly panicked.

'Where have you been?!'

'I'm fine!' I protested. 'Don't worry – no lifeguard delivery in the dunes needed today!' I laughed.

I think by now even he was slightly bewildered by my determination to keep moving! But I loved the familiar surroundings of Studland, where we had spent summer holidays every year when I was young, and so I had been picking up shells to keep as a reminder of this time. It felt extra special that my own child would be born in a place where I had so many happy childhood memories myself. I returned from my walk feeling energized and ready for anything.

Mum had to go home soon after. I had hoped her timing would coincide with the birth, but no luck; it looked like we were going to have to wait a bit longer. But, later that night, I woke up around 11.30 p.m. with what felt like serious period pains. I knew that these were often a precursor to labour and could last several hours, even days, before labour actually started, so I didn't wake Chris. I just tried to see the pain through as I would with any other period pain and go back to sleep. By 1 a.m., I realized sleep was not on the cards: the cramps were extremely painful. I had moved to sit on my birthing ball and began some breathing techniques to try to get more comfortable. By 2 a.m., the pain had really picked up and I woke Chris, desperate to get my hands on some paracetamol. It was like waking a crusty-eyed ogre on sleeping pills! He initially looked up at me as if to say, 'You've got to be kidding me – not at this hour of the morning, surely?!' But he quickly snapped out of it once he realized what was happening. We didn't have any paracetamol; Chris had finished the pack off trying to get to sleep the other night and had forgotten to replace them. He ended up calling some people who lived not far from the yurt and, as sheer luck would have it, one person answered at that ungodly hour and came to our aid!

Over the past weeks, I'd made him a to-do list for labour, combined with notes listing my wishes for the birth in case I needed to be taken to hospital. He woke Dizzi and Ralph in the house to alert them that it was D-day and we may soon need to start filling the birthing pool.

I continued to manage the pain by walking around and bouncing on my birthing ball until about 4 a.m., when I decided it was time to call the midwifery team. I was told it sounded like I had gone into established labour when I'd first woken and a midwife was sent out. I was shocked there was no prelude – we were skipping straight to the main act! When the midwife arrived at around 5 a.m., I was 3 cm dilated. We refrained from filling the birth pool yet, given I had a way to go and the pool would need to be kept at a temperature of around 37 degrees for baby's arrival. Since we were in a yurt, it was going to be a challenge to maintain that temperature for a prolonged period of time. Ideally, I was to dilate 1 cm every hour, but six and a half hours after the midwife's arrival, I was still only at 4 cm.

At around 11 a.m., there was a change in shift and a new midwife named Julie arrived, who was very gentle, quiet and softly spoken. She checked to see if there was any dilation progress, but I was still only 4 cm. At this point, on her advice, we decided to start filling the pool in the hope that it might help move things along. Chris had practised this twice in the previous weeks, but the extension hose suddenly broke! So, it was back to doing it the old-fashioned way, filling it with buckets and kettles, one at a time. It was like a comedy sketch – Ralph based himself in the kitchen, furiously boiling the kettle and filling vast plastic gorilla tubs, while Chris ran back and forth with them from the main house to the yurt. Goodness knows what Julie made of this fiasco, but she maintained her relaxed demeanour, laughed along and made light of it to help me feel at ease.

The water definitely provided some relief and I was so glad to get in. My contractions had been full-on for twelve hours now and I was barely getting any rest between them – sometimes I'd have three in a row, with no break. It was a waiting game for everybody; the midwife would advise helpful positions to try in the pool, regularly check the temperature, and she'd help me get out every now and then to be checked again for dilation. Eventually, I caved in to needing extra pain relief and started using gas and air.

By 4 p.m., I still wasn't dilated enough and I'd been in labour for sixteen hours.

At this point, the fact that I was 'failing to progress' was beginning to agitate me. I was trying my hardest to stay positive and concentrate on the positive hypnobirthing mantras I'd stuck around the yurt walls while listening to the accompanying music, but none of it seemed to be working. I could feel my dream of a home birth slowly slipping through my fingers. We'd given the home birth every shot, but at this point the advice was to go to the hospital.

When we arrived, I had my waters broken to speed things up. I had really been against any medical intervention, so this felt like a bit of a let-down, but I knew I had to accept what was happening, and there was still a chance I could have a water birth, albeit not in the yurt. Luckily, there was an empty room with a birth pool available, so we tried again. Jet was being looked after downstairs in the hospital car park, with my mum, in her car. I'd called her in the early hours of the morning to let her know I'd gone into labour and she'd delayed going home so she could stay around and help if needed. However, it was too much for her with her disability to sit with Jet in the car overnight, so she headed to her hotel to get some sleep and a lady called Anna, who we'd become friends with, kindly took over to watch Jet in the car park.

Chris was by my side, holding my hand, passing me the gas and air and trying to encourage me to eat something. It was about 9 p.m. and all I'd managed to eat was a croissant and an orange in the morning. We had snacks in our hospital bag and Chris handed me two Fruit Pastilles. The contractions were so powerful that, as soon as I put one in my mouth, I spat it out in the pool! I simply couldn't eat. I was examined again and I was still only 5 cm dilated. I was really struggling with the intensity of the contractions and not feeling any improvement in my pain with the gas and air – so much so that I kept turning to Chris and telling him it wasn't working, insisting he check the mains because it mustn't be turned on! Knowing I'd only dilated 2 cm in twenty-one hours of strong contractions, I really didn't feel I could carry on at that pace.

Between myself, Chris and the midwife, we made the call to have an epidural, which meant waving goodbye to the pool. I opted for a lighter dose, so I could still feel my legs and contractions, and therefore the sensation of birthing my baby. But by 1 a.m. the relief seemed to have worn off and I was in such pain that I'd started throwing up.

I was given a top-up epidural at about 1 a.m. and, an hour later, I had finally dilated to 10 cm. We were elated. We seriously thought this was it now – I would push for a bit and we would meet our baby! But that didn't go to plan either: after pushing hard for two hours and being examined various times by two different consultants, as well as midwives, we were told the head wasn't moving down the birth canal. It was agreed I'd push for a bit longer to see if the head moved and the baby could be helped out by forceps/ventouse, but, if not, it would mean an emergency C-section.

KATE BARRON

I tried to keep pushing, but there was still no progress with the head and the pain was insurmountable by this point. I couldn't face it any more. The advice was still to keep going, but Chris had become increasingly worried. He'd briefly run down to check on Jet, and Anna expressed concern about how long I'd been in labour. She advised Chris to advocate for me, so, very worried, he collared one of the consultants in the corridor. 'Enough is enough, now,' he said, and the next thing I knew, a form was being waved under my nose for me to sign for an emergency C-section.

25

Birth Part 2

I was too ruined to take on board any understanding of what it all meant and what the procedure actually entailed. It had never been fully explained to me in the run-up to the birth – mentioned, yes, but never covered in any detail, given all my conversations had been about a vaginal birth. But it had to be done, a natural birth just wasn't to be, and I now needed to place my trust in the medical professionals.

At 5 a.m., nearly thirty hours after my labour had started, I was finally wheeled into theatre, screaming so loudly from the pain that I was asked to keep it down so as not to scare other patients! I arrived to be faced by an army of doctors, nurses, midwives, anaesthetists – I had definitely underestimated the intensity of the surgery I was about to have, but it made me feel safe knowing there were so many hands on deck looking after me.

It was explained to me what would now happen, and as I waited for the anaesthetic to take hold, I was glad to know I would be awake through the procedure to welcome my baby. I reminded them that I wanted delayed cord clamping and skin-to-skin straight after the baby came out, which I also repeated to Chris, so he could make sure it happened. What followed was so clinical – it was stark and bright in the room, with so many pairs of feet running about – and I certainly felt nervous about being cut open, but other than the odd glimpse of metal tools and blood-stained sterile gloves, I tried to keep my eyes firmly fixed on Chris for reassurance as I waited, silently praying and hoping for the safe arrival of my baby.

I'll never forget the moment they lifted our baby over the blue screen so we could meet them. Chris got the first view as he stood up to peek, and he was able to break the news to me that we had a boy! Then I saw him for the very first time and I couldn't believe just how perfect and chubby he was. Hearing his cry was such a relief and I was so elated to know he was here, safe and sound and healthy. I couldn't wait to hold him. The medics were brilliant at making sure my post-birth wishes were followed.

Chris went off to cut the cord and to hold him, then the baby was brought over to me. For so many months we had been one person, two hearts, one body, and now finally I held my baby in my arms for the very first time. My beautiful baby boy, the child who had made me a mother. We'd already decided on his name if he was a boy, and, looking at him, we were certain he suited it: Magnus Edward Arden Lewis, born on 1 May 2022 at 5.38 a.m.

But, all of a sudden, I started slipping in and out of consciousness. Magnus was taken and given to Chris, who was ushered quickly out of the room, and all I remember was the midwife standing over me saying, 'Stay with me, Kate, stay with me.' She repeated it over and over. I could hear her and see her face, but I couldn't control what was happening – one minute I was awake, the next I wasn't, and it just kept on like that. I could just about hear Chris through the double doors that separated us, constantly saying, 'I'm here,' and fast-talking voices with some worried chatter between doctors about a reaction.

I'd had an allergic reaction to one of the drugs I'd been given. I remember feeling scared, as I had no idea what was happening to me, and also really helpless, as I wasn't in control of it. I just kept looking at the midwife's face and trying to focus on what she was saying. From then, the next few hours remain really hazy and I don't fully recall what happened. From what Chris has told me, once I'd properly regained consciousness, Magnus was handed back to me and we were both tucked under a blanket so I could hold him to my chest before being wheeled out of the room on a bed trolley. I must have tried to feed him at some point, but I have no recollection of it. The next thing I remember is waking up in another bed in a very stuffy hospital room, on IV fluids, with Magnus in a plastic transparent cot next to my bedside. From what I was later told, it had been very touch and go at one point. The midwives said I'd given them all a big scare, and I know this episode really shook Chris up, as he thought he was facing the terrifying prospect of not only losing the woman he loved, but having to tackle fatherhood alone once again.

Once I was stabilized after the reaction, I was overjoyed to finally begin bonding with Magnus. I held him close to me, cradled in my arms, and gazed down at this astonishing new life we'd made. I studied all of his tiny newborn features, trying to cement the image of them in my memory so that I'd never forget: his long eyelashes, button nose, round cheeks, pursed lips, tiny fingers and toes, which I couldn't believe held such small nails, and the very fine, light-brown hair on his head. He looked so delicate, so beautiful, and the most surreal thing of all: he was mine and he relied on me for everything. It was love like I'd never even known existed before: all-consuming, overpowering, disarming even, one that rocks you to your core.

Physically, my body was a wreck; mentally, I was absolutely exhausted. I hadn't slept for three days, but the adrenalin rush of motherly love and fierce maternal instinct coursed through my body in the most powerful way. In that moment, I knew that his life would belong to him, to live as he pleased; but I was no longer free, for my life would always be bound to his.

Like any new mum, I wanted to be the very best I could be for him in every way that he needed. However, the next few days in hospital were a real challenge. I was so sleep deprived, utterly exhausted, and really out of it from all the drugs. I continued to be on IV fluids for another twenty-four hours, which seemed to numb the initial pain somewhat, and mentally I was very foggy. I remember talking absolute gibberish in front of Chris, my mum (who'd been allowed in to see me for ten minutes, given Covid restrictions were still in place) and a midwife. Once the IV fluid tubes were removed, I was relocated to a different room and began to feel really severe post-surgery pain; even small movements such as getting out of bed, taking a few steps and lifting Magnus out of the cot were extremely painful. Magnus was just beautiful, calm and peaceful, often asleep during the day.

Chris couldn't stay overnight with me as he needed to look after Jet in the yurt, so I was alone. Magnus didn't seem to sleep much at all those first few nights. He slept a lot during the day, but my body clock was all over the place and I struggled to catch up on any sleep while he slept. The pain of my C-section made it so difficult for me to pick him up, manoeuvre him from one side of my body to the other to try to breastfeed, put him back in the cot or change his nappy. I was really sore, grappling with feeding and terrified to go to the toilet after the surgery.

Before I was discharged, a few days later, Magnus and I were both given a check-up and a physio came to see me. She told

Above: Girls just want to have fun – me and Jet, in on an early morning joke while Chris slaved away making breakfast! It soon became apparent that Jet had a strong motherly instinct; during my pregnancy, she was constantly by my side.

Left: Packing up the tent at 4 a.m., soaked to the bone, ready to travel across the country for my twelve-week scan. It's not every mother's ideal pre-scan morning, but I didn't care – I got to see my baby for the first time ever, and nothing could have dampened my spirits!

Walking through the otherworldly Dungeness at thirty-six weeks pregnant. I probably was heavy enough to tip the boat, but just to clarify – it was already leaning that way!

Standing under the bright, twinkling lights of the yurt on my due date, wondering how long it would be before I'd finally meet my baby . . .

Of all the amazing things I've done in my life, nothing has or ever will compare to the feeling of being a mum!

Magnus on the walk at four months old – such a smiley, happy baby. We travelled with the absolute bare minimum when it came to baby paraphernalia, but we very quickly realized that all he really needed was us.

Above: Sunrises and sunsets were such a big part of daily life on the walk; it felt very special to share the slow unfolding of so many of Mother Nature's masterpieces with my baby.

Right: Bedtime with Jet and Mum. Wherever we slept, we always read a bedtime story, and would often make up our own to boot – *The Adventures of Magnus and Jet*.

I walked all seventy-two miles of the beautiful Isle of Wight coastline at four months postpartum with Magnus strapped to my front – it was hard going, but I really loved this outdoor start to motherhood.

Above: This lifestyle gave me the freedom to spend every waking minute with my son, which is all I wanted as a mum. Even better, we got to do it all outdoors, in some of the most beautiful places our country has to offer.

Tummy time, exploring the colours, shapes and textures of autumn leaves in the wood. Nature was his playroom, and it provided in abundance.

Chapman's Pool, Dorset, in December 2022. At six months old, Magnus slept better in a tent in winter than anywhere else, even with temperatures going down to negative figures. This was actually the first time he slept through the night.

Magnus's first birthday on the island of St Martin's in the Scillies. I could not have chosen a more perfect place to celebrate. The day turned out to be quite an adventure!

Below: Elation as we reached the southernmost point of the British mainland on the Cornish coast. It had taken longer than we ever anticipated to get here, but my word, we had overcome some hurdles to do so!

Below: A journey that started with one broken man alone ended with a family of four crossing the finish line at Llangennith beach. Only we really knew what it had taken to get there, but we had done it!

Above: Heading to the abandoned Scarista bus amid the snowy sand dunes of Harris. Chris and Jet had slept in there five winters prior; now we were all there, making our own memories as a family.

Above: Magnus and Jet had such a close bond. He absolutely adored her. Jet was the most gentle, docile and caring dog we could ever have asked to be around our son.

Magnus being inquisitive in nature. I felt very strongly that whatever route we went down when it came to his learning, the outdoors would be his living classroom.

After the walk, we decided to give our feet a bit of a break and take to cycling. Off-road mountain biking has already enabled us to explore some incredible places on family adventures.

It turns out that my son is an adrenaline junkie like his dad! Magnus got on his first off-road balance bike at sixteen months old, and hey presto – his first big passion in life was born.

Collecting razor clams for digging in the sand on Seilebost Beach, Harris. It's my hope that this adventurous, outdoor start in life allows Magnus to grow up always feeling connected to nature, confident in himself, wild in his heart and bold enough to follow his own dreams.

A quick pit stop to climb the rocks while cycling the coast and glens of Arran in January 2025. We were down to three now that Jet was no longer with us, but we were ready to begin a new chapter.

me to wait twelve weeks before I began to do any strenuous exercise and to ensure I saw a women's physio before setting off on the walk again. Yes, it wasn't an easy birth by any stretch, but at the end of the day I had a healthy baby boy and that was all that mattered. Birth is raw, unfiltered, complex and powerful, however it happens. I feel so grateful to have been in such good hands and lucky to live in a place where I can receive that kind of care. Not every mother in this world can. We were both alive and well to begin our journey together as mother and son, and that was everything. He was everything, and I finally understood the love a mother feels for her child. There is nothing else that comes close.

In that moment, I too was reborn – full of profound hope and unconditional love, with an endless depth to my heart. Of all the things I had done in my life up to this point, it was the birth of Magnus that gave my life a whole new meaning. I was a mother.

26

Bloody, Blistered and Blanched

Postpartum hit me like a bullet train. If I thought I was unprepared and naive about birth, I had absolutely no idea what was in store – for one thing, just how major C-section surgery is or how long it can take to recover. Looking back now, would I have preferred to know what lay ahead? I doubt I'd have been able to enjoy the pregnancy so much if I had! Either way, what followed ripped through me in a way I never saw coming.

The choice to recover from the birth in the yurt in Dorset had been entirely mine, and initially we'd only intended to stay there around two to three weeks post-birth, providing all was well. However, faced with the reality of my situation now, having had an emergency C-section, we realized we needed to stay longer. A Caesarean is major abdominal surgery, cutting through seven layers of tissue, including the uterus, as well as fascia, muscle and skin. I'd been very naive about the challenging recovery process, which involves significant pain due to tissue damage and requires a longer healing period compared to a vaginal birth. Twelve weeks was the very minimum for recovery: for the wound to close, the scar to form and bruising and swelling to subside. As I would soon learn, those twelve weeks are just the beginning. In my case, the aftermath of the surgery was a real shock to the system.

The Cygnet Homebirth midwifery team still came to visit me daily for the first ten days. I was so thankful for that extra level of personal care – I certainly needed it! In those initial days, they would check for signs of infection or poor healing in my wound, support me in re-dressing it and give advice for keeping it clean, dry and getting some air to it. For the first few days, they administered injections in my stomach to help ensure my blood didn't clot post-surgery and showed me how to do them myself so I could continue the routine on my own. They also assessed for signs of infection generally, blood loss and any post-operative DVT (deep vein thrombosis), and asked if my bowel and bladder were working adequately (which they weren't, and wouldn't for many months). They checked Magnus over for evidence of wellbeing, weighing him to track weight loss or gain, and supported me with trying to get to grips with breastfeeding.

It probably sounds very overdramatic but, despite the fact that I had Chris, Jet and an excellent team of midwives, as well as supportive messages from friends, family and followers online, I felt utterly lost, isolated and alone. Now, the simple conveniences of an everyday home, the things I had come to see as luxuries that I could live without, began to matter. The bed in the yurt only had a very thin mattress, and I could feel the wooden slats beneath me every time I moved. I had coped with it while pregnant, but it was agony post-surgery. The pain comes from the incision in the uterus and the ripping apart of the stomach muscles to separate them in order to enter the abdominal cavity and remove the baby. The skin on top is also multi-layered, with the cut having been made from superficial skin down to deep organs.

While all of that was at the very beginning stages of healing, I, like any new mum post-surgery, had no choice but to be mobile, caring for my baby, but also sleep-deprived, bleeding from the shedding uterine lining after birth, and producing milk, which is a calorific energy depletion in itself – around 300 calories a day just in production! I was also told by my midwives that there is some anecdotal understanding that those who have an unplanned emergency C-section experience post-surgery more acutely than those who have an elective C-section. The level of pain definitely took me by surprise – I'd never read or heard anything about the reality of it and I wasn't mentally geared up for it in the slightest. I endured six weeks before splashing out on a better mattress to alleviate the pain. I wish I'd done it sooner!

There was no fridge or freezer in the yurt in which to store breast milk, or even food, for that matter. I didn't have my own bathroom either, which made it harder to wash and change my dressings, which I mostly just did in the yurt, making do with a bowl of clean water, flannels and cotton-wool pads. There was a tiny compost toilet outside the yurt, but it was dark, suffocating in the heat of early summer and ridden with flies and spiders, and I often found myself confined to it for long periods of time. Other than that, I would send a message to ask or knock on the door of the main house, which was only a few minutes' walk away, to use the family bathroom, provided it was free. I was always welcome to do so during the day, but it wasn't the same as having one at my disposal any time I needed, particularly during the night. Post-surgery, I'd massively underestimated the need for an available bathroom around the clock.

The terrifying reaction I'd had to one of the drugs during surgery meant I ended up on IV fluids for much longer than most women post C-section, and that left some side effects, like difficulties going to the toilet. My psoriasis also broke out for the first time in seven years. There was no denying that my choice to be here had made my recovery experience harder.

However, for all the misery my surgery recovery inflicted upon me, I'd still rather have faced that ten times over than experience the battle I had with breastfeeding. The reason I had been so adamant on having skin-to-skin contact as soon as Magnus was born was because I knew it was beneficial for bonding, stimulating milk supply and helping him to get that first latch. But, due to the immediate complications following my surgery, we didn't get that time together known as the 'golden hour' (the first hour after birth, when babies are most alert and likely to feed, which evidently has a big impact on subsequent breastfeeding success). I felt a desperate and deep-seated instinctive need to breastfeed Magnus, but unfortunately it was a bloody and brutal ordeal from the get-go. We had it all: low milk supply, latching problems, tongue tie, breast aversion, slow weight gain, suck dysfunction, positioning problems due to my cut and, last but not least, nipple damage. We're talking bloody, blistered and blanched, shredded, maimed and minced.

The battle to breastfeed brought a barrage of extreme challenges and emotions, and Chris couldn't understand why I was so against ending all the traumatic pain and stress by switching to bottle feeding. I felt unsupported and misunderstood. He begged me to stop and turn to formula, but I was desperate to persevere. Chris also struggled with the sudden loss of sleep, both mother and baby screaming during feeds, and the fact that, two days after Magnus was born, he had to begin writing his book!

The difficulty I had positioning Magnus under such stress and tension also led to crippling repetitive strain injuries in both wrists, which meant I struggled to dress myself, open a door and even pick him up. Lyndsey always did her best to comfort me during her visits. 'Please try not to be so hard on yourself – birth is so complex and you have absolutely nothing to be ashamed of.' Deep down, I knew she was right, but, for whatever reason, it didn't stop me feeling the way I did.

One aspect that gave me some relief was the beautiful way that Jet had accepted our new arrival. When we introduced her to him, in the yurt, she was incredibly placid, stayed back a little at first, as if curious but slightly hesitant about how best to approach this tiny human, and then came forward, licked him as if to say, 'Welcome to the family, Magnus,' and then sat back to leave us to get settled. At times, when he lay on the bed to nap, she would lie down next to him, her head right alongside his body, an extra layer of warmth, protection and love. She accepted him immediately, just as she had me, and it felt so special watching their bond develop over those initial days. As Magnus's eyes began to focus, he would really hone in on Jet and study her.

I also appreciated her love and comfort now more than ever – she was so intuitive and I felt like she could tell I was in pain. Chris slept on a pull-out floor bed, and Jet would often cuddle up next to me and Magnus during the night while I was trying to feed him.

Mentally, I really struggled. I cried a lot, sometimes hysterically. It was the first time in my life I'd experienced feeling at rock bottom, and I hated myself for it because I was just so desperate to spend quality, positive time with my newborn son. It broke my heart that I felt unable to give him as much as I wanted and felt I should have been able to in those first few weeks. The extreme feelings of inadequacy, anger, guilt and grief at not being able to provide for my baby in the way I wanted were traumatizing for me. One night, while everyone slept, I went outside and howled hysterical tears of despair to the heavens, begging for any powers bigger than me to help me in some way. I felt my body had failed me when I needed it most, and I was angry it seemed unable to perform the tasks it was seemingly made for. The only relief, and thankfully the most powerful I could ask for, came in the form of the joy and love for Magnus.

We sought every avenue of help available to us, including a nearby lactation consultant, but after eight weeks, I was forced to accept that it was not possible for me to exclusively breast-feed. I was still determined to provide Magnus with whatever breast milk I could, so I turned to a combination approach of pumping and formula. I rented a Spectra electric pump, which I was able to use for as long as I had access to plug sockets, but that would obviously no longer be the case once we resumed the walk. We also bought all the bottle-feeding kit we now needed, including a sterilizer.

Even with all this going on, I still never thought, *Sod this, there's no way we can continue this walk with a newborn.* I was deeply committed to our mission, this life we had made for ourselves and the fact that I wholeheartedly believed with every bone in my body that our lifestyle would provide our baby with the very best start I could possibly give him. I didn't have any blueprints to follow, or advice I could take from others who had done the same before me; I could only trust in my instincts that, as a mother, I was doing the right thing, and I felt it very deeply.

One day, during a visit, Lyndsey gave me a note to read after she'd left. 'You are resilient, resourceful, fierce in your instincts and motherly protection of your baby, choosing to centre your life around his needs and I know it will be great.' Her words were a powerful reminder to me, during this hard time, of who I was and why I wanted this path. I found peace in picturing our life ahead. I was really keen to get back to feeling myself, to my outdoor lifestyle, and start living the way I had dreamed about with my baby throughout the pregnancy.

WILDERNESS MUM

Going forward, we had absolutely no idea how we would make this work on the move. It was far from the simplistic, practical 'shove him on the boob and let's go' picture that I'd envisaged. Truth be told, I'd imagined a scenario of me carrying a baby, feeding blissfully as we traipsed over the clifftops, Chris and I happily hand in hand together as a new family, Jet wagging her tail beside us – something akin to *The Sound of Music* but with far fewer children! That dream may have shattered, but I decided that I no longer wanted to wallow in tears and pain. I needed to accept the situation for what it was and focus on all the positives. Yes, we would now face a much more complex reality feeding Magnus as we continued our walk, but I decided to reframe it as an exciting challenge. Thankfully, when Chris's mum, Sam, and her husband, Dave, had come to visit, they'd brought us a second-hand pram. I'd fully intended on baby-wearing and assumed I'd carry Magnus close to my body in a sling most of the time. However, at this point, so early into my recovery, I was scared stiff about causing my scar to hurt even more and, with so much to contend with, I just couldn't get to grips with using one. The pram was a game changer for me and I was so grateful.

On advice from the hospital physio and the midwives, I had begun taking very short walks after week one. Those had grown slowly and steadily over time as I healed and got stronger. Come June, the weather was really warm and, when Magnus woke in the night or early hours, I found it easier and far more effective just to take him outside the yurt for strolls, looking up at the night sky or watching the dawn unfold while listening to the early-morning birdsong.

Magnus was such a healthy, happy, beautiful boy and so all of the above really was secondary, even if it didn't always feel that way in the moment. I have many unique and treasured memories of our time together in those early weeks: his snuggles in the yurt with Jet, who was so accepting, gentle and loving with him; his eyes focusing for the first time; his first smile; his first laugh; all the times he fell asleep on me after feeding; lying outside with him among the daisies and the bluebells; walks through the woodland; cuddles in a hammock; rocking on the garden swing. And then all of those I could never have gained elsewhere: the moments in the middle of the night when the rest of the world slept and we'd stand under the stars or walk around the yurt, Magnus's eyes mesmerized by the fairy lights and the bold patterns on the wall hangings; telling him stories in such magical surroundings; having him take all of his naps outdoors in nature; serenading him, with Dizzi playing the beautiful dulcimer, Ralph playing the kora (a West African drum) and Chris on the guitar; his first bath outside under the trees; keeping him warm at night via a log burner rather than central heating; and singing around the fire, surrounded by a truly kind and caring community of people.

To me, these moments felt like a snapshot of my years ahead as a mother and the unique early childhood I wanted for my son: a childhood surrounded by nature, community and family. I wanted Magnus to have unlimited space and time to play, explore and learn in nature, gaining a real sense of self and understanding of the world around him through so many rich and varied experiences. Having Magnus join us on the walk as a newborn baby was about laying the foundations from the very start for a childhood both steeped in and shaped by time in nature, in outdoor adventure and in cherished family experiences.

The fact that he wouldn't remember these first years was completely irrelevant. We believed and hoped that they would form the basis of his whole life ahead; that by raising him in the outdoors from the very start, we were ensuring he would always feel connected to nature, that nature would be so imprinted in his being that it would become a key part of who he was as he grew and developed as a young child and even into adulthood. Above all, I wanted him to have a sense of wonder in his life from the very beginning. Research tells us wonder leads to greater creativity, curiosity and connection, but it went deeper than that: I knew from my own experience just how powerful a sense of wonder can be in making a person feel truly moved and a life feel enriching, meaningful and fulfilling, and I wanted to give that to him. I wanted to bring magic to his childhood, and while I don't believe you necessarily have to be outdoors to do that, I do believe that the magic doesn't have to be created; it is already there in abundance.

Two months after Magnus was born, we had to leave the yurt, as holidaymakers had booked it for the summer season. Those first eight weeks were a minefield of stark contradictions: overwhelming elation and love, coupled with intense hopelessness and despair. I believe that the postpartum period is the most vulnerable time in a woman's life, particularly from a mental health point of view. With antenatal education now all but eradicated in the NHS and postnatal care stripped to the very bare minimum (in some cases, only three visits in the total postpartum period), women have never been more isolated and abandoned.

Even the initial six-week check-up at the GP surgery should've been a lot more thorough and as much about my mental well-being as how I was recovering physically. The concept that 'it takes a village to raise a child' has been somewhat lost in the West – too many women struggle single-handedly behind closed doors, without the extended help of the wider community. There's a bounce-back culture, particularly in those first weeks after birth, where women are expected to power through and get on with it in a broken system which then berates them when they face struggles or burnout.

Yes, it was a time of bittersweet memories in many ways, but I don't regret choosing to birth my son there. His arrival into the world and those first two months of his life had unfolded in a very unique and special place, born into the sights and sounds of nature as I'd hoped. It was the perfect initiation for his life outside.

After another month spent at my mum's in Worcester for me to sufficiently recover, we decided to head back to the coast where we'd left off to resume and finish what we'd started. This time, we were armed with a small van that Chris had bought with his book money as a safety net for Magnus if we needed it – it also allowed Jet a break. At this point, we had let her retire from the walk; her bit was done.

That first day back, we showed three-month-old Magnus the sea for the very first time. We had deliberately waited until we were ready to resume the walk before taking him to the coast. I could see how much it meant to Chris to have the now four of us back on the coast, safe and well, in the place where his soul belonged. Having to press pause at the yurt and then at my mum's for longer than we'd anticipated, both for my recovery and for Chris to write his book, had been tough on him. He'd written the whole of his book in Magnus's first months of life, and the difficulties I'd faced, having to look after our son so much on my own while he was cooped up writing, meant he'd felt a lot of pressure. He was thrilled and liberated to now bring his new, precious baby boy to the coastline and share with him all the wonders that had changed his life.

Excitedly, we pointed out all the things about our world here that were now so familiar for us but completely new for him. He was seeing it all for the first time: the sun that glistened on the water, the waves that lapped at the shore, the cliffs that towered above the sea.

WILDERNESS MUM

That night, it was a perfect warm August evening. I sat on the clifftops, my baby in my arms, watching the sunset. We sat there for two hours, just us. I breathed in his smell, kissed his head and watched him take it all in. I thought about the last time I was here, almost full-term and still yet to meet the baby that grew inside me. In the space of a few months, so much had changed. I'd been right, though; I was different now. The entire essence of me was wrapped up in this tiny baby I held. I looked down at him and said, 'This is your new home. What do you think?' I knew really that *we* were his home, and that, as long as he had us, he would be safe and happy, but in a physical sense, this was his home now: his ceiling was the sky; his living room the sand, the sea, the fields and the woods; his toys were the playthings of nature. It was a beautiful moment, so peaceful. The past few months had been a real challenge, but I felt finally able to take a deep breath and experience relief.

Being back outside in nature with my baby was what I needed; I knew it would do wonders for me mentally and emotionally post-recovery. *Nature is a mother too,* I thought. *She gets it!* I finally felt at ease, happy and relaxed. I couldn't wait to live this life with my baby. I was so excited to raise him on this adventure among the awe and wonder of nature and for us to have these first months together this way. Our time together was the most precious gift to me now, and I felt exhilarated thinking about all the ways this life would really make it count.

27

Go with the Flow

From Hastings Country Park, our last destination before we diverted to Dorset for Magnus's birth, we now had around 2,000 miles left to walk along the coastline of twelve counties, including the South West Coast Path. We also had around twelve islands left to walk, including all of the Channel Islands and all of the Scilly Isles. It was a massive undertaking with a newborn baby, with a lot of practical logistics to work out, but I knew we'd make it happen and, mentally, I was ready!

Returning with a van did make it a different experience as we set off. We had initially toyed with the idea of carrying on as we always had once Magnus was born – moving from place to place each day, living in a tent and carrying everything we had, Magnus included. However, we very quickly realized there was simply no way in this world we could manage, carrying everything we now needed. Not only that, but we strongly felt we needed the extra shelter in the inevitable case of bad weather, as well as the additional sense of security. If for any reason Magnus needed medical attention, with a van we had the means to get him to a doctor ourselves, rather than having to sit and wait for help to arrive. Essentially, the van meant we could be self-sufficient and responsible parents.

Magnus had his first inoculations in Dorset, and the second set at the GP surgery near my mum's before we resumed the walk. We had registered him there as a temporary patient for the few weeks we were there, but he was still formally registered in Dorset, where he would have his third set of jabs as we passed through on the walk. It made more sense that he was registered there, as we were set to be on the south coast for some time now. Practically, though, it was a little more difficult than being able to pop to a familiar surgery down the road.

The van was a small dark-blue VW T4. It was twenty-two years old and extremely basic inside, with nothing other than three black leather seats in the back that folded down to make a bed where Jet would relax in the day and where we would all sleep at night. There was no cooker, no sink, no heater and definitely no toilet. We couldn't even stand up in it. The amount of room left equated to the length of about two rulers. The thought of the four of us being cooped up in there for days on end in persistent rain and wind didn't bear thinking about. Yet, for all its shortcomings, it did have insulated walls covered in grey carpeting and a set of black curtains over the window, which made for an all-important blackout blind!

We decorated it with fairy lights to make it more homely and bought a night light with patterns that we could project on the ceiling for Magnus. It was all we could afford, but we'd made it our own and hoped it would be enough to get us to the end of the walk. For now, it was more a vessel in which to carry all our gear rather than somewhere to sleep, as the weather was still decent enough to camp, provided that we could find somewhere suitable to pitch. But that itself presented a huge logistical challenge – how would we get back to the van each day if we didn't retrace our steps in a loop?

That first week, we were full of optimism and tried to walk together as a family. It was a sweltering August and I carried Magnus in an ergonomic baby carrier on my front, but we hadn't been able to find any kind of shade contraption to attach to it, so we took off *My Fair Lady*-style, with me holding an umbrella to keep Magnus out of the sun. The heat meant regular stops and taking long breaks under the shade of the trees, but we were only planning on covering around 5 miles a day at this point, so we had all day to play with.

We would walk and then Chris would run the 5 miles back to where we had left the van and come and pick us up. I would wait with Magnus and Jet, although it wasn't easy. In the time he was gone, I often found myself desperate for the loo, with Magnus strapped to me and Jet pulling on the lead, trying to run after Chris. Now on the busy south coast, still in the height of summer, I wasn't in remote enough places to simply squat where I pleased, and I struggled to find anywhere with toilet facilities where I could also take Jet with me. At this stage postpartum, I more than once found myself unable to hold it along a public promenade or suchlike. It was pretty mortifying to say the least, but all I could do was look down at the ground, hope to God that no one noticed, and grin and bear it until Chris arrived with the van.

One of the other biggest logistical challenges was feeding Magnus. Determined to still provide as much breast milk as possible, I invested in two USB-rechargeable portable breast pumps. I used them as much as I could; while walking, in the van and tent at night, or pottering around cooking and washing up. However, they were nowhere near as effective as my previous one, which I'd been able to plug in; they often came dislodged as I walked, spilling the contents all down me, and were a nightmare to clean. The weather was hot and I needed to thoroughly clean and sterilize all the parts after every use, which was incredibly difficult on the move and a massive drain on our water supply and on our time. My efforts here were only enough to provide about 30 per cent breast milk now – if I was lucky – and for the rest we relied on formula, meaning we also had a lot of bottles to wash and sterilize. Magnus needed a minimum of eight feeds a day at this point. We couldn't wash up a bottle after every use while out walking, so we had to buy eight bottles and prepare them all in advance. To do this, we would boil enough water on the gas stove to pour into a foldable plastic bucket to wash the bottles in soapy water. We would then pour a second lot of boiling water into the bucket to sterilize the bottles. Finally, a third lot of boiling water would be used to fill the bottles to the right level. This water would cool inside the bottles, ready for the addition of formula while out walking. This way, we could cater for all of Magnus's feeds during the night and following day until we had to do it all again.

That routine played on repeat every single day and certainly even the most basic mod cons of a house would have really come in handy – a tap with running water, a fridge, a kettle, even a microwave. However, the situation couldn't be helped and we ran with it. We tried to share the load and tag-team on this as best we could, with one of us boiling the water while the other washed the bottles, for instance, but Chris definitely ended up doing the bulk of all this each day while I cared for Magnus. His daily chores on the walk had changed somewhat from the days of it being just him and Jet in the tent, that's for sure, but he never complained. By mid-September, I'd had to say a difficult goodbye to the pumps and accept that my breastfeeding journey had come to an end. From here on out, we could only use formula.

By the time we got to the end of the South Downs, we knew we had to change tactics. If there's one thing this lifestyle had taught us, it was the need to be flexible, to problem-solve and always be willing to adapt. As soon as we'd started walking again, Chris immediately noticed that Jet was limping; the time we'd spent stagnant over the past few months had made her muscles seize up and brought her arthritis to the fore. This, combined with her older age now seeming to catch up with her – along with the fact that she'd slowed down a lot following her major surgery earlier in the year – made us feel that we wanted her to rest as much as possible.

Her surgery had changed her, and it was clear she was simply no longer able to continue on as before. From now on, Chris and I would have to walk separately so that one of us could always stay behind to be with her in the van. Rather than walk miles, she would have plenty of rest, comfort, the freedom to bask in the sun and potter around nearby as she pleased. At this point, Jet and I were close enough in our relationship that she could stay with me for an hour, maybe two, before becoming very anxious about Chris's absence, yelping and crying endlessly.

There was absolutely no way we could consider Jet going to stay with someone we knew and trusted, because she would have been in terrible turmoil and anguish being separated from Chris for anything more than a few hours, never mind a few months. It would have been traumatic for her and for the people she stayed with. Whether she would have eventually got used to it in time, who knows, but for us it was beside the point – Chris had made a promise to Jet that he would always show her the same loyalty and devotion she had shown him, and there was no world in which they would or could separate; it was a 'til death do us part' scenario. Challenging as that made life, I understood, and my own love for Jet meant that I was willing to do what was needed.

We found the best way round it was for Chris to do the day's stretch first thing, and as fast as he could, to get back to Jet as quickly as possible; this often meant running. I would look after Magnus and Jet in the meantime and then drive the van to meet him where he finished. We would then drive back on ourselves to the day's starting point for me to walk that same stretch with Magnus, Chris ready to pick us up when we were done. Essentially, we were now doubling our mileage every day just so we could both walk. It might sound bonkers and unnecessary, but I felt strongly that I needed to walk and to do it with my son.

My motivation to do so came from the fact that I had given my absolute all to this walk; I'd given up my career to do it alongside Chris, but also so much more than that — I'd lived and breathed it for nearly two years now, all the highs and lows, the highlights and hardships, the laughter, the pain, the sweat, the smiles, the blood and the tears. It didn't just feel like something I was doing any more, it felt a part of who *I was*. I'd just carried my baby, given birth and become a mother on this walk — it was now deeply entwined with that huge life transition and all the emotions that came with it.

It felt sad that we wouldn't be able to do the walking aspect of this journey together as a family, but it couldn't be helped. From then on, I would walk with Magnus alone. Initially, that felt like a very big step for me. Just a few months before, I'd been terrified to leave the confines of the yurt even for an hour with Magnus due to the anxiety-inducing prospect of having to try to feed in public. Now, I was faced with rambling across the steep cliff paths for hours, tackling all the feeding, nappy changing and entertaining on my own with him. It felt daunting and very out of my comfort zone at this stage, but my maternal instinct kicked in very strongly; I wanted my baby with me all the time, and I simply couldn't leave Magnus all day with Chris while I went off walking.

The alternative was for me to stay with Magnus in and around the van all day. Well, I hadn't brought either of us back out here for that – if we were going to have him on this walk, then, whatever the weather, whatever the season, Magnus was coming on that coast path with me to reap all the benefits I knew it could offer. That was that. I just had to get comfortable with getting him in and out of a sling on my own, changing his nappy on the floor anywhere and everywhere, feeding him on top of a cliff, on a slab of concrete, on a promenade or behind a boat, and finding ways to play and interact along the way. I quickly got used to my new reality. If it wasn't for the fact that Chris needed to move so fast to get back to Jet before she panicked, then he could have happily taken Magnus with him sometimes and we could have shared the load so much more. It saddened me that Chris wasn't able to have the same quality walking time with his son. I know it was hard for him and a far cry from the way he'd envisaged doing this walk once Magnus arrived. But such was his love for Jet, and I respected his loyalty to her.

In order to live this way, I had to embrace life with a go-with-the-flow approach, there was no room for scheduled wake windows, feeds and naps. I could appreciate fully why many women operate like that to make life easier; every parent needs to do what works best for them, and that looks different in every home. However, there was no way I could do that in our situation – everything was done on demand and on the go, as and when it was needed. Friends would often message me, 'How on earth are you doing this?'

I frequently thought about just how vastly my motherhood experience differed from that of my friends and other mums. Until I met Chris, I'd fully expected my path as a mother to be largely the same as theirs, in a house with a bedroom for the baby, having maybe nine months of maternity leave, then resuming my career and dropping my baby off at nursery. In absolutely no way, shape or form did I ever envisage anything like the version of motherhood I was now living.

The evenings were our time together as a family. However, the busyness of the south coast and, as I've mentioned, the laws prohibiting wild camping did make life frustrating. We would often spend a good hour trying to find somewhere quiet to park the van for the evening. A Park4Night spot might have worked for some, but they were often in busy locations, involved a cost, and were full of other campervans and motorhomes. With a newborn baby who was a long way off sleeping through the night, we wanted more privacy. The time spent driving around looking for somewhere depleted our fuel and ate into that precious family time we were no longer able to have together during the day.

Often during the night-time we were faced with boy racers doing doughnuts round the car parks, revving their engines and banging out tunes at full volume. It usually took us a while to get Magnus to sleep, so you can imagine our frustration when we had joy-seeking adolescents pull up right next to us.

To make life easier, we'd book into campsites, but again, at a minimum of £40 a night, they were extremely costly for us and we often found ourselves wedged like sardines between other campers having barbecues and staying up drinking and laughing late into the night. It wasn't our scene at all. It soon became apparent to us that the nomadic way of life as we knew it couldn't really exist in England; our options to live the way we were used to were so limited, and it was frustratingly difficult.

By October, we had reached the Isle of Wight. It was my first visit to the island and, having missed all of the islands on the west and north coast of Scotland, I was super-excited. The weather was great and, as usual, Chris and I took it in turns to cover the miles each day while the other stayed with Jet.

Walking-wise, the island felt like a big achievement for me. Now, four and a half months postpartum, I walked all 72 miles of it over two weeks, carrying my boy along with me, with some stretches being the steepest either Chris or I had walked in a long while! It was gruelling, sweaty and hard toil at times, on an island full of 'chines' (a local word of Saxon origin meaning 'a deep narrow ravine', formed by water cutting through sandstone as it flows to the sea), but the scenery was among the finest I'd seen on our coastline. The colours on the walk from Compton Bay to Chale over the cliffs were amazing: the reddish brown of the crumbling cliffs, rippled bronze sand below, miles of verdant green clifftops and the vibrant blue of the sea with her white-crested waves. Meanwhile, a section between Bonchurch and Luccombe made it feel like we'd suddenly entered the jungle, with its very own tropical microclimate; it was absolutely teeming with lush green vegetation, dangling vines and trees that twisted their way down the cliff face.

The following evening, as we headed towards the Needles, a row of three distinctive chalk stacks that culminate in a red-and-white striped lighthouse out at sea, we walked out of our way to find the best spot to enjoy the sunset. All four of us sat and watched the sky light up with soft hues of rose pink and tangerine orange, the iconic stacks in the distance. Chris took a photo of me holding Magnus up in the air, the two of us silhouetted against this natural masterpiece, and it remains one of my favourite images of us to date. We all played and laughed together, lost in the moment, free from all the logistical conundrums for a while, just grateful to be where we were, all together.

The next day, Magnus and I walked from the Needles to Freshwater Bay over the immaculately kept Tennyson Down. As we walked, I was doing my usual thing, singing and telling him stories, when a couple stopped me, staggered that I was attempting these inclines with a baby on board. He was certainly becoming a hefty load for his age, but it was still not as bad as carting a fully packed Bergen on my back! I was often met with quizzical looks or people stopping to say that I 'must be very fit' when I was out tackling steep terrain on my own with my baby strapped to my front and a 60-litre waterproof bag containing the supplies I needed on my back (it was never full or that heavy, but it was the only bag we had smaller than the Bergen). Given what I was carrying and the remoteness of where I was at times, it probably looked like I was aiming to cover some distance. However, it may have been to do with the fact he was still so little. The truth was, I wasn't very fit at all. In fact, I barely recognized myself in my postpartum body and I certainly didn't feel comfortable in it. For someone whose life had revolved around a high level of physical movement for years, my body had become intrinsic to who I was, the life I led and the life I desperately wanted to keep living. The slow journey back to strength and movement felt monumental. I didn't just want to feel strong physically, I needed it to feel like *me* again. And, instinctively, I knew this rebuilding had to happen here, on the coast.

The Isle of Wight gave me memories with Magnus that I'll cherish for ever. I wished I could dive into his mind and find out how he was processing it all. What did it look like through his eyes? How was his brain absorbing and making sense of it all? It was now autumn, and the woods were a blanket of colourful fallen leaves. One afternoon, we laid him on his sheepskin mat and he was mesmerized watching the leaves pirouette down from the treetops. On his tummy, he inspected their colours of gold, scarlet, russet and brown. He held them, crunched them, scrunched them. It was beautiful to watch. I had the helping hand of nature to keep him busy rather than wracking my brains for ways to entertain him in a house all day.

In fact, every day was full of moments like this. Everything for him was new and so I began to experience the world anew through him. I noticed how fixated he became on the breeze moving through the leaves on the trees above him, and every now and then he would erupt into giggles. The outside world was providing him with all the entertainment and joy he needed. I loved to watch it with him, talk to him about what he was seeing and hearing, let him feel different leaves, branches and the bark of trees.

Those moments of intense concentration were so powerful and I felt a great sense of being grounded as I watched nature capture his attention. It made me realize how the outdoors could provide for free what the baby industry makes parents believe they need to spend a fortune on. We were travelling with the bare minimum when it came to toys for Magnus – a small baby play mat, a few cuddly bears he'd been gifted at birth and some books. I also had an arsenal of songs and oral stories under my belt that I knew from memory.

The rest, we felt, nature could provide.

I began to read more into the science behind the benefits of babies being out in nature. In terms of physical development, there's a long list, but, to name a few, outdoor play helps babies develop gross motor skills through activities like reaching for objects, crawling and walking. Breathing fresh air helps strengthen the respiratory system, and vitamin D from sunlight is vital for immune function and bone health. The outside is full of sights, sounds, textures and smells which babies find exciting and enjoyable. All that sensory stimulation, which the indoors just doesn't provide, is brilliant for building synapses – connections in a baby's brain that are vital for cognitive development (observation, creativity and reasoning) as well as enhancing their understanding of the world. The outside also provides opportunities for talking to babies about what they can see, hear, touch and smell, and is therefore great for building new language.

Exposure to sunlight helps our bodies secrete melatonin, often referred to as the 'sleep hormone'. A 2004 study in the *Journal of Sleep Research* found that babies who slept well at night were exposed to significantly more light in the early afternoon period. Even on a cloudy day, being outside helps to regulate their circadian rhythms far better than if they're inside all day. At this point, I could certainly see the benefits in Magnus's sleep – all his naps were taken outdoors now and he was sleeping more soundly. As for his language, I was certainly very conscious and active in using our daily experiences to develop that, but only time would tell.

I also read that spending time in nature encourages babies to be curious, explore and connect with others, which is a big part of their social-emotional development. It reduces stress and anxiety in babies, promoting emotional wellbeing. Finally, as I'd hoped, early exposure to nature is said to nurture a lifelong appreciation and connection with the natural world, helping to foster a sense of stewardship for it in later years.

Looking ahead, when it came to the question of his education slightly further down the line, I felt very strongly that I wanted significant time in nature to play a key part. My teaching experience meant I felt well-placed to decide his education, whatever form that might take. Obviously that would be a joint decision I made alongside Chris, but we were very much on the same page when it came to exposing Magnus to the benefits of the outdoors. One thing was for sure – the chance of me becoming a typical school-run mum was slim!

28

At Dancing Ledge

By early December, we were on the South West Coast Path, which runs from South Haven Point in Dorset to Minehead in Somerset, getting our teeth firmly stuck into the Dorset seaboard, where Magnus had been born. It is a beautiful coastline, but very steep in places, the path becoming more precarious now, given the mud and the rain. We were in another winter on the walk, and our first with a baby. While staying at my mum's in August, I'd thought ahead and, with some of the money from Chris's first instalment of his book advance, had invested in a few key pieces of winter baby clothing, namely some merino-wool underlayers, a Patagonia down all-in-one snowsuit, and a specialist down sleeping bag that supposedly saw him good to minus 6 degrees and which had to be shipped over from the States. Magnus also had a group of truly wonderful ladies knitting fabulous woollen hats and jumpers for him out of the kindness of their hearts and sending them to us, particularly a woman from Shetland named Nan.

A lady named Bev who we'd met in the New Forest National Park in Hampshire had gifted us a fleece-lined waterproof cover, complete with hood, designed for babywearing, which, combined with my body heat, was fantastic for keeping him warm and dry while we were out walking. During the day, I would dress him in merino base layers, which are warm, moisture-wicking and temperature regulating, followed by a fleece or wool mid-layer, his down snowsuit (which was perfect, as it wasn't too padded or bulky) and a woollen hat. As I carried him, I'd make sure to check his onesie wasn't pulling on his toes at all (which can inhibit circulation) – we'd often make it footless, and he'd wear a pair of merino socks and a pair of boiled woollen boots he was gifted. I'd also regularly check the skin on the back of his neck for his temperature: if clammy, I'd remove a layer; if cold to the touch, I'd add another. With all the practice I was getting, I quickly learned how his body responded to different weather conditions, and dressing him accordingly became second nature. We had no heating in the van, which we were very conscious of as the temperatures dropped quite low at night. Occasionally we'd have to run the engine for a while to heat up before we turned it off to sleep. Without the ability to have a fire outside, it was our only source of warmth. That said, Magnus was now six months old and actually seemed to sleep far better in the cold weather.

It was here, in December, on the Dorset coast, that we filmed an episode for the Channel 5 show *New Lives in the Wild* with Ben Fogle. Support had continued to grow across the country as our walk progressed, and we were always keen to use every available opportunity to raise awareness about SSAFA. Our BBC documentary had brought in an extra £40,000 almost overnight in donations, and we hoped this would do the same. Ben came to join us as we walked some of the fossil-rich Jurassic coast between Studland Bay and Lulworth Cove. The coast was largely deserted at this time of year, so we had more opportunities to find really secluded spots to wild camp. We found a fantastic remote spot with spectacular views down at Chapman's Pool, where we cooked by a fire and slept in the tent. Getting there was an adventure in itself and, at this time of year, it was sensible for one of us to test out the terrain first, before the other attempted to take Magnus.

The temperature dropped as low as minus 2 degrees and Magnus slept soundly through the night for the very first time. He had just turned seven months old. I'm sure many people had dropped jaws, shocked that we had our baby camping in a tent during winter. Yes, small babies have a thinner insulating layer than adults and aren't able to regulate their body temperature. But, by nine to twelve months, they should be able to fully adapt their body temperature to the external conditions. One thing that was certainly evident with Magnus was his amazing adaptability – he had never known anything different but he was incredibly easy-going, flexible, tolerant of change and, in general, a very happy baby. To be honest, given our experience with him outside, it did seem there was a lot of overhyped worry and misconception in our society about the need to keep babies warm and indoors all the time to build their immune system and protect them from colds and flu.

In fact, the opposite is true, and there is plenty of excellent research to back this up: germs and bacteria circulate in enclosed spaces. Viruses that are spread by other human beings and cause colds and flu thrive indoors, making it a far more likely environment for young children to get sick. Time outdoors develops a stronger autoimmune system and a resistance to allergies. It's also better for a child who's already sick to be outside breathing fresh air rather than rebreathing air already full of germs. In Scandinavian culture, it's commonplace for babies to nap outside in sub-zero temperatures. The key is being properly dressed. I could see all this manifesting in Magnus – he slept far better in the cold and he'd never been ill.

WILDERNESS MUM

Ben interviewed me sitting on the edge of the cliffs near Dancing Ledge, and he asked what this walk meant to me. It surprised me how emotional the question made me. Even though I'd been walking for over two years, the fact that I hadn't been there from the beginning meant our charity endeavour was still always perceived as Chris's walk. I understood that, but it was no longer just a walk for me – it was a lifestyle. And because I had become a mother on this journey, it ran much deeper for me now. It wouldn't only be years of fantastic adventure and meaningful fundraising that I'd look back on later in life. It was tied up in all the core-changing transformations of becoming a mother, and I'd chosen to do it all this way based solely on my own instincts. There was also no doubt the walk had helped me to feel like myself again. Now seven months postpartum, physically there were big improvements. My wrists were still an issue and I sometimes wore splint supports on both. But I was finally off all the medication, which felt like a major breakthrough, and my psoriasis was much better. The healing around my C-section scar had come a long way and, although I still had some lower tummy swelling, as Magnus grew bigger I felt no pain carrying him.

Mentally, I had also come far. Initially, I'd barely been able to face looking at my scar, wincing every time I did, but, once we were living outside again, we didn't have a mirror, so it was more a case of out of sight, out of mind. Now, I realized there was absolutely no shame in a Caesarean abdominal birth – the fact that it's often stigmatized as either the 'easy option' in birth or a failure on the part of the mother is both completely wrong and very damaging. I had battled the repercussions of that stigma myself, but now I knew my scar was a sacred line, which told a beautiful and powerful story of my child's entrance into the world. It was also the result of a sensible decision, the only one I could have made at the time to ensure my baby came out alive and well, and all of that deserved to be celebrated.

I'd come to realize that there is so little education or preparation about Caesarean birth beforehand and not enough support after. The stories of our scars need to be seen, shared and normalized so that the women who bear them don't feel so alone. The walk also gave me a daily sense of purpose other than my son, a different goal to focus on and another feeling of reward at the end of the day.

From conversations I'd had with other mums, it seemed like a lot of new mothers struggled to find a purpose and identity for themselves beyond looking after their new baby, which can be extremely overwhelming and anxiety-inducing. Nothing could have prepared me adequately for what came next as I navigated this whole new focus and set of priorities, which centred around the need to care for my baby around the clock amid all the major physical and emotional challenges going on in my body.

I was more than happy to dedicate my whole self to Magnus, I wanted to do that for him as a mother; it's a mother's instinct to do so. But, in all the immense changes I'd undergone in the past few months, I did think it was taking a long time to feel like me again. Although Magnus would always be my priority now, I began to feel like it was important to have some kind of other purpose beyond him. Most mums I spoke to found that purpose in trying to carve out dedicated time to pursue a hobby they loved during their maternity leave or in resuming their careers, but, for me, that purpose was found in walking and continuing on this mission to raise money for charity.

I'll admit that the nature of being pregnant on the walk meant I was more unprepared than most. I didn't meet any other mums in antenatal classes, I didn't have a new mums' group chat on WhatsApp, no circle of new mums to meet up with. Whenever I did meet other mums on the coast, who sometimes invited us into their homes to shelter in bad weather, have dinner or enjoy a passing play date or a coffee, it was always a welcome opportunity to share, exchange tales of motherhood and take on board any tips and useful advice for the current phase. There were times when I did ponder the reality of raising Magnus on the move beyond the walk as he grew up, especially given we were often asked how we would ensure he was 'socialized'. It wasn't an issue at this point, and developmentally speaking wouldn't be for another few years, but I definitely didn't want him to grow up feeling isolated.

Although he probably wouldn't attend a typical nursery or school setting in his early years, I was certainly conscious that I wanted him to socialize in order to develop all those early associated skills, such as cooperative play and empathy, and to eventually make friends. To do that, I would need to find ways to integrate those opportunities into our lifestyle and I intended to start now, signing him up ad-hoc to various playgroups as we moved. Certainly, if Magnus ever did express the desire to attend school, we would absolutely take his feelings into account and adjust our lifestyle if need be. However, community was a huge part of our current adventure, whereby he was meeting lots of people and children. Hopefully, with some creative thinking, we could still build and access community in some way on our travels post-walk.

Once Magnus turned six months old, we began his transition to solid foods. It was a relief to think that this would eventually mean fewer bottles as he got used to eating three meals a day. However, laborious as it was, we were now at least comfortable in that routine. Baby-led weaning, which was the approach I wanted us to use, was now a whole new dynamic to contend with. I spent hours in the back of the van at night researching it all and considering how best to go about it under our circumstances. We didn't have a blender, a fridge or a freezer, or an oven – just a few basic kitchen tools and a gas stove. Initially, I introduced him slowly to one food at a time: mashed broccoli, cauliflower, carrot, parsnip, avocado, sweet potato and so on, mixed with a little of his milk. It took him a month or so to take to it at all, but we soon began to introduce finger foods.

Weaning him meant food shopping had become costlier. It was easier in winter, when we could keep food cool, but even then, without any means of storing or refrigerating food, we had to buy fresh almost every day. We bought a brilliant portable, foldable highchair, and he mainly ate outside, which was definitely handy when it came to cleaning up!

29

Blonde Hedgehogs

Two days into 2023, we broke from the South West Coast Path and set sail from Portsmouth to walk the Channel Islands, an archipelago in the English Channel that's located off the north-west coast of France, but which are dependencies of the British Crown. They include two main islands, Jersey and Guernsey, along with several smaller islands: Herm, Sark and Alderney.

Just before we left, Janice and Astrid, the two ladies from the Williams Gansey knitting project whom we'd met on the Blyth Tall Ship in Northumberland, sent Magnus his very own gansey knit, which had been made in a traditional pattern of a tall ship, with the cable depicting the ropes, and a ladder to represent the rigging, all in a beautiful sea blue. We were so honoured: it was such a unique garment, linked to great history, and the timing of its arrival was perfect, given where we were heading – the gansey originated in Guernsey, made from wool imported from England by the local fishing communities there.

Arriving in Guernsey felt like stepping back in time, with the old-world charm of St Peter Port and the island's narrow winding lanes and cobbled streets. Yet, despite our excitement to explore somewhere that felt completely new, the first few nights were among the hardest we ever experienced with Magnus. The only place we could find to park was a clifftop hotel car park on one corner of the island, which wasn't a problem as, over winter, the hotel was shut and the car park was empty.

However, the weather was atrocious – raging winds, rain and hail, and absolutely freezing – and it was impossible to light our gas stove outdoors to boil the water to wash, sterilize and fill Magnus's bottles. And it was too dangerous to light a propane gas stove in the back of a cramped van, especially with a small baby.

His feeds were obviously crucial and we were now faced with a dilemma. We needed a larger space or somewhere with a kettle, but, given the hotel was closed, this meant driving around to find another hotel or a pub that was open. We didn't want to drive around for ages only to find that all the other hotels were also shut this time of year, so we debated what to do, while doing our best to stay sane and entertain Magnus. At this rate, it was looking like we might end up awkwardly banging on a few doors to ask for help.

All of a sudden, I noticed a light turn on in the hotel. I decided to try my luck. I knocked on the door and, thankfully, it opened. I asked if we could perhaps have the use of their kettle to prepare our baby's milk, and, luckily, they were really accommodating. Both nights we stayed, they allowed us to use their facilities to do this, and it was a godsend. The weather remained like this, day in, day out, for our first two weeks, and Chris and I took turns to walk in the downpours and hailstorms, while the other entertained Magnus and Jet in the van. I would take Magnus out with me whenever we had a break of calm, but by and large we would alternate walking and childcare. I would walk very briskly to get back to Magnus as soon as possible, and we both did shorter distances in the bad weather. That meant getting creative to maximize the interior space for Magnus's tummy time and suchlike.

For his Christmas present (which we'd spent on the Devon coast in a little holiday-home cottage right by the sea in Salcombe that a lady had kindly offered us), I had made him an under-the-sea themed wall hanging. I'd found some blue, sequined, sparkly material in a charity shop and bought a load of brightly coloured felt. I stayed up until 2 a.m. on Christmas Eve sewing a variety of stuffed sea life to hang from it, including coral and seaweed. Now, it was really coming into its own as I hung it across the van, and I was glad I'd gone to the effort!

After a week, the island's soft-play area fortunately reopened, so we decided to take Magnus along. It was our first time at one and it became such a blessing, giving him extra space and play time when the heavens opened. He'd just turned eight months old and, although not quite crawling yet, he was well on the way. We quickly became acquainted with the woman who ran it and she even let us put all our bottles through the dishwasher each time we visited, which was a huge help. A few days later, a local woman named Hannah, who had no idea who we were or what we were doing, spotted us sheltering from the rain in our van with the baby. Without hesitation, she offered us a shed in her back garden, which doubled as her physiotherapy studio, for Magnus and me to sleep in (Chris, of course, insisted on staying in the van with Jet, parked out front). Hannah and her partner, Steve, were incredibly kind. They welcomed us into their home and gave us free rein to come and go, and their two young children, Hattie and Teddy, became brilliant playmates for Magnus. As a mum herself, Hannah instinctively understood the wild rollercoaster of early motherhood. I think she also sensed I'd been through a tough time. She ran hot baths for me after long, wet walking days and insisted on watching Magnus so I could take half an hour to just breathe. What I loved most about Hannah was how unflinchingly real and honest she was about it all. I felt safe opening up to her. Even though we'd only just met, for our remaining time walking Guernsey she became a friend, and one I remain in touch with to this day.

Although winter was hard on us, my years so far on the walk had taught me to appreciate and embrace all the seasons for what they offered. The rain would stop eventually, and meanwhile we had empty coastal paths to explore! There was also something seriously special about these islands, which already had such a different feel to the mainland. Along with that, we could satisfy our love of history by exploring the only British soil to have been occupied by the Nazis during the Second World War.

Between June 1940 and May 1945, the islands experienced a brutal occupation which led to severe restrictions, including curfews and censorship. Many islanders were subjected to extreme hardship, forced labour and imprisonment. Due to their proximity to Britain and their perceived strategic importance, the islands, particularly Alderney, were also heavily fortified as part of Hitler's Atlantic Wall. The evidence was absolutely everywhere in the form of bunkers, artillery batteries and foreboding concrete observation towers.

We heard stories so different from anything we'd heard previously on our journey. One was told to us by Des, a ninety-five-year-old islander who'd been evacuated from Guernsey just before the German occupation. Right before, a newspaper ran an article warning that German forces were coming, so, with only twenty-four hours' notice, parents were left with the unthinkably difficult decision of whether or not to evacuate their children from the island, with absolutely no idea what the future held. The boats carrying Des and the other children set

WILDERNESS MUM

off for the mainland that same night. As a mum now, it's impossible to imagine how terrified those parents must've been watching their precious children sail into the distance, not knowing when they'd return. It made me feel so privileged to have my little family beside me constantly.

Finally, after more than two weeks, we got a break in the weather and were able to head to the smaller islands of Herm, Sark and Alderney.

Herm is the smallest publicly accessible Channel Island, small enough at 1.5 miles long and 0.5 miles wide that we were able to walk it together. It lies 3 miles off the coast of Guernsey and we caught a small boat to get there. It was so quiet that we didn't see a single other soul while there and we skipped carefree along the sandy beaches feeling like we had the whole island to ourselves. While exploring Herm, I discovered fascinating stories woven through centuries of island life. For around 200 years, until 1736, it was the private playground of Jersey's governors; wealthy men sailed over to hunt pheasants, partridges, swans and rabbits in abundance. During the Industrial Revolution, Herm's famously hard granite was quarried for major projects like London Bridge. The island buzzed with life for the first time since prehistoric times, becoming home to 400 workers and facilities like a bakery, brewery, harbour, road and even a prison.

In 1889, a Prussian prince whose grandfather had fought at Waterloo with Wellington fell in love at sixty-nine, married a fellow royal and brought her to Herm. Their son, the future Kaiser of Germany, wed Princess Sophie of the Netherlands, and the two couples lived peacefully on the island until the First World War forced them to flee. During their time, they introduced red-necked wallabies, though sadly their descendants reportedly became rations for German soldiers during the Second World War. It was also here on the sandy beaches of

Herm that the Nazis trained and prepared for their invasion of the United Kingdom, known as Operation Sealion.

The following day, we got the boat to Sark and struck gold with the sunshine. 3 miles long and 1.5 miles wide, Sark consists of two main parts, Great Sark and Little Sark, connected by a narrow isthmus called La Coupée. It is also one of the few places left in the world where motorized vehicles aren't allowed, which most definitely adds to its charm. You can cycle around the island, although even cycling is forbidden on La Coupée because it's so narrow, with 80-metre sheer drops on either side. For many years, La Coupée was believed to be haunted and residents thought their donkeys refused to cross the rocky ridge because they were frightened by the presence of a ghostly dog the size of a calf, with blood-red eyes, named Tchico! Sark also happens to be both Europe and the world's first Dark Sky Island, meaning there's no public lighting and the starry Milky Way is so clear that locals can navigate by it.

So that we could both walk Sark before the last boat back to Guernsey, I had to power the whole way around it with Magnus in plenty of time to get back and stay with Jet so that Chris could get round it too. There were a lot of steep climbs, which made for hot, tiring work carrying Magnus, but I was really bowled over by the amount to see. We passed Window in the Rock (a square hole cut in the cliff face, with a sheer drop and epic cliff views), the Venus Pool (a natural swimming pool accessible at low tide), a Neolithic dolmen, Sark Henge (nine stones of Jersey granite, previously used by tenants as gate hinges to enclose their fields, now erected in a ring to represent the nine medieval territories), old silver mines, a Buddhist monument and two harbours.

*

WILDERNESS MUM

In the summer, you can explore Sark by horse and carriage, and there are signs in places declaring designated pulling-in spots just for those! They don't operate in winter, so the very few people we saw were either on bikes or on foot like us. The coast was wild and dramatic, with loads of high cliffs, winding narrow paths and very secluded bays, which made for exceptional scenery all the way round. I fell in love with the island, and all the more because I was exploring such a uniquely special place with my son.

Sark has its own share of fascinating wartime stories, particularly involving espionage – one of which helped inspire the creation of the nation's favourite secret agent, James Bond. Like the other islands, in 1940 Sark was occupied by the Germans. In October 1942, twelve British commandos led by Major Geoffrey Appleyard landed on Sark as part of Operation Basalt. In the dead of night, they worked with brave local informants Dame Hathaway and Mrs Pittard to gather intelligence from enemy maps to give information on German locations. Ian Fleming, then a naval officer and colleague of the raiding team, used Appleyard's daring bravery as inspiration for his soon-to-be iconic character, 007. As someone who grew up watching Bond films with my dad every Sunday and later collected vintage editions of the books, including a first edition miraculously found in a charity shop, uncovering this link while walking the island made the history feel all the more exciting for me.

After Sark, we only had one island left to walk – Alderney. But getting there was proving impossible. Because we were walking the coast on one continuous journey, it meant taking on islands when we reached them, irrespective of season. However, we'd forgotten to consider the difficulty of getting boats in January. Boats simply didn't run to Alderney at that time of year. Private boats might make the journey in the right conditions, but only with enough people on board to make it financially worthwhile – a minimum of eight, which we didn't have.

Eventually, thanks to Hannah and the local airline, Aurigny, Magnus and I were able to fly to Alderney on a tiny nineteen-seater plane, his first-ever flight. Meanwhile, a couple from Alderney, Caroline and Roland, did everything in their power to make sure we got to walk the island; Caroline came to pick me and Magnus up from the airport and waited with us while Roland did a six-hour round trip to pick Chris and Jet up on his rib, because Jet was too heavy to be carried in the tiny aircraft.

Once we'd conquered the logistical feat of actually getting there, we began our walk around Alderney – the closest of all the Channel Islands to France (only 8 miles away from the Normandy coast). I loved every moment. For me, Alderney's beauty was in how rugged, natural and untouched it felt. I particularly loved Saye Bay – a crescent of very secluded white sand – and Corblets Bay, with Mannez Lighthouse in the distance. The south side was more dramatic, with sheer imposing sea cliffs and tiny coves.

Alderney's Second World War history stands apart from that of the other Channel Islands. While the others endured life under German occupation, Alderney was the only one to be fully evacuated in 1940. With the civilian population gone, Hitler seized the opportunity to transform the island into an impregnable fortress. He ramped up construction of military fortifications, using prisoners of war and forced labour to build them. Alderney was so strategically valuable that it earned the nickname 'Adolf Island', soon becoming home to the western-most concentration camps of the Third Reich. Today, only three gateposts remain of Lager Sylt, one of four Nazi labour camps established on the island in 1942. Two of those camps, including Lager Sylt, were run by the SS and are the only concentration camps ever to have existed on British soil. When the islanders returned after the war, it's said that the birds didn't sing. Despite such a haunted chapter in its history, Alderney felt like a peaceful place to me. You can walk among the dark relics of the past and be reminded of what happened here but also feel at peace in this very beautiful and tranquil place.

As we were leaving, Caroline came to drop Chris back at the harbour to meet Roland and to take Magnus and me back to the airport. She gave Magnus a furry blonde hedgehog cuddly toy; blonde hedgehogs are generally only found on Alderney and are incredibly rare elsewhere in Europe. The story goes that they arrived on the island back in the 1960s after one was smuggled over inside a Harrods shopping bag!

Once we'd hugged Caroline goodbye, Magnus and I waited in the tiny airport, which even has a box of unfinished knitting to help you pass the time while you wait for your flight! Just the two of us on that tiny aeroplane was a great experience in itself. I really loved being on these islands. They have a very unique cultural blend of English and French influence – English-speaking, but with French street names and Norman law. Collectively, they all possess an old-world charm and offer a hauntingly preserved glimpse into the past, yet each island has its own distinctive personality and very strong sense of identity. Yes, we'd taken a beating from the weather, but that didn't take away from a strikingly varied coastline and an amazing chapter in our adventure. We'd made new friends we knew we'd stay in touch with, had a jam-packed month full of unexpected twists and turns, explored a far-flung corner of the United Kingdom – and survived January on the walk with a baby! As a family, we were leaving in really high spirits.

With Alderney completed, the Channel Islands were now in the bag and we headed back to the mainland, ready to resume where we'd left off and crack on with the rest of the South

West Coast Path, the Isles of Scilly, and over the Severn Bridge into Wales in the hope of finally crossing the finish line by summer. Our morale was high, ground was getting covered and our little man was taking it all in his stride, extremely content, always smiling and laughing. He was a very happy baby and I took great comfort in knowing that he was thriving. Our bond was just as I'd hoped it would be, and the end of the walk was in sight. But a grey cloud loomed in the distance. Life was about to take a turn for me . . .

30

Sod's Law

We were so excited for Devon and Cornwall, convinced it would be the best coastline we would see now until the end, and we were keen to soak it up and enjoy it. However, as we came through Sidmouth and round the estuary at Exmouth, past Topsham and into Dawlish, I found myself beginning to limp.

Please, no, I can't have come this far only to fall at the final hurdle!

Since returning from the Channel Islands, I'd started to notice a slight discomfort in my right Achilles tendon. At first, I thought I'd just overdone it and that, if I took it a bit easier over the coming days, it would sort itself out. I ended up doing a longer day than anticipated on my own with Magnus to the end of Dawlish Warren and the long sandy spit that looks over Exmouth. The following day, as I carried him through Dawlish and into Holcombe, I began to feel more and more pain with every mile, limping so much by the end that I was visibly struggling to walk. From then on, for many weeks, even when I wasn't walking, I was permanently in pain to the point where it stopped me from sleeping.

Suffering an injury that now hindered me walking was an incredibly hard pill to swallow, and I felt crushed. After everything I'd been through to get me to this point, and being so close to the end, I couldn't believe it had happened. I was desperate to grin and bear it and just carry on, but I knew I had to accept that I needed to rest and recover before I did any further damage. 'What the hell are we going to do now?' I asked Chris as we sat in the van together, very tired after a sleepless night of pain. 'I can't believe this is happening!'

I could see Chris was gutted both for me and for all of us – we'd been through a lot and had finally found a good rhythm that was now working for us, only to be hit with another major setback. He rubbed his forehand, eyes to the floor, deep in thought for a few moments, then he looked up at me and put his hand on my knee reassuringly. 'We'll find a way,' he said. 'We always do.'

One option was for us all to stop for a while, until I was ready to go again. However, we didn't know how long that would take and we also had nowhere to stay. We both knew I couldn't rest and fully recover cooped up in the van; it was simply too cramped. We also felt that, for the sake of consistency and particularly for the fundraising, Chris needed to carry on with the walk. If we started again months later, we would be heading into another winter, by which time Magnus would be well and truly on his feet, making it even harder in a tiny van. There was another reason too – Jet. We needed to get this walk finished now, for her, so she could rest and put her paws up in more relaxing circumstances. We felt that, if we pressed pause for any considerable length of time, there was a chance she could pass, and we wanted more than anything for Jet to cross that line, too. For all her incredible efforts, she deserved it as much as any of us. I also couldn't imagine Chris crossing that finish line without Jet. Physically, I knew he would do it, whatever it took, but mentally I knew it would break him into a million pieces. There was only one viable option left to us.

'I'll keep going on my own, with Jet. God knows how, but I will,' Chris suggested. 'But there's no way I can be without you or Magnus until the end – no way.'

So, we found a solution, of sorts. Magnus and I went back to my mum's for a few weeks, while Chris pushed on with walking the Devon coastline. It wasn't easy, though. He had to find a spot to park up, leave Jet in the van, then run as fast as his legs could carry him to cover that day's distance before getting back to her as soon as possible. It meant he was retracing his steps daily, but it was the only way he could make sure she was okay and also complete each leg. We considered trying to find someone each day through his social media to drive the van so that he could reconvene with Jet at points along the way, but it was too difficult logistically and we knew Jet would never have taken to being driven off by a different stranger each day.

I felt for Chris; what was once a carefree journey of self-discovery had become a nightmare for him. The South West Coast Path alone is 630 miles of mostly steep and undulating terrain. There was then roughly another 245 miles to reach the walk's final destination of Llangennith, including completing the Scilly Isles. If I couldn't recover before the end to help by driving the van to pick him up after each day's leg, he'd be looking at well over 1,000 miles to run.

He was exhausted and incredibly stressed by the pressure of finishing the walk while caring for Jet, missing his son and worrying about me. Equally, I was now left to solo parent for who knew how long, while in constant pain and barely able to walk. I did seek medical help and, back at Mum's, went to revisit the same women's health physio I'd seen before resuming the walk after Magnus was born. She wrapped some kinesiology tape around my ankle to help support the affected area. I had no choice but to move, and she gave me some daily exercises. My mum helped us so much in inviting Magnus and me to stay, but she couldn't help me with childcare – her disability meant she couldn't pick him up or keep up with his crawling. While I was there, I will admit I definitely enjoyed the luxury of a comfortable bed, a bath and some kitchen facilities. I'd always loved getting creative with cooking outside when time allowed, but often cooking was more about necessity, getting something made quickly to sustain us on the move. Now I had access to all the normal mod cons, I really enjoyed experimenting more with recipes for Magnus; having a child who was on his own journey with food had made me incredibly conscious about nutrition and was definitely pushing me to become a more thoughtful cook.

I also made the most of being in one place for a time and took him to various sensory and messy playgroups in the area. It helped break up the day for me and provided Magnus with a different kind of sensory stimulation and more exposure to other babies. My mum hadn't moved to the area until after I'd finished university, so I had no friends around to catch up with, unfortunately, but I busied myself doing my exercises when Magnus napped, and doing drawings of Jet and favourite places along the coast in the evenings while he slept. Chris and I had faced plenty of adversity in our two and a half years together, and, while this separation was different from dealing with food shortages and high winds, it was simply another hurdle to cross. We were ending the walk together, whatever it took.

It was now that Chris decided on a date to aim for to cross the finish line – 29 July, almost exactly six years to the day after he set off from Llangennith. 'There, now we have to do it!' he said, laughing nervously. Chris has always used humour to help him cope with stressful situations. This entire journey from the beginning had been full of challenges and the need to problem-solve, and this was no different. One thing I knew was that he would make it happen. We could only hope I'd recover quickly and be able to rejoin him on the coast as soon as possible.

Not long after, we received a message from a lady called Gaynor who had come out to walk a stretch of the South Downs Way with us, back in the summer. She was conscious of the fact that our family unit was now operating as two halves and there was too much geographical distance between Devon and Malvern for Chris to be able to afford the fuel to come back and see us regularly. Testament once again to the wonderful people we'd encountered, Gaynor offered to put us up in her holiday home in Goldsithney, not too far from Penzance, Cornwall. We didn't see much of Chris the first month we were there – he was still walking a good few hours' drive away, around Torquay, Salcombe and into Plymouth – but we were so grateful, because it meant we could reunite as a family on the rare occasions he could break the walk to visit us.

Gaynor's holiday home gave me the extra space I needed with Magnus. He was a speedy crawler now and I spent most of my days hobbling after him or chasing him around the place on all fours. Although I'd never actually taught early years, I found my primary teaching experience came in handy and I would get my creative hat on to think of more messy-play activities to do. Also, from a weaning perspective, now that I had access to a cooker, plenty of pots and pans and a fridge, it was quicker and easier for me to prepare meals. On the days my ankle felt okay, I would take him to a beautiful butterfly house down the road, to the park, the beach or on the bus into Penzance, where there was an occasional soft-play event put on in the church.

However, after so many years of moving each day and living in the open air, I found it hard to be so housebound. I didn't have a vehicle, and public transport was very limited, and the fact that I was injured meant I couldn't go far on foot. It also chucked it down for the whole of March, and entertaining Magnus indoors all day was so much harder than being outside with him.

Then, a lovely lady called Cheryl got in touch. I think she felt for me, being injured and housebound and on my own for weeks with a baby, and she kindly offered to drive us to Newlyn so Magnus could attend a 'mini artists' messy paint play class. She also took us to see his very first theatre performance at the Tremenheere Sculpture Gardens, brought home-made bread and soup over for lunch one day, and took us for a beach stroll and a coffee overlooking St Michael's Mount at Marazion. She even drove me to see a physio so I could seek some professional advice. It was lovely to have these opportunities to go out. Cheryl could tell I was struggling emotionally with my change in circumstances, and her support and friendship helped get me through those tough weeks while Chris was away.

It was really special to feel this sense of community on the walk. I certainly didn't have a close-knit village around me to help raise my baby; no family or friends alongside us to regularly lend a hand; nor did I have the connections that come from putting down roots in one place for a time. Often it definitely felt like we (particularly me, at this stage) were tackling it all alone. However, gestures like this were a reminder that there was a sense of a village out there, people who wanted to help, and it was all the more touching when I'd never even previously met them. I was glad to experience a taste of that, given I wasn't leading a routine life.

As soon as I'd seen another local physio, I was incredibly diligent at following the exercise regime they gave me to help speed up my recovery. There seemed to be little doubt that my injury was linked to childbirth. When pregnant, the body produces a hormone called relaxin, which loosens and relaxes muscles, joints and ligaments to help the body prepare to give birth. It can affect all ligaments in the body, not just the pelvic area, and takes time to return to normal again, which can lead to a higher risk of injury during the postpartum period.

It was clear that, even though I'd felt healthy and strong while walking these past months, I had pushed myself too hard too soon. I'd never anticipated carrying Magnus every day – we'd always envisaged Chris would carry him to allow me more time to ease into walking again without the additional strain of extra weight. However, that hadn't happened because we had ended up walking separately so Jet wasn't alone in the van. It wasn't her fault, but the honest truth was that I resented Chris for putting Jet first, to the point where he hadn't been able to support my recovery in the way I needed.

That said, the only person I could really blame was myself. It was me who'd insisted on carrying Magnus, because I'd wanted us to continue as a family rather than be separated in those first months of his life, and I couldn't bear the thought of him cooped up for hours in the van while we waited for Chris to walk. I'd done it because I wanted to be the best mum I could, but in doing so I'd pushed my body too hard before it was ready and I was paying the price. The more time went on, the more I realized how much more information I should have been given when leaving the hospital to support my recovery. I was told nothing other than to see a women's health physio after twelve weeks, which I did. I didn't know anything about scar care and massage once the bandages were off, about diastasis recti, about the hugely important need for breathwork or gentle movement in those early weeks, which I now know are crucial for recovery.

Ultimately, my body had needed more tender loving care, with regular physio check-ups and a specialized exercise programme, rather than just ploughing up and down the cliffs every day with another human strapped to my front! I realized that being determined and resilient can be a strength, especially doing something like the walk, but it can also drown out the voice that says it's *not* a sign of weakness to prioritize self-care.

31

Birthday in the Scillies

By April, Chris had reached Cornwall and was now within shooting distance of spending most evenings with us. Our time together increased as he got nearer – and then he made it to Penzance! His arrival made such a difference. He could now look after Magnus for stints while I dashed off on trains and buses to see various physios for various treatments all over the county; I was determined to recover and get back on the walk.

I was advised to start incorporating some walking into my days to avoid my ligaments weakening from too much rest. So, we tackled Lizard Point as a family to celebrate reaching mainland Britain's most southerly point, and I did other walks around Kynance and Mullion Coves on my own with Magnus, always careful never to do more than a few miles. The scenery was stunning and I was just so grateful I was no longer missing it all; I'd been looking forward to Cornwall for a long time!

It was almost May, and two months since my injury. While it was by no means better, I was seeing signs of improvement and getting desperate for a change of scene. The Isles of Scilly were coming up and we agreed we should try to get there before the ferries became entirely booked up by tourists and prices rocketed. Magnus's first birthday was approaching and the Scilly Isles would be a magical place to spend it, so the decision was made – we would all go together.

Chris got the ferry a few days ahead with Jet, to get a feel for the place before we joined them. My dad and his wife had decided to come and see us down in Cornwall, so we planned to head out by ferry to join Chris and Jet in time for Magnus turning one on the first of the month. If only it were that simple. It just so happened our timing had coincided with the World Rowing Gig Championships, meaning thousands of people had flocked to the islands! It was a disaster transport-wise; all ferries and flights appeared to be fully booked for weeks to come. But we *had* to find a way to get across, otherwise Chris was going to miss his son's first birthday.

Fortunately, while we panicked on the mainland, on St Mary's Chris met a born-and-bred local called Fran who was married to the harbour master, Dale. Thanks to her, we got our lucky break, and a boat was arranged to bring me and Magnus across from St Ives. Our departure was about as stressful as it gets. We'd had next to no sleep the past two nights due to Magnus teething, then my attempts to pack in the morning were thwarted when he refused to nap and spent hours screaming instead.

I was told the journey to St Mary's would take just under two hours on calm seas and that there was access to indoor seating in the small and cosy little boat. And, for the first half or so, it was lovely – blue skies, still seas and beautiful headlands behind us. Then, the sun disappeared on us, the clouds drew drearily overhead and the waves got choppy. Magnus was sleeping and I'd covered him in a water-resistant blanket, but it was obvious we would soon be in for a soaking. I decided to take refuge in the only option that turned out to be available – the driver's cabin. The sea was by now very choppy and, within five minutes of gazing at a very lopsided horizon, I felt extremely sick. 'How much longer?' I asked. I was expecting to be told twenty minutes – instead, the conditions and the size of the boat made it nearer ninety!

I had no idea how the hell I was going to manage giving Magnus a late lunch and a nappy change. Not to mention the fact that I was now holding him while turning a very pasty shade of grey. I managed to stick it out for about half an hour before I was sick over his shoulder. Thankfully, the lovely lady next to me offered to hold him and I was given a green bucket to continue with, which the driver then disposed of over the side. Yet Magnus was so unfazed by it all that you'd think he was the captain!

Once we'd finally made it back onto dry land, I knew the journey had been worth it. I was immediately taken aback by how beautiful St Mary's was – lovely white beaches, with other islands in view showcasing their own stunning creamy sands. Chris came to meet us off the boat, running up to us in excitement before we all embraced, overjoyed to be reunited again and just in time for Magnus's first birthday. The couple he'd met, Fran and Dale, had offered us a shed in their back garden which had been converted into a sleeping space for their son who was at university. This was wonderfully helpful for us. The laws against wild camping on the Scilly Isles were as strict as anywhere we'd seen and we'd also been warned it was extremely frowned upon by locals. It was just no go. We weren't permitted to bring the van because of the vehicle ban, and the campsites were all fully booked due to the gig championships. But, as an added bonus, Fran was a nurse and could administer Magnus's one-year inoculations!

On the day, Magnus woke up to a birthday breakfast, opening presents given to him by some islanders, who all sang 'Happy Birthday' to him, and we shared the special birthday banana muffins I'd made with Fran and Dale's son the night before. Dale then gave us a private boat ride to the island of St Martin's.

When we arrived, we just couldn't believe how tropical it looked: bright sunshine, empty white sands and turquoise sea – it was the Caribbean on British shores! We were like kids on Christmas morning. We plonked our bags down on the beach and, for a few good hours, played in the water and on the sand with Magnus and Jet. It was heaven – beautiful, peaceful and, best of all, relaxing. Things had been so full on for us over the past year that it had been ages since we had taken a pause. This was like a little family holiday and we cherished every moment. In motherhood, there are so many moments that you wish you could freeze in time and this was one of them.

Out of nowhere, a man came by on his boat and asked if we had anywhere to stay for the night. It was mid-afternoon at this point and we thought we'd head to a campsite, but hadn't organized anywhere yet. He told us his name was Tony and invited us to pitch our tent inside his polytunnel – a steel frame covered in polyethylene, used to grow plants. An hour later, he rocked up on the beach on his quad bike with a metal trailer attached. He was in his late fifties, short, stout and scruffy-looking, with tanned skin, kind eyes and a beaming smile. We loaded all our bags and ourselves onto the trailer and set off to our newest temporary accommodation. As we bumped along in the trailer up the hill to his set-up, we found out that Tony had come to the islands years ago in search of a simple, quiet life and lived in the tiny annex of a house that belonged to an elderly gentleman he cared for.

He told us about his day-to-day life as a carer, cooking, cleaning, taking phone calls with nurses, organizing doctors' appointments and administering medication. We sensed he was really excited to have us around as new company, particularly the joy, light and laughter of a now one-year-old child.

Tony was such a star. He said he needed some time to clear the polytunnel out for us, so, once we'd dumped the bags and checked out our digs for the evening, he then took us to another part of the island. On the way, we ended up with a punctured tyre, but the ride was so fun and so random, we just laughed through it and it got sorted in the end. Waking up from his nap suddenly on the back of a trailer, Magnus was again completely unfazed – there was no doubt this nomadic life of ours had made him very 'go with the flow'!

We spent the rest of the afternoon on another gorgeous beach, where we set up some birthday bunting and had dinner, and Magnus blew out the candle in his birthday muffin before sunset. I just loved the fact that we'd come to a place having absolutely nothing planned and no idea what to expect (which sometimes with a baby can be a little daunting), and we'd ended up on our own private boat ride, bombing round the island in a quad-bike trailer, having Bahamian-style beaches to ourselves, eating birthday cake while watching the sunset and preparing to pitch our tent in a random polytunnel, Magnus clapping along to songs sung by Chris and Tony on the guitar. It was such a vivid reminder that, when nothing is planned, it leaves it open for anything to happen – and, for us, that's real adventure.

We couldn't have wished for a more perfect first birthday for our son.

Birthday celebrations over, we decided to take our time on these islands so that I could do some easy walking and get a bit of headspace to come to terms with what was coming. Given each island was only a few miles to circumnavigate, I was confident I could manage to see them all without overexerting myself. Once we'd ticked off St Mary's, we headed for Bryher, the smallest of the islands, with a coast path of just 3 miles, and scenery which meant it lived up to its name – Bryher is a

Cornish word meaning 'land of hills'. We got pitched up at the only campsite on the island and took the afternoon to enjoy ourselves. The first beach we stumbled upon down by Fraggle Rock was simply stunning, with brilliant views of Hangman's Island (said to have been a site for executions during the English Civil War), and it proved a total hit with Magnus – he had a whale of a time zooming up and down the sand on all fours, scouring for shells and seaweed, clambering on lobster pots and boat trailers, dipping his hands and feet in the water and exploring the rock pools, as well as taking some sandy siestas!

That afternoon, I ran into the water for my first wild swim of the year. Fresh from the Atlantic Ocean and off the back of a winter, it was far colder than it looked! The icy shock to my system was exactly what I needed – a refresh, reset and a feeling of liberation I'd been craving after a few stagnant months. The next day, I took it easy walking the rugged western side on my own while Chris stayed on the beach with Magnus and Jet. I stopped and sat on a rock for a while to take in the view of the cliffs surrounded by sea pinks. Having been so busy with Magnus, it felt like the first 'me time' I'd had in a while and I got teary.

Now Chris had committed us to crossing the finish line on 29 July, we *had* to get there. That meant covering hundreds of miles in just under three months. There was no way I could do it all with my injury, and certainly not at the pace needed. For us to make it, I could do intermittent stretches here and there, but I wouldn't be able to cover all the miles to the end. I would have to accept that the walking side of my journey was largely over and that my role now was to support Chris in every way I could so that he could finish what he started almost six years prior.

I knew I hadn't failed, and I certainly hadn't quit, but it was soul-destroying nevertheless. I'd put too much into the past two and a half years not to finish: battling through the baltic winters, summer saunas, living full-time in a tent and occasionally sleeping on garage floors, in barns, stables, sheds, polytunnels, boats, never mind persevering through nine months of pregnancy, childbirth and my first year of motherhood. I'd given it everything – blood, sweat and tears, quite literally.

It wasn't just the pain of stopping that made me cry – I felt a crippling frustration that my body was the barrier when my heart was still all in. I wiped away the tears and stood up. I didn't want to wallow in self-pity; I'd done enough of that these past months. I had to remind myself what joining this walk had given me, put my own feelings aside and do what was best for all of us as a family.

32

Salted and Sun-Kissed

Once back on the mainland, we made it around Land's End and waved goodbye to our little cottage base in Goldsithney ready to resume proper outdoor life once again. The place had been such a lifeline for me with Magnus during the worst of my injury, but I was now desperate for the sense of movement, freedom and ever-changing surroundings that the walk provided. I adapted into my supporting role. Now that we no longer had to double back so that I could walk it all with Magnus, Chris was able to cover the miles much quicker. I'd drop him off at his start points, pick a spot down the coast in which to meet, drive Magnus and Jet there and wait together for him. We were also able to find pockets of time together when he could take a break before his next leg.

Meanwhile, Magnus and I played on practically every beach along that coast path, from Porthcurno to Sennen Cove, Pendeen to Porthtowan, Holywell to Perranporth, Padstow to Port Quin, Port Isaac to Tintagel, Boscastle to Bude. I found this transition stage, between Magnus learning to crawl and learning to walk, one of the most physically demanding as a mum. So much of it was spent doubling over, holding his hands to help him keep balance so he could explore on his feet. It certainly felt backbreaking at times, but here on the beaches, we had ample space in beautiful surroundings, without having to do 90-degree turns every time we hit a wall. He had so much time and opportunity to freely move and crawl, exploring how his environment changed with each new bay we visited.

While other children learn to crawl and walk on carpet or wooden floors at home, and pull themselves to standing using tables and sofas, Magnus raced along the sand on all fours, pulling himself up on rocks, using them for support and balance as he practised standing and taking steps on his own. I watched him press his hands firmly into the warm sand, then grab chubby fistfuls of it before watching the way it sifted through his fingers, creating cones of sprinkled towers. His tiny fingers traced lines like little drawings in the sand, while his toes danced and splashed in the shallows. He investigated shells, seaweed and stones like a detective chasing clues on the sandy floor, poring over their shapes, textures and patterns. His hair was salted and sun-kissed, swept wild by the sea breeze. We sat together as I made up stories of mermaids, pirates and sunken treasure, his eyes wide with wonder as he looked towards the horizon. I watched this wild baby, his growth shaped by sand and sea, so at home here. Even though I wasn't walking the miles any more, I was still able to enjoy and bring the coast alive in a different way with Magnus, and that was no small silver lining.

In the late afternoons, we would reconvene and find a campsite where we could enjoy some family time together before it all began again the next day. When we reached north Devon, it was getting too hot to leave Jet in the van for any length of time. But it was also impossible for me to look after her and Magnus at the same time when I was out and about all day – she would pine and pull on the lead in one direction to get to Chris, while Magnus would zoom in the other. That said, when she felt calm and settled in the presence of Chris, the relationship she had with Magnus was so special it often brought tears to my eyes. Jet was Magnus's introduction to the magical world of dogs and the perfect first dog for him to be around, thanks to her extremely gentle and placid nature. She was very relaxed and content around Magnus, often leaning forward to give him an affectionate nudge or lick.

Likewise, Magnus absolutely adored Jet, laughing hysterically whenever she shook her hair off, yawned, rolled over in play, wagged her tail or stretched. We made a big point of showing him how to be gentle and respectful with her, how and where to stroke her, and, although we trusted Jet implicitly, we were always on hand to support the development of their relationship under supervision. To him, she was loving, interesting and entertaining, and Magnus loved giving her cuddles, often nestling up close to her or lying with his head on her. Trust, love, loyalty, protection and comfort oozed from Jet to Magnus with the result that she made him incredibly gentle and caring around any other animals he came across. I knew it was one aspect of a beautiful legacy she would leave him.

The only option now was for Chris to take off at sunrise, do as much as he could in the early morning before the heat set in, meet up with us for family time during the bulk of the day and then set out again in the late afternoon or evening when it was cooler. The problem was, I couldn't do the usual drop-off and pick-up that early and that late, with Magnus asleep in the tent. So, back to the drawing board. In the end, we decided we'd spend the days together playing on beaches, Chris waiting with Jet in the shade to allow me time to walk the incredible Valley of the Rocks with Magnus, and even taking our son up the world's steepest water-powered funicular railway in Lynton. Then, in the cooler late afternoon, Chris would go off in the van with Jet to keep working through the coastline. He'd leave her for short periods in the van to walk, then would run back to her. Then he'd find a spot to park up and sleep in the van with her overnight, wake up at the crack of dawn and do the same again before coming to find us mid to late morning.

In all honesty, it was tricky having to prioritize Jet's needs so much, and it put a lot of pressure on us both to work around her separation anxiety from Chris; they were just too tightly bonded. It felt cruel to try to keep them apart, and neither of us could ever inflict that upon Jet. This meant I was camping on my own with Magnus every night. I had to cook, clean up, entertain him safely around the site, warm his milk, get him to sleep and do the morning hours alone, moving between different campsites every day. The hardest aspect was getting him to sleep, with it being so warm and light in the evenings – it would often get to around 11 p.m. before he went down for the night, which, coupled with already intermittent sleep, made for some long days. My crazy camping antics in Hawaii now seemed like a breeze compared to camping solo, night after night, with a baby!

On the last day of June 2023, we finally finished the South West Coast Path at Minehead. We certainly wouldn't be known for completing it the fastest; in fact, it had taken us seven months, through three seasons, with the ever-changing needs of a baby. We should have been euphoric for finishing it, but our sense of achievement was dwarfed by what loomed on the horizon – Wales, and the finish line!

From Minehead, things changed again. Chris now had a month to get to the finish line in Llangennith, with approximately 220 miles still to cover. The landscape also shifted significantly. Gone were the punishing gradients of the South West Coast Path and scenic cliff-top views; the land was now flat and characterized by industrial activity all the way into

Wales, including Hinkley Point power station. Chris had no time to drop us off and pick us up from campsites each day, so I couldn't continue camping alone with Magnus, as I had no means of travelling between places.

We were, however, receiving kind offers from people inviting us to stay in their homes, some of which Magnus and I accepted. Chris would then return late in the evenings in the van to park up and sleep on their driveway, but more often than not Magnus and I would stay for a few days, enabling Chris to make greater progress before coming back to pick us up and move us all on to wherever he'd reached.

For two nights, we stayed in the home of Rob and Karina, near Bridgewater. Rob was a woodworker and had designed and built their property himself from scratch. His craft was visible in every detail, from the bed frames and spiral staircase to the fireplace surround and the garden greenhouse. It was extraordinary. His work had then evolved into creating magnificently intricate 'Bough-House' sculptures, huge fairy-house structures made from tree branches, which stood proudly in their home for us to marvel at. However, after a car accident in 2012, he'd lost a lot of the feeling in his hands and was unable to make them any more, essentially losing both his passion and his livelihood.

Struggling to come to terms with his new reality, Rob had tried to focus his mind on those whose struggles seemed far greater than his own. At the time, servicemen and women were being repatriated from Afghanistan and he began to think of the sacrifices given by those in the armed forces. His mind then went further back, to the soldiers who gave their lives in the World Wars. I know this is something Chris always did when things were hard on the walk – he would think back to the horrors those men faced and realize that his own struggles paled in comparison, and he found strength in that to keep going.

Rob began looking into some of the figures of losses from the First World War and discovered that, on the first day alone of the Battle of the Somme, 19,241 British men lost their lives. That gave rise to his idea to commemorate them and somehow physically represent those individuals and the scale of that loss. So, he crafted 19,241 plastic figurines – each one matched to the name of a soldier, and each one unique to represent individuality – and hand-stitched shrouds to cover them, one for every British man lost that day.

These were then displayed at various locations in the country to commemorate that fatal day. But it didn't end there. Spurred on by the 19,241, Rob then did some more research and found that a total of 72,396 soldiers who died in the Battle of the Somme had no known grave because their bodies were never recovered from the battlefield. He then committed himself to making tens of thousands more shrouded figurines to commemorate each of those men too. For many descendants, it felt as though their loved ones had at last been returned to English soil.

It was fascinating to hear about the project and even see some of his shrouds for myself. I felt real admiration for his commitment, creative endeavour and endurance to have seen all of that through. Rob had also raised funds for SSAFA in the process, as we were doing on the walk. There were some interesting parallels between our two stories and, at the end of our first evening staying there, our talk turned to endings.

'It's such a huge thing when something that's been your life for so long comes to an end. How are you feeling about that?' Rob asked me.

'Honestly, I don't know. Even though I know it's coming, we're still so deep into it that I can't even imagine this not being our life every day. Maybe in one sense it will be a relief, but I also feel like there's such a big question for us as to what's next. That's still undecided, which feels quite daunting with a baby.'

'Did you ever doubt you would finish?'

'No – we knew we could get to the end. Even when times are really tough, it's just been a case of one foot in front of the other, then one day at a time. There's never been a doubt that we'll get there, we might just need to make peace with it taking a little longer and looking a little different than we expected. But to not finish has never been an option.'

'I totally resonate. It was very much like that for me with the shrouds project – I just had to keep going, day in and day out, until it was done. And now I've got these shrouds sitting in my garden shed. The relics of this huge project. Sometimes I go down to look at them, but mostly they just sit there.'

I noticed a glimmer of sadness in his eyes then, and I sensed it was grief. It was the first time I'd even had five minutes to contemplate what was coming and I realized that this ending wasn't just going to be a celebration. We too were going to grieve that our epic journey was over and I didn't know if we were ready for it. I felt like Rob really understood the predicament we were soon to find ourselves in and I found myself wondering how Chris would cope at the end, and how we'd cope as a couple.

Rob and Karina cooked for us and set us up in their own bedroom upstairs. Their three daughters, Lily, Rose and Daisy, were so brilliant with Magnus too. It was one of the first times Magnus had been content to be held by someone else, which meant I could finish a drink for once! Rose even knitted him a woollen hat, a present that he wore many times afterwards.

We also stayed for two nights with a lady called Sarah, near Weston-super-Mare. Sarah had been a foster carer for nine years, during which time she'd looked after sixteen children of all ages, from newborn babies to teens. As we talked about her experiences, it took me back to my teaching days and why I'd chosen to go into that world in the first place – to make a difference to children's lives, just as she was. It reminded me how dramatically different my world had become since I'd left. I loved this life and was deeply committed to making our lifestyle of wild family adventure work going forward, but there were aspects of teaching that I missed and I was excited to soon have the opportunity to put the best of what I'd learned over the years into practice with my own son. Whatever route of education we chose for him, I would always be an eager participant in doing my very best to provide a fun, holistic, effective learning experience for him, wherever we were in the world.

It was around this time that I had an idea to involve people in the finishing celebrations on a wider scale. I invited anyone who wanted to join in to create a piece of fabric bunting and send it to the King's Head Inn in Llangennith; I would then string them all together to become part of the official finish line. The bunting would then become the decoration for the festivities afterwards. Given that this walk had now covered the entire coastline of all four countries in our United Kingdom, and with so many fantastic people being a part of it in varying ways, be it virtually or in person, I felt this would be a really meaningful, creative and inclusive way of celebrating that. It was open to anyone of any age and was also a way for those who would like to be there but couldn't for whatever reason to still be present in a very touching way.

Once we crossed the Severn Bridge and made it into Wales, we were on the home run. Magnus and I stayed with various friends and family of Chris's to allow him to continue on with Jet, pushing through the miles to get us to the end. We did walk through Swansea, Chris's home town, as a family, and it was here that Magnus took his first unaided steps. We all erupted into gasps, big cheers, claps and smiles. It was such a huge moment, and what a time for it to happen – when we crossed the finish line in a few days, Magnus would be able to walk over it himself with some of his very first steps!

Walking was his rite of passage between babyhood and toddlerdom. I knew that this was the start of a new era, the very beginnings of him walking his own path, charting his own course and setting his sights upon his own mini horizons. I couldn't help but wonder what those were going to look like once we'd finished. It's perhaps the greatest irony of motherhood: you wait patiently for these milestones, celebrate them when they happen, then mourn the loss of the era that's just come to an end.

Now we'd made it into the Gower, we decided to all walk the last 14 miles between Port Eynon and Llangennith together. As we came nearer and nearer to the final day, it still didn't feel real in the slightest – we were still walking miles each leg, still dodging downpours, still wondering where on earth we were going to spend the night. It transpired we were also set for some sleepless nights during our final week, with another tooth for Magnus coming through. In some ways, it just felt like any other week walking the UK coastline, and I really struggled to get my head around the fact that, in just a few days' time, we wouldn't wake up and say, 'Right, where do you think we can get to today?!'

33

There and Back Again

The penultimate day of the walk, Chris spent some time on his own with Jet at Rhossili Bay Beach, overlooking the final mile of coastline. I knew it was a huge amount for him to process, and I left him to it while I walked along the clifftops with Magnus to watch the wild ponies that roamed nearby. I stopped and sat down with him for a while too, marvelling in peace at the view. This walk had opened my eyes to so much beauty in my own land I never even knew existed; my appreciation for this tiny speck on the world map ran much deeper now the adventure of a lifetime had unfolded for me on my own doorstep.

Most significantly, this wild and windswept coastline had cradled my very first experiences of motherhood. At times, it had felt as punishing as the storms we'd had to endure, as chaotic as trying to pitch our tent in high wind, and as unpredictable as the weather in winter. It had also felt as beautiful as the sunsets, as powerful as the tides and as grounding as the vastness of the horizon. Motherhood was as ever-changing as the clouds and as fleeting as the birds. But one thing was for sure: it was also a constant, as consistent and reliable as the rhythm of the waves and the rising of the sun. To experience this first taste of motherhood on this wild coastline had felt like meeting it in such a raw, instinctive form – without walls, routines or schedules. It had meant learning to nurture in rhythm with the weather, to soothe beneath open skies, to carry, feed and comfort surrounded by wind, waves and dramatic headlands.

It meant discovering the primal, physical and emotional strength of mothering in extreme circumstances, when I had been laid bare as a mother with only my gut instincts to follow. Motherhood is tiring and testing however you look at it, and I learned I'd much rather do the bulk of it outdoors, where I was the best version of myself and therefore the best mum I could be.

Above all, the walk had given me the greatest privilege of all – the ability to spend all my time with my baby, free from distraction. In stripping myself of material wealth, I had become rich in time, and that time as a mother was more precious than anything else in this life. I had traded the security of a salary and the stability of a home for the privilege of an extended maternity leave and the ability to give my boy security and stability in the form of a mum who was always present in every sense of the word. His babyhood was so fleeting; he was already on his way to being a toddler. The gambles I had taken enabled me to have this. I would never have that time again, but I had lived it in the most magical way. This adventure, these memories and this time would always be ours.

It had given me clarity about how I wanted us to raise Magnus moving forward. Although there were plenty of challenges, there was no doubt that we had become our truest, happiest and healthiest selves living a simple, uncluttered life in the outdoors, fuelled by the thrill of adventure and helping others along the way. I knew I wanted to find a way to continue living this wild life that we loved, prioritizing time and experiences in the outdoors together. We'd raise Magnus in a life of adventure, making unforgettable memories along the way while raising money for charity as we went.

There was no denying that getting to this point had been made easier by the fact that we had a very happy, curious baby who took everything in his stride. He loved nature, loved being active and outdoors, and had endless curiosity for the world around him. I knew I wanted to keep and expand on that as he grew up, for him to feel bound to the natural world. I didn't want his childhood stolen away by screens and social media, watching on the sidelines as life became a spectator sport. I wanted him to live it. I wanted his childhood to be one of liberated and unbridled joy, freedom and adventure, where he had space and time to explore, discovering in his own way, at his own pace.

I envisioned his childhood tramping carefree through forests and woodlands, building forts and dens, rolling down hills and through long grass, eating around a campfire, splashing in streams and rivers, jumping up and down in waves, climbing trees, admiring views, standing awestruck before towering peaks. I wanted him to marvel at and feel connected to the wonders of the natural world, be it the miniature world of minibeasts or the majesty of the mountains.

The night before we crossed the line, I opened the hundreds of boxes of bunting that had been sent from all over the UK and abroad, even from as far away as Canada and California. I was bowled over by the creative effort people had made to mark the end of our journey. Nearly every piece came accompanied by a personal card or letter and I photographed every single piece so I had a record for life of who it came from and to show Magnus when he was older. Post-finish, I would store them all until we could one day make some sort of patchwork wall hanging or blanket from them to keep as a treasured memory of our adventure.

The bunting would serve as a beautiful reminder of the amazing community that had been brought together by our walk and whose breadth was evident in the artistic nods to national and local heritage – from Harris tweed, Fair Isle knits, Scottish tartan, Welsh dragons and pasties from Cornwall to various flags, maps, shells, beach huts and lighthouses. Now, all those people and places were coming together to be represented as one. We may live in a very divided world in lots of ways, but there is still so much connection and so much unity that binds us, and I was moved by how much hope exists in us. For me, these handcrafted flags made especially for us were a powerful creative representation of human and community spirit.

Finally, the day had come . . . the finish line.

We arrived at Rhossili Bay car park an hour before we were scheduled to walk the final mile. SSAFA had told us we were going to meet a few charity personnel and some dignitaries, but we had no idea exactly what was waiting in store for us when we arrived.

As we approached, we were heralded by a brigade of trumpeters in ceremonial uniform, followed by the bagpipes, and formally welcomed by the HM Lord Lieutenant of West Glamorgan; the Lord Mayor of Swansea; the then head of SSAFA, Sir Andrew Gregory; a number of military personnel including the Paras – which meant so much to Chris, given it was his old regiment – and a huge crowd of people already cheering in celebration.

We then gathered together on the clifftops, with Rhossili Beach in the background, to hear from Sir Andrew that we had indeed made our £500,000 target from all the JustGiving donations, Gift Aid and donations made directly to SSAFA in our name! I was elated. We had worked so hard over so many years on this walk to raise as much as we possibly could, and to hear we had hit our goal was unbelievably rewarding. We were also regaled with huge flags representing the nations by one of our followers, called Bryan, who had travelled all the way from Newcastle and who'd been a brilliant support to us on numerous occasions.

After a number of speeches, the Lord Lieutenant proceeded to open and read a letter of congratulations sent by King Charles III himself. Given he is Colonel-in-Chief of the Parachute Regiment, in which Chris served, and head of the UK's armed forces, and the fact that Chris had met him briefly when he was invited to lay a wreath at the *Iolaire* memorial ceremony up in the Isle of Lewis during the walk, it felt very meaningful to receive that recognition from him. We were then swept off to do a ten-minute radio piece and an interview for SSAFA to help even more donations roll in on our last day, before coming back out to walk the final mile.

When it was time, the crowd had organized themselves down either side of the cliff path and cheered us to the front. We led the way over the clifftops and, as we reached the bottom, I turned to look behind us – and was utterly gobsmacked. Hundreds of people were piling down the coast path behind us in a long line, like we were the Pied Piper! I was completely awestruck by the number of well-wishers who had come to walk that final mile with us.

As we poured onto the beach to walk en masse, more people joined us. We now had a flood of a thousand people walking that final mile with us. The atmosphere was truly electric – it felt like positive vibes would be etched into that beach for ever.

One of the greatest things about this walk for me was that

I always felt it was so much bigger than us – that it was about helping people, inspiring and uniting them in all sorts of ways. As the walk had gone on, it had often felt like we had a nation behind us; here, on this beach, it literally did feel like that!

Once we reached the sand dunes at Llangennith, which led to the finish line, the crowds went on ahead. We took a moment to ourselves before following, with our flag bearers behind us. The crowd filed into two lines, gathering on either side of us to cheer us to that final finish line, where Chris had started on his own all those years ago. Seeing the huge arch of bunting made by our supporters stretching across the finish line made me well up and I would've broken down completely had I not been so conscious that Magnus was half asleep. The excitement of the morning and all the clapping and waving to his public from his carrier had got the better of him!

Then, just as we arrived at the very end of the walk, Chris and I hand in hand with Magnus and with Jet trotting beside us, the heavens opened. It only rained for the exact minute we crossed the finish line, but how fitting that we would finish a walk around the coastline in typical UK weather fashion!

We walked through the bunting to raucous cheers and were greeted by the proud and smiling faces of our family and friends, and an array of media capturing the moment on camera and film. As we hugged each other and Jet and Magnus, I was filled with love and pride and respect for what we'd done. This was a once-in-a-lifetime achievement. Only we knew what it had taken to get here and only we knew how monumental it felt. Feelings like that cannot be bought, they are earned.

Now, we had a choice: to end our adventure story right there, or to begin writing a new chapter.

34

Cool Your Jets

The walk had finished. Just like that, it was done, and life as we knew it was suddenly over. The next day, waking up in a hotel room at the King's Head in Llangennith, the pub that had very kindly offered to host a party in our honour after we'd crossed the finish line, we were completely overwhelmed and disorientated; so many years spent moving from place to place with a strong sense of purpose had ended abruptly. This journey had consumed my life for the best part of three years and Chris's life for six. Every day, we'd walked, always by the coast, but our surroundings were forever changing. Each morning, we'd wake up in one place and, each night, we'd go to bed in another. We felt like a boat that had been surging through the sea en route to its destination, only for the engine to now suddenly stop, and so we found ourselves bobbing around aimlessly with no direction. When you pour yourself into something, as we had for so long, it becomes you.

I knew, once the shock had subsided, we'd be asking ourselves, 'Who am I without this?' Yes, the end had been expected, we'd known it was coming for years, but when it finally came into view, we weren't ready for it. The rug had been well and truly ripped from under our feet. We were faced with one question: 'What now?'

For Chris, it was both a welcome relief to have finished and a disappointment that it had ended under such strain and duress for him, given how much inner peace he'd found along the way. During the earlier stages of the walk, Chris and I had spoken a lot about what we could do next for an adventure; we had so many dreams and high expectations of ourselves, and really felt like we had the world at our feet. The future for us had seemed so bright and so promising, we truly believed that anything we set our minds to achieve was possible. However, the last 1,000 miles were so all-consuming, certainly with little Magnus, but more so with Jet, that our sole focus had been simply getting to the finish line. As a result, in the days that followed the walk coming to an end, we found ourselves quite frankly clueless. Once the party was over and everyone had headed home, we were left standing there with no idea where we were going to go next or what to do. Looking back now, it seems absurd that we had no plan whatsoever, long or short term.

Given the situation with Jet, diving into a new adventure wasn't an option – we had no choice but to hold off, and that hit hard. Stopping wasn't something we were even sure we knew how to do any more. After years of constant movement, staying still in one place felt completely at odds with who we'd become. We didn't know where we were going next, or how we were going to get there. The only certainty was that Chris had a month to deliver his second book and he needed to get cracking.

We stayed around Llangennith for a few days, in the King's Head, to catch up on some much-needed rest, trying to process the mania of the past few days and the fact that the walk was now over, before heading back to my mum's in Malvern. For me, it was a relief to be in comfortable, familiar surroundings while we regrouped and made a new plan after such an overwhelming period. And, when Chris told me he needed a few weeks in the Scottish Highlands with Jet, so he could have space to write, I knew there was no point trying to stop him.

When he returned two weeks later, I realized that he'd needed time away, and, importantly, alone, to come to terms with the fact that the walk was over, to process that the past six years had just come to an end. He needed to say his own goodbye to it all. But the other main reason was the speed at which Jet was deteriorating; she didn't have long left. That trip was his last chance to be alone with her and revisit some of their favourite memories.

While walking the south coast, we'd become friendly with Tim and Rebecca Peake. Rebecca was from Scotland and, while we were still mulling over what to do next with our lives, she recommended a place she felt we'd be able to get some much-needed headspace after the craziness of the finish line. We headed to the small Scottish town of Comrie, Perthshire, which lies on the banks of the River Earn, nestled on the edge of the Scottish Highlands. It's about a forty-minute drive from Loch Lomond and the Trossachs and an hour south of Glen Coe, surrounded by huge hills, with a 6-mile freshwater loch nearby. It was a beautiful spot, with a great community spirit and plenty of outdoor-orientated fun for Magnus. As soon as we arrived in Comrie, it felt like we were finally able to take a deep breath and relax – it was exactly what we needed to reconnect as a family.

In a very random twist of fate, we were invited to stay in a small wooden cabin located at Comrie Croft, a reimagined farm with eco-camping, Nordic katas (a kind of teepee tent), a market garden, forest school, weddings on site throughout the year, a small farm shop and brilliant mountain-biking trails. The cabin was essentially seasonal accommodation for crofters that come to help tend the land here over spring and summer. It was tiny and very basic, but we had all the space we needed outdoors; it would be a brilliant short-term base while Chris worked on his second book, and we felt at home there very quickly. While Chris wrote, Magnus and I were out the door at 8 a.m. exploring the woodland, waterfalls and walking trails round about, and we'd often stay out exploring until dinner time. When it rained, I bundled him in waterproofs and wellies and we usually went out regardless.

There were lots of other tiny toddlers in the area, around the same age as Magnus, and a group of very welcoming outdoor-enthusiast mums who were active in organizing nature-themed playgroups throughout the week at different locations. We'd go on hikes, make little boats to watch sail down the river, plant trees, garden or just do outdoor free play. For the first time, Magnus had loads of opportunities to socialize with other children his age, and I was able to make other mum friends I could see and interact with regularly. Developmentally, the children were all too young to play with each other as such – they would play near and next to each other in what's known as parallel play – but it was a refreshing and welcome change to have the frequent social familiarity of a group we could get to know on a more personal level.

This time certainly made me reflect more on how I could ensure that Magnus maintained opportunities to socialize with other children moving forward on our travels. For the moment, he was still only one, and attending a wide variety of playgroups around other children on a regular basis was more than adequate. However, it did make me think ahead: over the next few years, our intention certainly wasn't to move every day as we had on the walk. We enjoyed the slow nature of travel that walking offered and perhaps we could stay in places we liked for longer periods, a number of weeks, months even, where he could establish deeper connections.

He didn't need to be within a mainstream school environment in order to develop social skills. Our life had been very social on the walk and Magnus was very comfortable around people and other children. A childhood of travel would involve all sorts of fantastic and enriching social experiences for him, with the wider benefit of being immersed in different cultures. At the end of the day, I would follow the lead of my child to guide our life in whatever way made him happiest.

Chris rented a mountain bike with a trailer attached so that he could take Magnus on the trails when he needed a break from writing. It was evident from the get-go that Magnus loved it. He was a thrill-seeker like his father! When he turned sixteen months, he had his first go on the skills pump track on a borrowed balance bike, and his first-ever passion was born – mountain biking. We got him his own balance bike as an early Christmas present and it immediately became his favourite thing to do. I would spend hours with him every day on that track, supporting him as his skill and confidence grew. As a little treat to himself for finishing the walk, as well as two books, Chris bought himself his own bike and took breaks to join Magnus on the tracks and show him the ropes. For Magnus, watching his dad zoom around the tracks, doing jumps and enjoying himself, was a real inspiration, giving rise to an 'if Dad can do it, so can I!' mentality. For me, watching Magnus be inspired by his dad, following his lead, copying his moves and listening to his teachings, really did warm my heart.

We both had an approach that meant not wrapping Magnus in cotton wool. We wanted to embolden our boy to take risks and, by eighteen months, he was whizzing down the big hills of his own accord. He had great balance, coordination and ability to assess risk, and he quickly became very proficient – a real head-turner for anyone watching! Now a year and a half old, it was clear that our son was incredibly happy. Obviously, I couldn't miss out on the action, so I got myself a bike too and began to learn how to ride it. I'd never been confident on a bike at all, but watching my man and my son was all the inspiration I needed!

In all, we spent three months at Comrie Croft and, once Chris had finished his book, we had fun as a family, walking through forests, mountain biking, playing by the loch and engaging in community life. It marked the first period of time since Magnus had been born that we'd actually been able to kick back and just enjoy being a family together, with no pressure to move forward or write. For Chris and me, it was our first time 'off' in four years and we soaked up every moment. However, the cabin was not feasible for winter living because it had no heating to stop the water pipes from freezing, nor did we want to overstay our welcome – so, by early December, it was time to move on.

Chris had told me a story about his time back on the Isle of Skye, pitched up on the side of a mountain during a storm. He told me how scary that night had been and how uneasy he'd felt. Never one to overplay these things, I knew by now that, when Chris used the word 'scary', it equated to 'bloody terrifying' for the rest of us! He hadn't been able to sleep for fear the tent would break and he and Jet would be stranded 300 metres up a mountain in a deadly storm.

All of a sudden, in the middle of this storm, Jet had rolled on her back, stuck her legs in the air and given him the goofiest smile any dog could muster. Laughing, Chris had grabbed his phone and taken the photograph that would become his profile photo on his 'Chris Walks the UK' social media for the remainder of the walk. He told me it was then he'd made a promise to Jet that, whatever happened, he would stick by her side, as she had to his until her very last day.

It was a promise we were determined to fulfil. This was Jet's time to rest as much as she desired, in as much comfort as we could offer. Our lives and any further adventures were on hold for her.

Chris and I had both become keen photographers during the walk and were eager to turn our hand to filming as a more in-depth way of telling stories about the wild, beautiful places we visited, the people we met and our adventures as a family along the way. We'd been approached by a TV producer asking if we were potentially interested in filming a series, and Chris had spent many hours writing the proposal for the entire ten episodes, which would see us revisit his favourite parts of the walk in the most remote places in the UK, particularly the Outer Hebrides.

The idea was to document the places that very few even know exist and to tell the lesser-told stories, while sharing the realities of life in the wild as a family raising a young child in the process. The producer was really enthusiastic, so the plan was to head out and film a pilot. We too were full of enthusiasm, if very wet behind the ears. Learning to write, film and produce our own videos was something we really wanted to do, wherever our future took us. Even if the series was never commissioned, we concluded it would be a good learning curve and we could always upload our efforts to YouTube in the hope that they'd do well enough to become a source of income. It was time to trial being an adventuring family outside of the walk.

It was around this time, too, that we decided to rebrand. Given the walk was over, we felt we could no longer remain as 'Chris Walks the UK' and 'Kate Walks the Coast' on social media. Those names had been perfect during the journey, but we were stepping into a new chapter. Over the past year, we'd noticed more and more of our followers referring to us as 'Wilderness Family'. It was a name that seemed to stick. To many, we'd become synonymous with the idea of wilderness because of our clear love for the wild and the way we chose to live. We were a little apprehensive at first; after all, we weren't planning to vanish into the most remote corners of the earth and live solely off the land for ever. But, to us, wilderness didn't have to take on such an extreme meaning: it was more about our way of life and what we loved, our deep connection to nature, our choice to live outside the norm and the freedom we found in wild spaces. In the end, we felt it encapsulated who we were and what we'd become. If we were going to choose a new name, this one felt right. We decided to keep our separate pages to reflect our different perspectives, just as we had on the walk, and so I became 'Wilderness Mum'.

We knew our trusty little T4 van that had loyally carried us from Dorset to the finish line, and then all the way up here, was no longer going to cut it. We were two grown adults, an active toddler and a 27-kilo dog, confined to a space the size of a wardrobe. Aside from that, given it had no amenities whatsoever, it was never going to cover us for a winter on the Outer Hebrides: we needed an upgrade. As soon as Chris got paid royalties from his first book, *Finding Hildasay*, we bought a second-hand Fiat Ducato long-wheelbase van. It had been beautifully renovated, but most importantly it was three-berth, with an oven, a proper bed and a diesel heater to keep us warm. Pure luxury, as far as we were concerned! It cost £20,000 and nearly wiped us out.

To some, that money could've been a big chunk to put towards a deposit on a house or even some land. However, we wanted a life for ourselves as a full-time adventure family and, to make that work, we needed to be all in. Fortune favours the bold, as they say. I think my parents were concerned that we weren't choosing to invest everything we had in securing a house for ourselves. And, while they wanted me to live my dreams, this lifestyle I had adopted was so far removed from their own personal life experience, they found it hard to relate to. In terms of the wider family dynamic in raising their grandchildren, we were very much a world apart from my brother and stepsister. My parents were also concerned about how on earth we were going to make an income from this lifestyle – what if we weren't able to make it work?

All our remaining funds went on filming equipment, including a mini drone, a GoPro and a sturdy camera stand. We were taking a big chance on the pilot and it wasn't a decision we made easily, because it wasn't just about us: Magnus's welfare and being able to provide for him was always at the forefront of our minds.

I did have one major concern, though. By now, it was December, and the Isle of Harris in winter with a one-year-old in a campervan would be daunting because of the weather. Early that month, we had bid goodbye to Comrie Croft and set sail for the Outer Hebrides, catching the ferry from Oban on the west coast to Lochboisdale in South Uist. One hour in, I was already on the outside deck being sick as a pig, while Chris stayed inside with Magnus and Jet, watching the ferry's Christmas tree fly back and forth across the floor. Thank goodness Magnus had better sea legs than me!

Docking in Lochboisdale, it was clear winter was in full force. After a few beautiful but very windswept days in Uist, we headed down to Harris to begin filming. The landscape was stunning: dramatically rugged, wild and among the most beautiful I had ever seen. It was especially magical to see it in winter. During our time there, it snowed heavily, which was very rare; coincidentally, the last time they had seen snow like this was five years previously, when Chris and Jet were last on the island. On the one hand, exploring and filming in an empty Harris transformed into this Narnia-like wonderland was incredible. Beaches, half white, half golden, lay at the feet of snow-capped mountains that loomed over the island like sleeping giants. The skies shifted from dark and brooding, heavy with storm clouds, to soft hues of pink and gold, while double rainbows arched across the sky several times a day. The natural light here was ethereal. We walked incredibly scenic stretches of the island, played on its world-class beaches, and Chris and I took turns to swim in the sea (wetsuits firmly on!). We revisited the weather-beaten Scarista bus, which sits abandoned in the sand dunes, where Chris and Jet took refuge during a storm one night as they passed through, years before, and we even managed to wild camp amid magical sunsets on the very few occasions the wind allowed. It was fantastic to share all of that with Magnus.

However, the winds were fiercer and more intimidating than anything I could ever have imagined. It was like being at the mercy of a relentless beast. Most days, we faced ferocious, smash-you-in-the-face onslaughts, until, pretty soon, 50 mph wind speeds felt kind and 80 mph felt common! I remember turning to Chris and saying, 'How on earth did you camp in this?!' Bridges would shut and we could hardly open the van door for fear of it being ripped off!

Chris had had an entire winter's experience walking and surviving in a tent on Harris, and though we were all seasoned campers, hardy and used to the cold, five years on, doubtless he had looked back on his time here through rose-tinted glasses when it came to the weather. Looking at the forecast, it felt like we were set to have weeks confined to the van!

We tried to remain optimistic and would give filming our

best shot whenever there was a break in the weather, but the relentless winds made it largely impossible. Mostly, we had no chance of getting a drone up, we could hardly hear each other speak, and the noise and force of the wind was often too much for Magnus. Whenever possible, he was bundled up in his snowsuit, hat, neck warmer and gloves and enjoyed exploring the wild wonders of the island – he was a hardy toddler and used to the cold and being outside, but this was on the extreme end of the spectrum.

Chris received a message from a gentleman called Ian who he'd met back in January 2019, when he offered Chris a place to wait for the delivery of a new tent after the old one was obliterated in a storm. Aware of what we were contending with now, Ian offered us the use of his holiday home on another Hebridean island, the Isle of Scalpay, connected to Harris by a short causeway. It was just before Christmas. We were overjoyed.

It was a four-bedroom house with plenty of space for Magnus to run around, for Jet to stretch her legs and completely relax, and for us to celebrate the festive period without so much extreme-weather stress. We even had a surprise knock on the door on Christmas morning; it was a neighbour armed with a large box. 'Tina from the local shop wanted me to give this to you and wish you a happy Christmas and a big welcome back!' It was a hamper of delicious local produce, plus some Harris gin, locally made toiletries, hand-knitted jumpers and a teddy for Magnus with the words 'Happy Christmas Magnus, Harris 2023' embroidered on the front. I was so touched.

Chris had told me about the love and kindness he had received from locals while on Harris the first time round, and it was amazing to see that kindness continue, even though we had officially finished the walk. Given we had, we were extremely grateful for offers of housing for respite, as our outside life was no longer linked to raising money for the charity. It was testament to the community spirit on the island and the deep connections Chris had made with people while walking here years before. The islanders had really taken him and Jet into their hearts, and, as far as they were concerned, it was like Chris was returning home – but with his family in tow, this time. I felt really moved and proud that what he had done on these isles had touched and captured people in such a profound way.

But, no matter how hard we tried, it was a real struggle to make the filming work. In the end, the producer got back in touch to say that, unfortunately, the TV bosses had decided to go in another direction. It was a disappointing blow for us, as we felt we could make a fantastically unique series. We decided to turn our efforts to YouTube, although we knew this would be a very slow burn – we would need to set up a Wilderness Family channel and start completely from scratch, with zero followers. Any hope of earning any income stream from advertisements meant growing a big enough following to do so, which put a lot of pressure on us to make a lot of consistent and quality content. However, we had a bigger issue to contend with. Our beloved Jet was failing fast.

35

No Judgement, No Questions, Just Love

Jet's back legs had begun to shake uncontrollably at times. Each month she'd struggle a bit more, despite us trying everything we'd been advised would help her, including tablets for arthritis, painkillers, steroid injections and holistic remedies. None of them seemed to have any effect, and her limping was getting worse. She had always adored cuddles, but now we had to be careful where we stroked her – we'd started to notice her flinching and moving away more often. She was also struggling to contain herself when it came to going to the toilet. It was heartbreaking.

We both knew Jet's days were numbered. Now, we faced the agonizing decision of how long we would allow this to go on. We didn't want to cut her life short, but we also couldn't selfishly prolong her suffering simply because we couldn't bear to lose her. A few days later, with Magnus sitting on my knee and Jet on the sofa between me and Chris, her legs began to shake uncontrollably and she was yelping in pain. Chris and I turned to look at each other, our eyes filling with tears. 'Kate, I'm going to phone the vet,' he said. 'It's time.'

Two days later, I sat next to her on the sofa again, my hands stroking her and tickling behind her ears. Struggling to keep it together, conscious that we didn't want her to pick up on our sadness, I kissed her as lovingly as I would my child and told her how much I loved her and what an incredible best friend she'd been. With that, Chris gently put her in the van and set off on the hour's drive to the vet to say his final goodbye.

We had been told we could bury Jet here on Harris. It felt poetic in a way, to do so in a place where she'd been in her prime and had shared so many fantastic memories with Chris.

What felt the longest few hours of my life ticked by, then, finally, I got a call from a distraught Chris. 'I can't do it, I just can't. It doesn't feel right,' he said tearfully. 'I've changed my mind about burying her on Harris. She hates being cold, and the thought of leaving her body in the ground on a wind-battered coastline out in the Atlantic, and us only able to visit her grave as and when we can make it back here, feels wrong. I want to cremate her instead and keep her ashes with me until I decide where to scatter them.

'But the vet's just told me that the only pet crematorium in Scotland is over in Elgin, which means I'd have to take a five-hour ferry, then a four-hour drive on the mainland to get there. It'll be shut by the time we arrive, so I'd have to do it all with my best mate dead in the back of the van and then next to me overnight. I just can't do it. I'm sorry.'

I got it – I couldn't have done that either. It would've been unbearable having to transport Jet's body like that. So Chris brought her home and I hugged her as gently as I could. Even though I knew we'd still have to say goodbye at some point and it would be even harder the second time, I was relieved to have her with us still.

The next day, I suggested we phone Dr Scott Miller. He knew Jet well and understood just how much she meant to us. He really was the only person we trusted to do what had to be done in the best possible way. Without hesitation, he offered to travel up to Scotland. 'I'll fly out to you if need be and we can do this whatever way is best for you and Jet,' he told Chris.

We felt strongly that we should take Jet back to the mainland, where it was warmer and easier for her to enjoy time outside for as long as she had. It was pointless persevering with filming, given the situation. In the end, we decided to head back to Llangennith, in Wales. It felt fitting to say goodbye to Jet in the place where Chris had set off for his six-year walk. Back then, he'd been a man in the bleak depths of despair; by the time the walk ended, in the exact same place, he was a man transformed, full of love, self-worth and purpose, with a family by his side – and much of that had been largely thanks to Jet.

We got her another injection to ease her pain and Dr Scott agreed to meet us in Wales. The night before we met him, we stayed once more in the King's Head Inn, Llangennith, the place we'd had our celebration party after crossing the finish line. We ordered two massive steaks for Jet and let her eat whatever she wanted. Then we waited for the morning.

It was a dreadful night. Neither of us slept at all. I watched Jet sleeping and couldn't get my head around the idea that, this time tomorrow, she would be gone. It also broke my heart that Magnus was losing his best friend. On the one hand, I was glad he was too young to understand what was going on, but on the other, I couldn't bear the inevitable – hearing him ask where she was and missing her, as we all would. By the time dawn broke, I had a migraine from crying.

We decided to keep Magnus away from Jet's final moments. I would say my own goodbye first and then take Magnus immediately to my mum's to do the best by him, while Chris and Dr Scott administered the injection and stayed by Jet's side until she passed. It broke me not to be able to be with her at the very end, but it was a sacrifice I had to make as a mum. Chris took Magnus, and I sat alone with Jet for a while.

It's really hard to explain the way a dog can have such a huge impact on a person. I knew, without question, that Jet had changed Chris's life in a way no human ever could, but what I hadn't realized until now was how deeply she had changed mine too. Jet had touched my life from the very first moment I saw her. It was Chris's love for her, and her quiet, unwavering devotion in return, that helped dissolve any hesitation I may have had about returning to Whaligoe Steps to camp beside them that night. From then on, it didn't take long to realize how special she was. Knowing her background, I felt incredibly honoured to be accepted by her so fully. Jet became our calm in the eye of every storm, never once faltering in her loyalty or love. I had come from a life where most of my decisions affected only me. But Jet quickly wove herself into every decision I made, from where we walked to where we paused and where we slept. She had become the heartbeat of our world for years, and, when our son came along, she willingly shared that space with him so naturally and gently. I had reached a point where I couldn't imagine life without her. She was our best friend, our guardian, our confidante and our free-spirited companion. Together, we shared the very best of life: freedom, the raw beauty of the land, adventures that shaped us and the family we became. For years, Chris, Jet and I lived and breathed every moment side by side. Saying goodbye to her would leave a void that nothing could ever fill. Time and acceptance would be our only allies now. A part of each of us would go with Jet, but our memories of her would carry us forward until, one day, we would meet again.

WILDERNESS MUM

I looked at her as she rested her head on my lap, hinting for a tickle. I rubbed behind her ears and in all the spots she loved the most, doing my best not to crumble under the weight of imminent uncontrollable tears.

'Jet,' I said to her quietly, 'I count myself among the luckiest to have been your mum and been loved by you. Thank you for accepting me and always being there when I needed a cuddle; no judgement, no questions, just love.'

The truth was, if it hadn't been for Jet slowing Chris down on his walk so he and I serendipitously ended up in the same place at the same time, Magnus would never have come to be. She had helped give me the greatest gift of all – a family and my boy. I thought back to all the ways she had comforted me while pregnant, how she had made me feel safe and the experience of bringing Magnus into the world all the more magical. 'You are the best of all mankind rolled into one: strength, compassion, loyalty, unconditional love, and you will forever remind me to be the best person I can be. Your legacy is us. You will live on in us, I promise. We shall never forget you, you will come with us wherever we go . . .'

Then, I knelt in front of her, gave her a soft kiss on the nose and looked her in the eyes, and kissed her forehead and told her I loved her one final time. With that, I took a deep breath and walked out the door. It was the last time I ever saw her.

Jet passed away peacefully with Chris by her side on 7 April 2024. We decided to keep her ashes with us always.

36

Wow

After Jet died, we knew the worst thing we could do was sit around moping. We'd made her a promise to live our best lives, and we wanted to honour our word. We wanted to go somewhere serene and beautiful; a place we knew we'd have peace, and space to grieve our loss; a place where Chris had many special memories with Jet; a place we knew we'd love as a family. We were also determined to give filming our series a fair try, so we decided to head back to Scotland. Our destination this time would be Barra and Vatersay, two small, quiet and lesser-visited islands joined by a causeway, the southernmost inhabited islands in the Outer Hebrides and the most westerly in the UK. It would be here that we would celebrate Magnus's second birthday.

We arrived in Barra at the end of April to significantly better weather. Both islands are unassumingly enchanting, boasting miles of white-sand beaches, clear turquoise waters and fields of machair (wild flowers), which were coming into bloom now it was spring. Some of the locals immediately recognized Chris from his previous time there. Helen, the local shop owner, insisted on giving us a free dinner and could not have been more accommodating during our stay, sharing tips and local knowledge, and telling me stories of when Chris and Jet were last there. It warmed my soul to hear about Jet when she was in her prime.

The first of May came and it was time to celebrate Magnus turning two, with a cake I baked in the van oven. Given he had spent his first birthday on the Scilly Isles, we loved that he was on another island for his second, and hoped to keep up this natural tradition. The past year had seen so many huge developmental changes, as he transitioned from his first tottering steps to running, jumping and kicking balls. His first word had been 'Wow', before the age of one, which didn't surprise me given how many times he must have heard me say it on the coast path. I felt proud that his early sense of wonder had manifested in this way. His incredibly content and easy-going nature as a baby had followed him through to toddlerdom, and he was very loving towards us, often putting his arms around both our necks and kissing us each on the lips in turn while embraced in a family hug.

He had his moments, like any toddler, and of course there were tears from time to time, but he very rarely had tantrums. I'd heard parents say, 'easy baby, difficult toddler', and I'd wondered if we were going to face some sort of terrible-twos transition, but there were certainly no signs of this yet. He was confident, bold, caring and very fun-loving, and it had been wonderful to watch his confidence and skill on his balance bike really soar. Beyond that, it was clear that he loved this outdoor life; he much preferred being outside than in, being active, exploring in the woods, splashing in streams and playing with whatever he found around him.

The one thing that I was mindful of was that he was yet to say more than four words: 'Wow', 'Jet' (his second word), 'Dada' and 'Mama'. It's easy to feel the weight of comparison around your child's development and I didn't want to fall prey to that, measuring his childhood by the standards of society's performance metrics. Time would tell and, if need be, in a few months' time, I would start to seek out support for speech and language therapy. He was visibly a very happy little boy, full of joy, curiosity and wonder, and that was what mattered most.

That day, we cycled round the island and spent the afternoon playing on a deserted beach, clambering over rocks, showing Magnus sea life in the clear water and running in and out of the dunes and over the hilltops. It was idyllic and exactly what I'd hoped the day would be, although he did cry the entire way through our rendition of 'Happy Birthday' on the guitar.

As the weeks went on, the weather swung between T-shirt warm and heavy downpours and strong winds, but we had enough spells of sunshine to make good progress with the documentary series. It was certainly less windy than Harris in midwinter! However, we wanted to be present parents for Magnus, not stuck behind screens, so busy documenting and editing our life that we weren't actually living it. I hadn't given up one rat race to enter another filled with an unmanageable amount of social media and content creation, so we soon established a balance, getting some filming under our belts without letting it consume our days.

It could get frustrating at times, and Chris often felt I was too quick to drop everything for Magnus. Filming this documentary was essentially our job now, even though we weren't getting paid for it. We just hoped it would be the start of a long process that would see us good financially in the long run. On the outside, it probably just looked like we were having a blast on holiday all the time, but there was immense pressure on us to make a living. We had to find a way to ensure longer-term financial stability. But, whichever way we went about that, it had to work around us being full-time parents and providing the best childhood experience for Magnus. That required time, dedication and effort, because we had no family or friends around to help. We couldn't just drop him off with a grandparent for a few hours, and he didn't go to nursery, nor had he ever had a babysitter.

Finally, a few weeks in, it felt like we hit a rhythm and were getting somewhere. We spent those weeks exploring every inch of Barra, from boat trips around its 'castle in the sea' to walks and swims in every bay, cycling the windy coastal roads, hiking over the clifftops and watching the aeroplanes land and take off on the beach – the world's only commercial airport with a beach runway! People come from all over the world to see this take place, and we were able to watch multiple times a day. Magnus also seemed determined to cycle as much of the island as possible on his balance bike. 'He's only two and he's done more of the Hebridean Way than me!' I'd joke to Chris. We worked tirelessly day and night to plan episodes, film footage, record narration and edit it all together. It felt like the documentary was finally coming together.

But, when our old friend the Atlantic weather front came rolling in, we had to press pause. Thankfully, Magnus could play at the children's centre, or we'd take him swimming at the public pool. Ian, husband of shop owner Helen, kindly offered us a caravan where we could take refuge and have more space, as well as charge our filming gear, given we had no off-grid charging equipment in the van.

Then, out of the blue, Chris got a call. He had been selected as one of six out of thousands to appear on the BBC series *Extraordinary Portraits* with Bill Bailey, in which artists create portraits in all manner of mediums to tell personal and powerful stories of everyday people. In Chris's case, the project was to be a sculpture cast in bronze by sculptor Hywel Pratley, who created the first permanent memorial of Queen Elizabeth II after her death in 2022: a 7-foot bronze statue that stands outside Oakham Library. It was a real honour for Chris to have been chosen, and of course he was thrilled to accept. I was thrilled for him, too!

There was a catch, though. *Extraordinary Portraits* involved six dates in total, spread out between June and mid-September, each about two weeks apart and in varying locations. There was no way we could afford to keep travelling back and forth between the Outer Hebrides and the south of England and Wales over the tourist season; it would cost us thousands, never mind the colossal travel distances with Magnus. But Chris wanted to do it, understandably, and I wanted to make it happen for him.

So, we said goodbye to Scotland again, and, over the next few months, Chris darted between Northampton, London and south Wales for filming, and then further around the country doing a few talks to keep us afloat. During those months, we were like ping-pong balls bouncing all over the place, filming, staying at campsites and visiting friends and family. It was at times like these that I craved a base of our own so that Magnus and I could have some familiarity while Chris was away.

During that time, I took Magnus on a week-long mother-and-son adventure, wild camping and staying in some of the bothies in north Wales. It was full on, going it alone with him in this way – spending days tramping through woods and streams and over hills, sometimes trudging through downpours in full waterproofs, trekking side-by-side with my big backpack stuffed with sleeping bags, roll mat and everything we needed for the night. I had wipes with me, but mostly we were muddy and feral, our hands and faces streaked with dirt. And yet, there we were, my just-turned-two-year-old attempting to help pitch our tent when we camped or puffing away as he tried to blow up the roll mat to lay on a wooden slab in a stone bothy, miles from anywhere. It was most definitely exhausting and certainly hard work at times, but I felt the benefits of experiencing those special moments together made it all worthwhile. He was happy as can be and so was I. I knew it was all those years of walking the coast that had given me the confidence to do this on my own with him, and I felt deeply grateful for that and for many more mother-and-son adventures that I knew were still to come.

On the day of the big unveiling, we found that the finished bronze sculpture was truly magnificent and moving – not only had Hywel really captured Chris's physical likeness, as well as his determination and nobility, but, to our surprise, he had also incorporated Jet, her head nestled under Chris's. I know Chris was over the moon to have her included, and it was a real testament to the two of them, their bond and all they had achieved together. We had struggled to find closure after such a life-altering chapter in our lives, but it felt like this commemorated the walk in such a beautiful way, making all the sacrifices worth it.

It had now been a year since we'd finished the walk and, aside from losing Jet, the hardest aspect had been this transitional phase between one way of life ending and carving out a new one. It was a quiet, disorientating hardship that evolved completely behind the scenes. We had lost the huge sense of momentum and purpose that came with the walk, and we grieved the loss of it. Our current situation didn't feel like a much-needed rest but rather an uneasy limbo, caught between the world of the walk and the world of what came next. We were untethered, restless and unsure which way to go, searching for a new meaning, a new path.

Of course, we were also parents to a toddler now. All that quiet unrest in our minds had to take second place to meeting Magnus's needs. He had started talking, which had opened up a whole new world for him – the words seemed to flood out of him like they had been there all along, behind a locked door, just waiting to get out. I felt such relief and joy at his sudden burst of language. For months, I'd been bombarded by posts and articles online insisting toddlers should have a certain number of words by a certain age – 'at least fifty words by age two, and be sure to seek help if not' – and I'd also felt the weight of family concern, worried he wasn't progressing as quickly as other children. I had even contacted the health visitor we'd stayed in touch with in Scotland, who passed me the number of a speech and language specialist for an initial call. At the same time, I had tried to hold on to the belief that he simply needed a little longer – especially as research shows boys often talk later than girls, taking more time to build vocabulary and form sentences.

I was conscious of walking a fine line: not wanting to ignore potential needs or be slow in seeking help, but also not wanting to buckle under pressure when I knew he'd had a strong diet of language since birth, and when my instincts were telling me he'd get there in his own time. Once the gates did open, his verbal progress was so fast. In early August, he had maybe eight to fifteen words. By early September, he was firmly engaging in role play and reenacting favourite scenes from stories. By Christmas, he was reciting large chunks of *Room on the Broom* from memory.

It was a powerful reminder to me to listen to advice and not dismiss concerns if I had them, but to trust my instincts too. With my own background in storytelling and oracy, Magnus had been constantly surrounded by books, stories, songs and words since day one. Deep down, I knew it was only a matter of time. His progress reinforced what I've come to believe again and again: children develop at their own pace, and parental instinct is often the most reliable guide amid the barrage of advice online.

Every day for Magnus was a myriad of wonderful experiences and adventures, but, once he was asleep, Chris and I felt the heavy weight of trying to work out where we should go from here and how we could continue to give him this life and support ourselves financially. One year on, we were still figuring things out.

Some people might've assumed we could just opt out of this lifestyle and settle for going back to a normal life. But I'd never once questioned our choice. I believed in it, and in us as a family. Chris and I wanted him to grow up watching his parents pursue their dreams, so that he too could learn to aim high, smash through the glass ceilings and be bold and courageous in pursuing whatever it was he wanted in life.

As we contemplated what to do next, we spent the autumn and winter months on mainland Scotland, with Magnus strolling through dens, hiking over hills and clifftops, ambling along beaches, running riot in the parks and tearing up all sorts of mountain-bike trails. I would also take him to toddler play groups each week, so he had opportunities to socialize with other children, as well as to forest-school sessions, castles, public gardens and museums wherever we found them. Now two and a half, he was so confident on his bike, taking to the trails independently and flying on ahead, me racing behind on foot. He even did his first jump!

Chris had got me a bike back in Comrie, but I was a total beginner – I didn't try to ride a bike until I was about eight, when I crashed and went head first over a gate and that was that. Nevertheless, I enjoyed being part of the fun; and if I was to keep up with my boys and not be left behind on these cycling adventures of theirs, then I had to learn. In January 2025, we headed to the Isle of Arran with the bikes to spend a week cycling its coastline. Arran has a 65-mile coastal path that goes all the way around the island, packed with fabulous scenery, with many fantastic trails for walking in stunning glens. It's one of Scotland's Great Trails, in fact – a network of twenty-nine marked, long-distance trails. It was winter, but we'd picked a week with relatively calm weather and spells of sunshine. What's more, the tracks are very well maintained and accessible for a toddler, which meant Magnus could walk and cycle them easily. We were having such a brilliant time biking together as a family that it sparked an idea. What if we put cycling at the centre of our next big adventure?

We'd thrown a number of crazy ideas into the ether during our transition year – everything from hiking the length of New Zealand to attempting the Trans Dinarica, a new 3,400-mile cycle route linking eight Balkan nations – but it all felt too impractical with Magnus at his age. We both wanted to be ambitious in our thinking but not gloss over the practicalities of a large-scale endeavour with Magnus and limited funds in the bank.

I began researching cycle routes, and one evening I landed on a page about Europe's Atlantic Coast Route. It is Europe's longest cycle route, following its mighty western border, stretching from Scandinavia all the way down to Portugal. It winds through the majestic fjords of Norway, the wild Irish coastline, the rough cliffs of Brittany and the sun-kissed coast of Portugal, covering nearly 8,000 miles in total.

As I shared what I'd found about the Atlantic Coast Route with Chris, we turned to each other, a glint in our eyes . . . 'That's not a bad idea,' we both said. The spark it lit in us meant it quickly became a strong possibility. Nothing we'd landed on yet had made us feel quite like this.

Then we discussed the major elephant in the room – how on earth could we make this work in practice? Thanks to Brexit and the new rules limiting the amount of time Brits could now stay in other countries, our only option was to do the expedition in legs rather than one continuous journey. Filled with enthusiasm, we decided to see this as an opportunity in itself – we could use the time between European legs to regroup, re-strategize and earn some money to keep us afloat.

We wouldn't necessarily do the journey in order either, but would work with the seasons to cover the distance. With that, the bones of a new fundraising adventure were formed: 8,000 miles cycling and hiking Europe's Atlantic Coast in aid of Make A Wish UK, who help families with critically ill children make special memories by granting their wish.

It felt very surreal to be heading off for new horizons without Jet. We'd thought briefly about scattering her ashes back on Hildasay, where she'd been so happy, but we just couldn't let go of her completely. We kept her ashes in a beautiful mahogany box, which accompanied us wherever we went. This way, it felt like Jet was still on the adventure, in her favourite place: right by Chris's side.

We planned to set off at the start of April 2025, just before Magnus's third birthday. Up until the age of three, the most important relationship is the strong parent–child bond, which we had obviously prioritized. Our lifestyle had made him incredibly adaptable, so we weren't worried about uprooting him for another long adventure. His roots *were* adventure. I was conscious, however, about the need to continue his social-emotional development around other children. So far, he'd had plenty of that on our travels, interacting with different people on the walk, joining various playgroups and even making a bubble of familiar friends up in Comrie. Finding impromptu pockets of community on the move, be it in the form of local playgroups or forest schools, was going to be a priority for me.

We were full of excitement and hope, with our sights set firmly on new horizons and a new sense of purpose. We decided to start in Norway, with its mind-blowing coastline, the right to roam and a culture of *friluftsliv*, a word that translates literally to 'free air life', but is actually much more than that – it's a culture, a lifestyle, that revolves around spending time outside and embracing nature as part of everyday life. This was us through and through. This was what we sought. We would start in Norway, diving in at the deep end.

37

New Horizons

We arrived in Norway at the start of April and, for once, we struck gold with the weather! On our very first night, we found an incredible park-up next to a lake, the sun setting beyond the hills before us. It was so peaceful, and I breathed a huge sigh of relief; I knew we were going to love it here. The scenery was jaw-dropping, and this was just the beginning. More than that, we immediately felt at home and we couldn't hold back the excitement.

We took a few days to get our bearings and enjoy some time together as a family before tackling the coastline. Refreshed and raring to go, we started the first miles of this adventure on the anniversary of Jet's death, 7 April, on the island of Flekkerøy, south-west of Kristiansand. It was the perfect start. The number of small islands scattered along the coastline, connected to the mainland, meant we could park the van and circumnavigate the islands easily on foot in a loop – Magnus often riding his own bike – before heading back to the van to sleep each night.

Logistically, walking around a small island made life simpler because we didn't need to double back to retrieve the van or leave it somewhere for a few days or weeks of bikepacking; we could simply park up, walk a loop of the island and head back to the van to sleep each night. The trails were well-marked but with plenty of scope to venture off the beaten track – we found ourselves clambering over big boulders to find secluded slices of paradise in the form of hidden bays and coves. This meant we were more focused on hiking than cycling to begin with.

A few days in, we came through a clearing in some woodland and stumbled on a truly fantastic spot: a crescent-shaped sandy bay with turquoise water, lined with grass and surrounded by woodland, with mountains on either side. There was a picnic table, a pristinely clean public toilet in a quaint little wooden hut, firepits and outdoor barbecues, all free to use. From what we'd seen so far, there was no doubt that Norway was incredibly well set up for people to enjoy outdoor life and spend time in nature, the way it should be – without having to pay for the privilege! That said, it was obvious that respecting and looking after the natural surroundings was deeply ingrained in the culture and psyche here. The sun glistened on the water and there wasn't a soul in sight. It was magical. This was exactly what we loved about adventuring: stumbling upon hidden gems and being able to take the time to stop and soak them up. So we did just that: we pitched the tent and set up camp, spending the next twenty-four hours wild swimming, exploring the woodland, playing on the beach and climbing boulders with Magnus.

That afternoon, we witnessed an early-years forest school taking place on the opposite side of the water. Children just a few years older than Magnus were throwing stones into the water, swinging in hammocks and cooking snacks over the firepit. If we ever chose to place Magnus in school, this was exactly the kind of experience I wanted for him. Scandinavian forest schools are holistic and child-led, and place huge emphasis on outdoor play – something very hard to come by in the UK. I was excited to see more of this type of schooling in action as we continued our Nordic adventure.

We pressed on and made our way up the coast to Stavanger. The villages and towns along the way were incredibly picturesque, with houses painted in whitewashed timber or striking reds and yellows that stood out so beautifully against the blue of the sea. The houses were large, often with balconies and amazing views, and it seemed almost a requirement of residency here to own a boat. It was also common to see houses perched on little islands in the middle of lakes. I couldn't help but imagine how idyllic it would be to have a base like this on the water, a boat ride away from civilization, surrounded by woods and trails. A place to pause between our travels, to work creatively and enjoy family outdoor life in beautiful surroundings before setting off once again.

We struck a good balance of hiking and cycling, with plenty of opportunities for Magnus to ride his own balance bike. He was clearly thriving out here. The weather being on our side helped a lot, but in general I could see he was absolutely loving life in Norway's outdoors: essentially one big, wild adventure playground. He was off-road biking along demanding trails with incredible skill and confidence for his age. His stamina and enjoyment when it came to challenging hikes was also surprising me more and more. One particular afternoon, he happily walked for nearly four hours up a small mountain, past streams, lakes and waterfalls, across wide wooden planks over squelchy bogs and up sheer cliff faces where there were huge boulders to climb. He was wide-eyed with excitement, almost squealing with joy, seeing each huge boulder as the next exciting challenge to conquer. We made a game of high-fiving all the trail markers painted on the rocks, and when we reached the top, I felt so proud that he had managed a surprising distance and challenging ascent on such little legs.

Once we came around Stavanger, we took our first ferry

across the water, arriving in Norwegian fjord territory – and, in this case, the hype we'd heard was not exaggerated. Lysefjord is the southernmost of all Norway's fjords (of which there are over 1,700), stretching 26 miles inland through the Ryfylke region, and is incredibly dramatic. It's flanked by mighty mountains over 1,000 metres high, sculpted and carved by massive ice sheets that covered Norway during the Ice Age. It is also home to two of the country's most iconic hikes: Preikestolen (Pulpit Rock) and Kjerag, known for their jaw-dropping views.

That night, we found one of the best – if not *the* best – van park-ups we'd ever had, right on the banks of the fjord, with enough space for just one vehicle, meaning no neighbours and a firepit ready and waiting. The view was out of this world – imposing granite peaks with sheer, vertical walls towering over miles of icy, clear blue water, like great giants standing guard. The nearby road was so quiet, and opposite were enormous sloping grey boulders we could climb, slide down and run across for hours.

Behind us was a small pebbled bay where we all played very happily before some locals handed us one of their freshly caught scallops to try – just collected on a free dive and prised open before our eyes. I watched as my son sat cross-legged on the beach, utterly absorbed in his world of stones. He raked his small hand through the hundreds of tiny pebbles that lay beside him, interested in the way they shifted, slid and jostled, before scooping up a fistful for closer inspection. I observed him as he pored over the selection in his hand, mesmerized by the differences in colours, shapes and patterns. He noticed that some were dry and dusty, some wet and shiny, glistening as if varnished by the sea. He smiled as he threw them down, enjoying the clatter as they hit the ground and settled into place. Before long, he was on to bigger stones, balancing them one on top of the other with careful precision; sometimes they were no longer towers but castles, cranes, giants and mountains.

Then, in an instant, he was up on his feet and heading to the water's edge. He picked up stones and threw them into the water, delighted with their splash and the ripples they made, each throw an attempt to outdo the last. Chris joined him, engaging in a contest for 'biggest splash', before showing him the art of skimming stones. Soon, they were hand in hand, walking up and down the shoreline.

A broad smile spread across my face as I watched Magnus playing carefree in such spectacular surroundings. Nature was allowing him to delve into the infinite freedom of his imagination. Watching his quiet joy in simple acts of play like this always made the world slow down for me, reminding me of the beauty of an unrushed life and, most importantly, an unrushed childhood. It was all the assurance I needed that the outdoor lifestyle we had given him since birth was working; he was as content and happy as I could have wished. He had certainly shown himself to be adventurous and bold, and now it seemed that his curiosity was developing too.

We stayed in our much-envied spot for a few days, during which time we got a local tip: there was another hike, on the other side of the fjord, which takes in the same incredible view as Preikestolen but without the crowds. We headed up there, and I understood why it's been named one of the most breathtaking views in the world: the scenery stretched for miles down the pristine blue waters of the fjord. Every now and again I'd notice swirling mist gathering below, thinking it would swallow the view, only for it to retreat and reveal the landscape anew, adding an extra layer of drama and surprise to an already breathtaking scene. It was another day in paradise. In the evenings, we began contemplating a way to make it around Lysefjord, somehow covering every inch of it with Magnus. But first, we would celebrate him turning three!

On the day of his birthday, the weather held, and we had an

action-packed day doing all the things he loves best. He woke up to a birthday breakfast on the banks of the fjord, followed by a morning on the nearby mountain-biking trails, with a picnic; the afternoon was spent Gruffalo-hunting in the woods; and then the day ended with some climbing and playing on the beach before blowing out his candles, the sun still glistening on the water. There was nothing lavish about it, no expensive toys or big party – just a couple of balloons, some wild flowers, a few small dinosaurs wrapped up and the all-important slice of birthday cake – but he was as pleased as punch. He'd had a fantastic day, and I couldn't help but stop for a moment and ponder just how much this child had seen and done in his three years, not to mention the birthdays spent in locations many would only dream of: the Scilly Isles, the Outer Hebrides and now Norway. We had made some questionable decisions at times, and we had a long way to go before securing any kind of financial stability moving forward, but I felt we had given our son the most fantastic start in life and that this had fostered his curiosity, confidence and creativity, as well as a deep understanding of the natural world that stretched beyond his years. I strongly believed that we were laying the foundations for a child who would grow up with a love of learning but also, and perhaps more importantly, secure emotional health and a passion for life.

I couldn't have imagined a more perfect day for him, other than perhaps the presence of some other children to share in his excitement. His ability to interact more regularly with others his own age was playing on my mind more now that he had turned three. On the odd days it had poured with rain, we had taken him to soft-play centres (which, out in Norway, are more like aeroplane hangars!). I could see his joy and excitement when he befriended others to play with, and I wanted more of that for him.

*

In spite of the wonderful scenery and bracing exercise, our time in Norway hadn't all been plain sailing. For one, Magnus was so used to riding his own little bike on off-road trails that he really didn't take to being in a trailer on the back of Chris's bike when we had to take to the coastal roads. When it came to busy main roads, for now, Chris tackled those on his own while I built up my confidence. The mountain roads were hugely intimidating in terms of blind bends, hairpin turns and steep drops, and there were long stretches of road where it was impossible to stop for a break. Norway's coast also has long, dark tunnels carved through the mountains, where bikes and pedestrians are often prohibited. Whichever way we tried to get around it, though, Magnus just wasn't keen on the trailer on the roads. It was an unanticipated problem.

On top of that, Chris got an excruciating infection in his back molar and needed two rounds of emergency dental surgery – a big blow to our budget! We were being incredibly frugal with our money, but food was eye-wateringly expensive. The free park-ups were fantastic – a far cry from how hard we had found it on the south coast during the walk – but we did have to pay for a campsite once a week in order to recharge our drone and laptop for filming purposes. At night, I'd stay up bleary-eyed until 3 a.m. creating a website for us. It included a shop where people could buy prints of our photographs, along with mugs, coasters, glass worktops and other items featuring photos taken on our travels. I had hoped this would become a second source of income to sustain us, but it didn't work, and our savings weren't going to see us through for much longer.

There was one other thing that weighed on both our minds: the pressure we had put on ourselves to cover every inch of coastline. We had set ourselves this huge physical undertaking in order to help raise money for charity, but forcing ourselves to get from A to B every day, with all the logistical challenges that involved, especially with a toddler, was proving too much.

As much as we were loving it out among the mountains and fjords, we made a call to head home, deciding to see this as a trial run and a recce of the landscape for our return one day. Disappointed as we were to leave earlier than we'd hoped, our time there had inspired us in lots of ways: a glimpse into Scandinavian forest school; the joys of van life, with access to unbridled natural beauty on our doorstep every day; and a daily reminder of how much wonder exists for us to explore in the world. For now, we would press pause on Norway and try again somewhere where we knew the coastal stretches would be slightly more accommodating for a young boy and more feasible for us all to do together. After all, for us, it wasn't about Chris and me pursuing adventure for our own ends – it was about incorporating our son into a lifestyle of full-time family fun and adventure, and being intuitive to his needs along the way. That was our goal. We decided to resume our journey closer to home, on a set of far-flung islands in the North Sea, geographically level with Bergen and with many cultural ties to Norway as well. A place that we'd been meaning to visit together since finishing the walk: Shetland.

38

Puffins

We arrived on Shetland with the aim of starting again on its Atlantic-facing west coast. Given we were well into May, we were hoping to take advantage of the British summer weather; and we now had a greater ability to earn money along the way, with Chris doing his paid talks. After Shetland and Orkney, we'd go down the west coast of Scotland from Scrabster to Cairnryan, taking in some of the Hebridean islands on our way. From there, we would hop on a ferry to Ireland to cycle the Wild Atlantic Way, returning to include sections of the Welsh coastal path and the south-west coast of England, before heading to Europe over winter.

We were super-excited to come to Shetland as a family for the first time, a place that held such meaning for Chris and had been pivotal to our family story – not to mention the inspiration behind Magnus's name. Both Chris and I had wanted a strong, distinctive Scottish first name, loaded with meaning, both personal and historical. Magnus means 'great' or 'mighty'. Originally a Nordic name of Viking heritage, it was brought over to Scotland from Scandinavia via Shetland when they invaded and is deeply rooted in the northern isles. We'd always been drawn to names with strong ties to the isles. When Chris was last there, he met a man named Magnus on the remote island of Foula who'd shown him black and white photographs of his family stretching back through many generations — each man bearing the name Magnus. Chris told me this story when we met, and it had stayed with me. I also loved the mythological connection: in Norse legend, Magni was the son of Thor. Together we'd felt the name was just right for our boy, and we couldn't wait to introduce Magnus to the place that was so linked to his identity.

As soon as we arrived, we got stuck into tackling the miles, working our way from north to south, but we were met with gale-force winds and torrential downpours (hello, Shetland summer). Chris took one for the team over the initial few days, starting the cycle in the northernmost point of Fethaland while Magnus and I took refuge with some friends Chris had made last time, James and Kathleen. They introduced us to life in the local community, taking us to various playgroups, a fantastic charity woodland with large-scale dinosaur models and the heritage museum in Lerwick.

When I saw a video of Chris trudging miles over Ronas Hill — Shetland's highest peak at 450 metres, covered in granite Arctic–Alpine tundra, with summit temperatures equal to those of the Cairngorms — it stopped me in my tracks. He was being battered by icy winds and rain, and I thought, *Hang on. Does he really need to be putting himself through all this again? He's already done this once!*

For six years, following the coastline so rigidly had been Chris's sole purpose every day, and now just being by the coast brought that deeply ingrained habit back out in him. But trying to do this new journey in the same way wasn't necessary; we were allowed to make our own rules now. Insisting on doing it that way meant so much of it would be off-limits to Magnus, and Chris would end up doing huge sections alone, which wasn't the family-focused lifestyle we were aiming for. I understood Chris's mindset – the walk had been such a profoundly powerful, soul-defining and enlightening experience for both of us, and even though we had tried to leave it behind and open a new chapter, it was clear we were still trying to keep it alive in some form; perhaps it was a way of keeping Jet alive too. But we needed to accept that it could never be recreated, nor should it be – nothing lasts for ever, and that journey had run its course. Chris realized that he needed to shift his outlook – we all did – if we were going to make this work as a family adventure.

Once the moody skies had cleared, Magnus and I were able to join Chris. First up, he took us back to Fethaland so that we could experience mainland Shetland's northernmost point for ourselves. Only accessible on foot or by mountain bike down a 3-mile track, Fethaland was an empty paradise, with twenty or so crumbling stone huts scattered across the green hillside leading down towards a pebbled beach. On one side lay the Atlantic Ocean, where a stack, a cone-shaped rock formation known as the Witch's Hat, took prominence, and on the other side was the North Sea. Once Shetland's biggest *haaf* (deep-sea) fishing station, in the eighteenth and nineteenth centuries up to 400 men lived and worked in Fethaland, setting out on perilous expeditions to catch the fish that paid their rent. They lived in stone huts or booths with temporary roofs of turf.

Over the summer, these men would head 30–50 miles offshore in open wooden rowing boats. Cloth sails were used, but more often than not it was sheer manpower that drove the boats through the waves. They had no cover, and the men were forced to fish in all weathers, spending two to three days at sea at a time, completely exposed to the elements, risking it all every time they left the shore. Some never came back. It was impossible to come here, surrounded by the relics of stone huts, and not feel so close to the island's history.

The pressures of modern life seemed a world away; Shetland was a haven of natural beauty and tranquillity where you could press the reset button. Magnus loved trying to befriend the local sheep, wandering among the old stone huts and peering through their open windows out to sea. There was mile upon mile of space for him to run and cycle, flat green grass now carpeted with sea pinks, dramatic high cliffs to explore and a lighthouse perched right at the edge of the mainland. Down in the pebbled bay, beachcombing quickly became the prime activity. The rocks were perfect for climbing, the water was clear and turquoise, and a curious grey seal kept popping its head up to say hello. If we'd had enough food with us and a reliable weather forecast, we would have pitched the tent right there and stayed for days.

As we continued south together, we were having a whale of a time riding our mountain bikes off-road along the stunning north-west coast, weaving across the clifftops. The cliffs of Eshaness made for a stunning coastline and a centrepiece of the island's unique geology, with white waves crashing against rugged red-hued cliffs formed by volcanic eruptions 350 million years ago. Beneath us lay sea caves, one of which, Calder's Geo, is the largest in Britain – and we cycled past a multitude of dramatic stacks, arches and windows that still stood strong against the relentless sea. Set back from the cliffs, we even stumbled upon a set of stepping stones across a loch near an Iron-Age broch (a circular stone tower).

It was clear that our son absolutely loved the thrill of riding up front on Chris's bike, even over bumpy and boggy terrain, and got very excited believing that we were moving over the top of a once-erupted volcano, and that the broch was the home of a sleeping giant. These incredible surroundings never failed to inspire his imagination – how could they not? Now that he was so verbal, I loved hearing how his mind perceived it all, bringing a whole new sense of wonder to the way I now travelled. 'We're cycling over a volcano!' he shouted gleefully against the wind. 'It erupted with lava and fire and there were dinosaurs here too!'

We soon heard the puffins (or 'tammie norries', as they're known up there) had arrived at Sumburgh Head, Shetland's southernmost point, where they return each spring to nest and breed in the cliffs after a winter at sea. Only around 10 per cent of the world's puffin population come to the UK, the rest residing in Norway and Iceland, so to see them here was a real treat. We watched them sit on the cliff edges amid the blossoming sea pinks, emerge from the burrows, take flight and land with sand eels firmly clamped between their beaks to feed to their pufflings. Magnus stood giggling at their quirky, comical charm, especially their wobbly landings.

They were smaller than I'd imagined, but no less beautiful, with their colourful beaks and bright orange feet splashes of vibrant colour against their black and white feathers. We learned that the black allows them to blend in with the inky blue of the sea to protect them from predators above, while the white blends with the sky to protect them from predators below. Puffins can flap their wings up to 400 times a minute to stay airborne, but are most impressive underwater, using their wings like flippers to push to depths of 60 metres – 20 metres deeper than recreational scuba divers!

I turned to see Chris and Magnus immersed in a head-to-head dinosaur battle, Magnus now a horned triceratops squealing with laughter and excitement as he rolled around on the floor with his dad. It was a wonderful reminder that, when we slowed down, without needing to push from A to B each day, we made time for more connection, presence and joy.

A thought hit me. *What if we took a step back from feeling we needed such a huge challenge to deserve to live this life?* Was suffering and hardship the only way to adventure? Did we always have to make it such a slog? It was evident that Chris had been finding the pressure of it all too much: the intensity of the day-to-day adventure combined with looking after Magnus; our limited finances and trying to work full-time on the side in the evenings; organizing and doing talks as well as creating content for our various social-media channels. We had also launched a Patreon channel by this point – a platform whereby people could subscribe monthly in return for extra, behind-the-scenes content – hoping it would make all the difference, but we quickly realized this wouldn't be enough.

Chris felt very overwhelmed at times. Adventuring with a young child was very different from travelling alone, where any mistakes you make are yours alone to bear. That overwhelm was manifesting in dizzy spells and a real struggle to focus. And while he was incredibly creative, he could only focus with time and space to think, and we were hardly getting any. He was also suffering the consequences of lugging an extremely heavy backpack for miles every day and living in a tent for so long – his neck and shoulders were incredibly tight, causing him crippling pain that affected his sleep and his daily mood. For a man who had been in peak fitness all his life, he really struggled with feeling that this was beginning to slip away. We needed to strip this journey back and simplify things.

We had been used to unplanned, extreme adventures that unfolded quite literally step by step, but adventuring with a very young child doesn't work like that. It requires so much more foresight and preparation. Having a small child dependent on you in the wild is a huge responsibility, but that doesn't mean it's any less enjoyable. If anything, our days were now far more meaningful. We just needed to find a rhythm that allowed for more choice and flexibility.

With Magnus now three, questions around his education were taking up more and more space in my mind. He was still very young, and I certainly didn't want to push academia on him too soon. In the early years, play is paramount; it is through play that children learn. I'm troubled by the ways in which child-led play has been increasingly stripped from early-years education in England. Many reception classes go from self-directed play to Year 1 desks and formal learning before every child is ready. Suddenly, children are expected to sit still and focus for an entire school day, which is so at odds with their proven need for physical movement and active play. By the end of that year, they're already facing the phonics screening test, and then it's straight on to SATs in Year 2, forcing far too much academic pressure on them at such a young age. In mainstream settings, there is so little time spent outside, where I have come to believe that the most meaningful learning happens – where children learn to become thinkers, problem-solvers, explorers, risk-takers, nurturers and leaders. From improved communication and concentration to stronger self-belief, physical confidence and emotional resilience, learning outdoors equips children with the tools they need to thrive in life, as well as the time and space to just *be*. Before the walk, I never envisaged myself as a parent who wouldn't send their child to school. However, the closer we now came to his school age, the more my experience as a teacher was making me feel sceptical. Truthfully, I felt very uneasy about outsourcing and entrusting my child's education to a system I didn't necessarily believe was the best option I could offer him.

I am also mindful of the fact that we are living in a new era of crisis for our children, with mental and physical health at an all-time low. One in six children aged five to sixteen is likely to be affected by a mental-health problem, and the likelihood of it happening has risen by 50 per cent in the past three years alone. Today, in a typical classroom of thirty, five children are likely to be struggling with their mental health.[1] In terms of physical health, obesity, short-sightedness, asthma, vitamin D deficiency and a decline in cardiorespiratory fitness are all increasingly common. A growing body of research links this to a lack of time spent outdoors and, in my view, the two have to be linked. The quality of a child's early years is vitally important, having a huge impact on their health and wellbeing for years to come, even into the next generation. 90 per cent of brain development occurs by the age of five, and the benefits of secure parental attachment even by the age of three follow children throughout life. Our children are this world's future; time spent in the outdoors and establishing a personal connection to nature are absolutely crucial for their mental and physical wellbeing. By recognizing and nurturing this, we support not only them but also the wellbeing and health of the planet they are set to inherit. If we don't, then their ability to face the challenges of the world they will live in feels deeply uncertain. I believe that a more holistic approach for both parents and children, whereby joyful living and learning can be beautifully intertwined, is the way forward.

When it came to Magnus's future, I kept asking myself: *Is there a better way?* It seems I'm not alone, and many parents are asking themselves the same thing. I began looking into a number of alternative approaches: home-schooling, worldschooling and unschooling. Home education is rising by 21 per cent each year

---

1   The Children's Society, 2022 (https://www.childrenssociety.org.uk/what-we-do/our-work/well-being/mental-health-statistics).

in the UK, and many of those parents are ex-teachers. Family, friends and followers often assumed I would home-school Magnus. However, I certainly didn't want that to mean sitting in a van teaching him alone each day, and I wasn't keen on using online lessons, textbooks or worksheets to support me in that either. I wanted his learning to be very hands-on, experiential and collaborative, while also fostering friendships and learning with others.

To home-school him this way would mean finding a permanent or semi-permanent base so that we could become part of a strong community. In order to keep travelling, the best way I felt I could meet those needs while on the move was through 'worldschooling' – combining immersive learning in different cultures with longer-term travel, which can be done in all sorts of ways. Some families plan their own learning experiences as they go, others join pop-up hubs to find community, and an increasing number now take advantage of organizations that offer formal schooling in set locations across the world, which run from a few weeks to three to four months at a time. Some of these schools follow rolling curriculums, allowing parents to move on to new destinations while staying in step, often with dedicated work hubs for digital-nomad families.

Worldschooling holds a lot of appeal; not just because of opportunities for diving into learning other languages and broadening Magnus's exposure to other cultures and lifestyles, but because our world is changing so rapidly – I believe our current education system is too outdated to effectively equip our children to thrive in the future they will face. For me, education needs to be innovatively reimagined, and I feel that connecting learning to nature and engaging with real-world problems in cultural contexts is vital.

There seemed to be an endless number of 'worldschooling hubs' being advertised on social-media community pages in locations all over the world. They were mainly run by parents doing the same thing: looking for connections to other families and a way to make a bit of money at the same time. Opting for hubs like these would certainly take extensive research and it was a big gamble on whether it would be a good fit. Personally, I liked the idea of more in-depth, child-led, enquiry-based projects rooted in the outdoors that ran for three months or so at a time and were curated by specialist educators in different locations around the world, catering to those who wanted an alternative education model. However, all this would also mean ensuring we had an established, reliable income to fund ourselves.

Perhaps we could find a base in Scotland for four to five months a year where we could set up a small outdoor family business. Given our unique personal story, in particular Chris's unmatched knowledge of the UK coastline, we could run trips for people that included hiking, bushcraft and responsible wild camping – adventurous experiences that chimed with what we valued and stood for as a family. With our combined love for photography, we could also make promotional content for tourist boards and self-publish adventure-photography books, and I could even do some outdoor or online teaching. Meanwhile, Magnus could attend an outdoor, nature-based early-years or forest school setting, where play, self-direction and community were central. Perhaps we could then spend three to four months a year worldschooling abroad, immersing ourselves in different cultures, exploring different languages, foods, history, landscapes and traditions. We could use the remaining three to four months a year to travel together as a family, living wild adventures.

39

My Soul and My Song

As we left the puffins behind us and drove off in the van, Magnus sandwiched between us waving goodbye to the sheep on the roadside, I turned to Chris. 'Chris, what if we cut out having to walk and cycle the full 8,000 miles? What if we took all that pressure off ourselves? We could still follow the rough route we'd planned, but just be us – travelling more leisurely, picking and choosing the places we actually want to spend each of our days rather than being beholden to a mission and forcing ourselves to take the hardest route every time. We can still fundraise, but we can make it work for our new little family. We could do micro-challenges along the way, each one raising money to make one child's wish come true through the charity.

'Between challenges, we just travel. We spend our time adventuring in whatever way works best for all of us; whatever excites us most on the day. For some reason, we always feel guilty about just enjoying life, like we only deserve this if we're putting ourselves through such a demanding slog at the same time. But maybe . . . maybe we've done our fair share of that now.'

Chris turned and looked at me, nodded in agreement – it

was written all over his face. Subconsciously, we had still been modelling our pursuit of adventure on the lifestyle we'd come to know on the walk, and it had taken all this time and experimentation for us to realize that what came next didn't need to mirror that. Before he could answer, my phone rang. It was a man called Adam from a company called Promote Shetland and he wanted to know if we would make three short documentary-style films to promote the islands. It would be paid work – not much, but enough to tide us over. We were thrilled, and replied with a very enthusiastic 'Yes!' This would be our first paid gig showcasing a part of the world we loved so much, and a foot in the door that could then get us further paid work with other tourist boards. The timing felt like fate had stepped in; it was so fitting that, just as we were setting ourselves a fresh intention, a new opportunity had come our way. If anything, it gave us a confidence boost that our new life could still work out going forward.

We now had a work purpose that very much aligned with our passion – highlighting wonderful places, history, geology, nature and people, while improving our filmmaking craft at the same time. If we did a good job, we really hoped this could open the door for similar opportunities elsewhere and offer a way to keep building this life we so wanted.

I still pinch myself when I think how dramatically my life has changed over the past six years, swapping a very conventional London city life to live as a full-time nomadic mum in the great outdoors. Somewhere along the line, living in a tent for years in all weathers, moving on foot each day around our incredible coastline, I have begun to feel more at home outdoors than anywhere I've lived in my whole adult life. It's changed my outlook on life so significantly; the very deliberate choice to navigate first-time motherhood on a walk around the UK coastline felt instinctive and natural to me. The deep sense of groundedness, connection and fulfilment that I find in every day is what keeps me on this journey.

We are now years deep into full-time van life with a toddler. People often say to us, 'You're living the dream,' but make no mistake: every dream has its drawbacks in reality, and life nowadays certainly comes with its challenges. The constant compromise on space alone can be stressful and chaotic, certainly with a three-year-old staging dinosaur fights at your feet while you're cooking dinner in the confines of a box, rain pounding down outside – I could go on! Nomadic life is certainly not for everyone – but then, every lifestyle comes with its trade-offs. When people tell us, 'You're so lucky,' I often want to remind them that luck has nothing to do with it. It takes sacrifice and continued courage to pursue a life that goes against the grain, and constant commitment to make it work. Chris and I firmly believe that the way of life we have chosen gives us something far more important than the comfort, luxuries and commodities chased by so many; in sacrificing how much we own, we have bought ourselves the freedom to choose how we spend our days. Most importantly, it has bought us time and presence with our son. Life is so fragile and so short; Magnus's first years have passed in the blink of an eye! To have been able to spend every day of those years with him is a blessing I count greater than any other, and one I believe we have bestowed upon him as well. As long as we're able to meet our basic needs, it's our view that time is our most valuable currency.

Over the past two years, Chris and I have been working out our new path. There has been lots of trial and error; after all, life is unpredictable at the best of times, especially when you're forging an unconventional path as a young family with no textbook to follow. If anything, the past few months have taught us that what matters isn't the distance travelled or how thrilling (or gruelling) we made the endeavour; what matters is staying true to ourselves and pursuing the life we want in a way that's right for us. I have no doubt that, as life progresses, what we want and how we live will evolve and change with the seasons as new horizons come into view. What's important is that we are open to that, willing to adapt and see positivity, learning and growth in that process, staying conscious of the idea that adventure can be found wherever you choose to look for it. That is the real journey, after all.

I do not call myself Wilderness Mum because I want to live every day of my life in extreme wild places and remote outposts. I call myself that because, no matter where I am, I will always love and look for wild places. One day we might sleep under the stars in the mountains, the next my son might be splashing through rivers in a forest school. Humans and nature are inextricably connected, and we don't need to be in the middle of nowhere to find a sense of it in ourselves. We can appreciate wilderness in Mother Nature all around us, be it the birds in the sky, the food in a woodland, the sea life in a rock pool. We are all wild in our essence – it is our ancestry, our history, our identity. It's there to be connected with at any moment. For me, a love of wilderness has become a part of who I am – my spirit, my soul and my song. I will always turn to it for inspiration, peace and a wider sense of belonging, both as a person and as a mum, for as long as I live.

Acknowledgements

This book was written under some pretty crazy circumstances: here, there and everywhere, whenever I could find the time and space, given our lifestyle – by head torch in the front seat of the van at night; in notebooks, sitting on camping chairs by Norwegian lakes in the evenings; in cafes, ferry terminals, hotel lobbies and public libraries; on boats and bathroom floors; in the studies and spare rooms of kind friends and acquaintances, especially those in Shetland; all typically late at night when Magnus was asleep! It's been a real journey, and I'm so grateful to everyone who's helped along the way.

Thank you to always beloved Jet, for being the most loyal and loving dog anyone could wish for. Thank you for your unconditional love, constant friendship and all the ways you supported me without even knowing it. We all love and miss you so much, but we carry you with us on our adventures and we know you are watching over us from above.

To Chris – thank you for your patience, love and support. I know it hasn't been easy at times, and the past five years have certainly been a rollercoaster! Thank you for seeing life outside the box, standing with me in refusing to give up on our dreams and for being by my side throughout this parenting adventure, making our son laugh as much as you do.

Thank you to my mum and dad for supporting me, even if some of my decisions and antics have left you terrified at times! You inspire me in many ways as parents, ways I know I will mirror in the way I bring up my own son. Thank you for being rocks I know I can always count on.

Thank you to Chris Smith, director of Storytelling Schools and my mentor for seven years, for recognizing my potential as a young, newly qualified teacher and supporting my passion for storytelling, teaching and teacher training.

Thank you to Lydia at Pan Macmillan for being such a supporter of my story and taking the chance on commissioning me to write my own book – it means so much, and I will always be grateful! Big thanks also to my two editors who came on board towards the end, Michelle Buckeridge and Richard Walters – your feedback and input was invaluable. Thank you also to my desk editor, Rosa Watmough, for taking the time to chat through my final edits at the end!

A *huge* thank you to all the wonderful people of the UK who helped us on our walk and supported us in whatever form over the past few years. You are a testament to the fact that there is so much kindness, community and humanity out there, and still so much good in the world. I wish I could mention you all, but please know that we are forever grateful – in many ways, this book is for you. A special thanks has to go to Steve Rooke for being that friend you can call at 3 a.m. whatever bind you might find yourself in; to Bill and Katrina Castles in Aberdeen; to Mick and Vicki for your help in Essex; to Mark Tuff at Clarty Commandos; to Dan Davies for being a great friend generally and for your creative genius and sand-art expertise; to Anna Stiles for being such a rock on the south coast, especially sitting all night in the car with Jet while I was in never-ending labour! To Dizzi and Ralph for giving me such a memorable place in which to birth my son; to Carol and Mike Cole; to Marjorie Edwards for being a big help on the south coast; to Gaynor for kindly putting me and Magnus up in Penzance while I was injured; to Theresa Flatley for her support and generosity; to Anne Robertson and Sarah Fowlie, who have been so active in rallying support behind the scenes; to all my wonderful friends who supported me both on the walk and from afar, especially Sophie Tring and her family, Verity Douglas and Sam Atiko-McQueen, Amy Ejvet, Saraya Cortaville, Francesca Byrne and Tracey Saunders.

I also want to thank Keith Thornburn for being an absolute hero and helping me at all hours with his technical expertise on the website. Thank you to Tim and Rebecca Peake – Tim for so kindly endorsing my book and Rebecca for being a very appreciated, continued source of support and advice ever since we met on the walk.

A real heartfelt thank you to the communities of Gourdon, Johnshaven and Inverbervie for your support throughout our woodland lockdown. To Rosie Frampton and Ali Monset, as well as Gill and Simon Lee-Atherton, who so kindly helped us with the offer of extra shelter during autumn and winter in Scotland with Magnus last year. To Kathleen and James Williamson, Rob and Nan Mort and Dan Ward for being all-round wonderful and welcoming us into your homes during our time in Shetland whenever Chris had to work, so that I could tackle the ending of this book with the use of plugs, wi-fi and a bigger play space for Magnus. Your help meant so much to us. An extra thank you to Nan, who has knitted so many beautiful woollen Shetland garments for Magnus since he was born and continues to do so – he is extremely lucky! We are so very grateful to *all* of you who in any way have supported and continue to support us in our endeavours. We can't thank you enough.

Last but by no means least, I want to thank my wonderful son, Magnus. You bring endless joy and meaning to my life. More than anything, I have written this book for you, as a memoir of your early childhood, a chronicle of all your amazing first adventures that you won't be able to remember but have undoubtedly formed the blueprints for who you will become. I hope to give you the most magical childhood, and hope that we continue to have fun-filled adventures together for the rest of my days.